D0464133

Praise for

Pension Dumping: The Reasons,
The Wreckage, The Stakes for Wall Street
by Fran Hawthorne

"Having lived through the S&L crisis, I can't help but wonder what policy makers might have done had they been presented with a concise, cogent description of the gathering of the perfect storm before events unfolded. Fran Hawthorne has written such a book for pension policy makers. Let's hope they take heed."
> OLENA BERG LACY
> Former U.S. Assistant Secretary of Labor for Pension and
>   Welfare Benefits (now EBSA), 1993–1998

"Fran Hawthorne provides a thought-provoking and lively analysis of bankruptcy laws, specialized investment and capital market strategies, and where pensions fit into the strategies to move troubled companies forward. She discusses how the bankruptcy laws focus on the business in the future and how these laws ignore the rights of employees. She also suggests areas for policy change."
> ANNA M. RAPPAPORT, F.S.A., M.A.A.A.
> Anna Rappaport Consulting
> Past President of the Society of Actuaries

"Will retirement security be an oxymoron for most Americans? Fran Hawthorne's *Pension Dumping* offers a clear-eyed, provocative look at the critically important world of pensions."
> BARBARA RUDOLPH
> Author, *Disconnected*
> International Editor, *The Deal*

"Employer involvement in traditional pension plans has been supplanted by a massive shift to 401(k) plans where employees are responsible for their own retirement savings and dependent on their own investment skills to assure an adequate retirement. *Pension Dumping* is a must-read for those trying to understand why. Fran Hawthorne gives the ordinary reader insight into the mysteries of our nation's pension and bankruptcy laws, as well as accounting, corporate finance and investment principles, in straightforward and readable terms. Hawthorne has reached out to a broad group of stakeholders—from investors to union leaders, from pension experts to the skilled corporate and bankruptcy lawyers involved in major cases, from the policymakers who wrote the laws to the workers who lost their pensions and health benefits despite those laws—to tell this compelling story. With clarity and even humor at times, Hawthorne examines a complicated, multi-faceted, and often troubling phenomenon with broad current and future implications for companies, workers, retirees, taxpayers, and society as a whole. It is a cautionary tale well worth reading."

PHYLLIS C. BORZI, J.D., M.A.

Research Professor, Department of Health Policy, School of Public Health and Health Services, The George Washington University Medical Center

Former Counsel for Employee Benefits, U.S. House of Representatives, Committee on Education and Labor, 1979–1995

Pension Dumping

A complete list of our titles is available at
www.bloomberg.com/books

Pension Dumping

The Reasons
The Wreckage
The Stakes for Wall Street

Fran Hawthorne

Bloomberg Press
New York

First edition published 2008
1 3 5 7 9 10 8 6 4 2

Library of Congress Cataloging-in-Publication Data

Hawthorne, Fran.
   Pension dumping : the reasons, the wreckage, the stakes for Wall Street / Fran Hawthorne. -- 1st ed.
      p. cm.
   Summary: "Pension Dumping is the story of how terminating the pension plan has become a knee-jerk strategy for bankrupt companies that hope to attract big investors to help them restructure"--Provided by publisher.
   Includes bibliographical references and index.
   ISBN 978-1-57660-239-3 (alk. paper)
1. Pension trusts--United States.   2. Pension trusts--Termination--United States.
3. Pension trusts--Termination--Law and legislation--United States.   4. Corporate reorganizations--United States.   5. Bankruptcy--United States.   6. Investments--United States.   I. Title.

HD7105.45.U6H39 2008
331.25'240973--dc22   2007050623

Acquired and edited by Mary Ann McGuigan

To Pete and Joey

Contents

Acknowledgments

THIS BOOK would never have come into being if Jared Kieling and Mary Ann McGuigan of Bloomberg Press had not been able to extend our meeting back in October 2005.

The three of us were meeting in Bloomberg's futuristic headquarters in midtown Manhattan to kick around ideas for a book on pensions. We spent about an hour mulling over the dangers of 401(k) plans and how absurd it was for the entire retirement security of America to rest on the average person's eagerness and ability (or lack thereof) to play the markets. This had been a longtime concern of mine, but we couldn't seem to turn these ideas into a book that would be right for Bloomberg. Clearly, we were getting to the point where one of us would have to say, "It's been great meeting, let's stay in touch." It was well past lunchtime, and I, at least, was feeling a little weak. I was even starting to put my papers back into my briefcase. At the last minute, I tossed out a vague thought: What about this new trend of companies filing for bankruptcy and dumping their pension plans?

So first of all, I have to thank Jared and Mary Ann for having the patience that October day to linger a little longer, and for their guidance and help in shaping this book.

Of course, so many thanks go to the scores of people who were willing to take the time to talk with me for my research. I particularly want to acknowledge Bill Beyer of Keightley & Ashner in Washington, DC, who not only met with me for a long interview but also answered my (many, many) follow-up e-mail queries with detailed and documented explanations. Special thanks as well to Lynn LoPucki and Joseph Doherty of UCLA, who ran an analysis of Professor LoPucki's bankruptcy database for me to single out companies with underfunded pension plans. Similarly, Steve Kerstein at the Towers Perrin consulting firm produced a series of graphs of corporate financial indicators specifically for my research for this book. And, also, thanks to Joel Zweibel, the veteran bankruptcy lawyer, who went to the trouble of digging out his old LTV files for me.

Three old friends assisted in this endeavor: My former colleague from *Institutional Investor* magazine, Hilary Rosenberg, did some of the earliest reporting on distressed investing in her 1992 book *The Vulture Investors* and was willing to dig through those old memories to help me understand the beginnings of this phenomenon. Tom Gilsenan, my colleague from even farther back at the *Sun* newspaper chain in Silicon Valley, helped me find families who were hard hit after the Minneapolis-Moline pension plan shutdown in 1974. And labor lawyer Larry Magarik, whom I've known since our eldest kids were in preschool together, filled my notebook with a list of must-read books.

Finally, to my family, especially my husband, Pete Segal, and my son, Joey Hawthorne—thanks, as always, for putting up with my long nights and weekends at the computer, my moments of panic, and my obsessing as I actually pulled this together.

Introduction

*"Bankruptcy is about shedding your old debts, and an un-
funded pension plan is just another big pool of debt. I can't
think of a good reason not to do it."*

—MIKE JOHNSTON, RETIREMENT PRACTICE LEADER, HEWITT
ASSOCIATES LLC

WHEN I was first introduced to the pension industry as
a junior writer at *Institutional Investor* magazine in the
mid-1980s, a book like *Pension Dumping* would have been unimagi-
nable. First of all, thanks to a new federal law, pensions were rarely
dumped. And second, investors wouldn't be interested in companies
that dumped them.

The pension arena was a predictable, if boring, world. With a
defined benefit pension plan, you worked at a company until you
were sixty-five; then you retired and the company gave you a gold
watch and a check for a few hundred dollars every month, year in and
year out, until you died. My grandfather, a retired engineer for New
York City, received one of those pensions; my father and mother, an
engineer and a college administrator, respectively, would get theirs
when they retired; and I'll even be entitled to one from *Institutional
Investor* someday. Oh, a handful of companies at that time offered
something known as defined contribution plans, which provided personal accounts into which employees contributed their own money.
One version of these plans was called a 401(k). But they played a
pretty insignificant role in the total benefits package and were usually tacked on as supplements to defined benefit plans.

And pensions had become solemn and eternal promises. That
had not always been the case. The nation had just gone through a
series of wrenching catastrophes in which companies had abruptly
shut their pension doors and declared they couldn't afford to pay
retirees any more benefits. The trauma had prompted Congress to
pass a law in 1974, the Employee Retirement Income Security Act

(ERISA), to guarantee that such shutouts would never happen again. Because these pension promises were now so sacred, the money that companies put aside to fund them had to be stewarded with extreme care: no messing around with exotic or risky instruments like small-cap stocks or international equities. Virtually every pension officer allocated the assets exactly the same way: 40 percent in AAA-rated bonds, 60 percent in blue-chip stocks. Some funds were even 100 percent invested in bonds. Safe and secure.

In another corner of the financial universe lived creatures called distressed investors—or, less fondly, vultures. The basic philosophy of investing in distressed properties had been around at least since the Depression, when Max Heine first popularized the concept of finding hidden value in the difference between the price of a distressed company's securities and the true worth of its assets. Distressed investors bought up the debt of troubled companies at huge discounts from creditors who didn't want to be stuck holding the hot potato. Over time, the pool of potential investments grew and shrank, depending on the economic situation. The sector thrived when crises—the bankruptcy of the Penn Central Railroad in 1970, the recessions of the early 1980s, the stock market crash of October 1987—pushed companies into financial turmoil. And when other investors were flourishing, the vultures withered. A new national bankruptcy law in 1978 also gave a big boost to the distressed-investing philosophy, although it took Wall Street about a decade to wake up to the implications. The 1978 law made it easier for managements to bring their companies out of bankruptcy, thus making it more feasible to file for bankruptcy to begin with.

But even the new law couldn't make distressed investors respectable. There is, after all, something a little creepy about people who clap when the economy collapses. The nickname said it all: *vultures*. It's not easy to warm up to those hulking black monsters with their ugly, bald heads poking out of stark white necks—and those beaks! The Wall Street variation of the species is ready to pounce before the body is even cold, eager to gobble up poor, failing companies for a fraction of their true value. The vultures tried to claim that they weren't tearing living flesh. It was exactly the opposite, they argued: By their willingness to invest hard cash, they were in fact *saving* dying companies. They just had to cut off the sickest parts in order to save the rest.

These arguments generally fell flat, however, and vultures remained on the fringes. Certainly, they had nothing in common with sober, careful pension managers. Vultures didn't need to know anything about pensions, and pension managers could safely ignore the distressed sector. There was no need, in short, for a book like this one.

Making Pensions Passé

As the 1980s rolled on, I went on maternity leave—doing my bit to improve the nation's future worker-to-retiree ratio, as one Labor Department official teased me. When I returned from my leave, I switched to covering state and local governments and the Washington regulatory scene. By the time I came back to pensions, as an editor, in the early 1990s, the mindset had drastically changed.

Defined contribution plans, especially the 401(k) version, now dominated the corporate retirement scene. In 1979, just 7 percent of the private-sector workforce had a defined contribution plan, while 28 percent had a traditional defined benefit pension, according to the Employee Benefit Research Institute, the Washington, DC, nonprofit organization that the pension world considers the ultimate source for data. Less than twenty years later, in 1998, the numbers had flipped: Some 27 percent of American private-sector workers had a defined contribution plan, and 7 percent had a traditional pension. The big mutual fund houses like Fidelity Investments and the Vanguard Group were climbing over each other for this part of the business, offering dozens of different investment choices, from staid corporate bonds to super-risky tech stocks. Bookstores were filled with guides about how to invest your 401(k) money and become a millionaire.

Companies had come to realize that defined contribution plans were a lot cheaper for them: They could limit the amount of money they were obligated to pay, yet still claim to be providing a pension—of sorts. This new type of plan also fit in with what seemed to be a growing do-it-yourself trend. Americans were going to Ikea to assemble their own furniture and surfing the Internet to do their own medical research. So why not decide how to invest their own retirement money? If they could build a dining room table, couldn't they read the stock tables? Defined contribution plans were now sexy, and defined benefit plans were boring old dinosaurs. In my pensions beat, my in-box was swamped with ideas for stories about 401(k) plans, and it was getting harder and harder to scrounge up anything new to say about defined benefits.

Traditional pension plans were certainly not disappearing en masse. Indeed, with the market boom of the 1990s, corporate pension trusts were earning such high returns on their investments that companies didn't need to take a penny out of profits to fund their payment promises (what's known in the business as a "contribution holiday"). By 2000, defined benefit systems were wallowing in more than $1.2 trillion in assets for barely $1 trillion in expected payouts. So there was certainly no reason to get rid of these golden eggs. However, there was very little growth in the number of employees enrolled in these plans. Almost no companies except the very smallest were introducing defined benefit plans—and the small plans were usually just glorified IRAs for the mom-and-pop owners. A significant number of companies took a middle-of-the-road approach, maintaining their plans for people already on staff but not letting new hires join. Occasionally, a flailing company in bankruptcy—Pan American World Airways in 1991, Sharon Steel Corporation in 1994, Eastern Air Lines in 1996—closed down its pension plan because it owed hundreds of millions of dollars in funding that it just didn't have. In those extreme cases, the federal government insurance agency called the Pension Benefit Guaranty Corporation (PBGC) took over the plan and kept on paying retirees most of their benefits. But on the whole, it was more or less assumed that these plans would hang on until the last surviving employee died off, maybe in the late twenty-first century.

Everything changed once more with the multipronged catastrophes of the early 2000s: the terrorist attacks of September 11, 2001; the tech-stock collapse; the scandals at Enron, WorldCom, and other big companies; the war in Iraq; and Hurricane Katrina and the ensuing jolt to the price of oil. All these calamities were piled on an economy whose manufacturing sector was already weakened by low-cost foreign competition. Company after company tumbled into bankruptcy, especially in the airline, steel, auto-parts, and textile industries.

And pension promises tumbled with them. Never mind a slow, gradual fadeout of defined benefits until the last retiree died. Never mind a solemn and eternal promise. Companies were throwing their pension plans overboard as fast as they could bail—Bethlehem Steel, LTV, Kemper Insurance Companies, US Airways, United Airlines, Kaiser Aluminum, Polaroid, Consolidated Freightways, National Steel, Weirton Steel. In each case, the company had promised its workers hundreds of millions or even several billion dollars in pensions. Now, in bankruptcy, the company said it could no longer afford to keep those promises and handed the obligation over to the PBGC. When Steven A. Kandarian became executive director in December 2001, the agency had a surplus of $10 billion to cover the pensions of people whose plans had been shut down. By the time he left a little more than two years later, it had a deficit of about $11 billion, having taken on all those abandoned pension plans.

Silver Lining

There was more to the story, however, than misfortune for retirees. Pension dumping wasn't always a total disaster. Indeed, it could be a central element in a company's potential recovery from bankruptcy. These multihundred-million- or multibillion-dollar pension promises were a fairly huge chunk of the company's overall liability—sometimes even the largest—so dumping them could improve the financial picture dramatically in one blow.

Although companies were loath to admit it publicly, their obligation to pay defined benefit pensions to their retired workers, year in and year out until the workers died, was turning out to be one of the easiest of their prebankruptcy debts to get rid of. It was certainly easier to escape than their tax bill, which the government never let a company skip, or payments to secured creditors. Unloading a pension commitment was often easier than trying to wriggle out of a trade debt or an unsecured loan. ERISA, the federal pension law, even had provisions explaining exactly how to escape the pension obligation it was supposed to protect. Companies might face opposition from their unions, but the sentiments of the unions themselves were often split, with workers who were still on the job willing to give up the pensions in a trade-off to protect their wages. The PBGC would pick up the full payment to retired workers 90 percent of the time anyway.

In other words, a company in bankruptcy could actually have its pension and dump it too: It could look like a nice guy to the vast majority of employees, telling them they'd get their full payments, while in fact wiping the whole hundred-million-dollar burden off the debt side of the ledger. This was a complete win-win. As Mike Johnston, who heads the retirement business at the big Illinois-based benefits consulting firm Hewitt Associates, puts it: "[Dumping a pension] is just part and parcel of the bankruptcy. Bankruptcy is about shedding your old debts, and an unfunded pension plan is just another big pool of debt. I can't think of a good reason not to do it."

Meanwhile, the world of bankruptcy investing had become larger and much more sophisticated. The bursting of the tech-stock bubble in 2000 brought in a slew of new acquisition candidates. A secondary market had developed in the 1990s in which investors could buy and resell their holdings. By the late 1990s, all kinds of players were piling onto this terrain, including private equity and hedge funds fat with cash and no place to put it. Their strategies varied, of course. Some were there for the quick profit taking; some looked for a long-term relationship; some even aimed to play an active role in managing the revival. Investors might debate the merits of staying public versus going private, taking a seat on the creditors' committee, or maintaining their freedom to trade, firing the old management or keeping it.

Few, if any, of these investors had ever put the pension fund into their fancy analytical calculations. After all, until ERISA in 1974, there had really been no structure for dumping a pension plan while in bankruptcy. And during the first post-ERISA decade the companies doing the dumping were small ones, not the type that big-time market players were likely to be interested in. Throughout the booming 1990s, of course, hardly any companies felt a need to terminate their pensions. However, as the 1990s slipped into the sagging twenty-first century and more and more big companies were dumping their pensions as an automatic part of bankruptcy, vultures began to pay attention. The defined benefit plan might be another morsel of hidden value in the bare corporate cupboard. If the company could save a few hundred million dollars by dumping without too much trouble, if the PBGC could be counted on to take over the debt, if there were no banks or other strong creditors to fight it, then in one swoop a savvy distressed investor could get rid of a huge chunk of a target company's liabilities, virtually cost free.

Suddenly, there was a new and very large piece of data for the vultures to chew over. In fact, sometimes vultures even demanded that a plan be dumped before they would consider investing. Suddenly, the worlds of vultures and pensions were no longer so far apart.

Backlash

As it turned out, the vultures were out of their league. How little they realized what they were getting into when they latched onto the pension fund ploy. They thought this was simply a new cache of hidden assets, but once they touched a company's pension plan, these investors were moving out of the shadows and into the klieg lights, beyond the realm of numbers and into the world of politics. That's because pension plans are as much about social policy as they are about finance.

Of course, thoughtful investors, including vultures, have always had to deal with social policy to some extent. They know that a company's prospects for successfully reorganizing out of bankruptcy depend on intangibles like employee morale and public reputation as much as on the numbers on a balance sheet. But pension dumping raised issues far beyond the investment norm. For instance, even if most retirees in a pension termination still get their full payment from the federal government via the PBGC, the company has outright announced that it has no qualms about breaking a promise it had once solemnly sworn to uphold. Whatever bond existed between the company and its employees has been transferred to the government. What does that do to the employees' faith in the company or their willingness to work hard? Pensions are also a key issue in union negotiations; so what kinds of pressures might the company's unions bring? Were the vultures making things worse by demanding that the pensions be junked? Was it really necessary to cut off the pension in order to keep the rest of the company alive? Most important, pensions go to the elderly, and the elderly vote. They are the single most powerful demographic force in U.S. politics. Tangling with Grandma is a far more risky venture than devouring a corporate carcass. This callousness was the public image the vultures had to counter: They were proposing to beef up their bottom line by stealing Grandma's pension check.

Vultures may have been clueless about how to cope with the political pressures of pension land, but pension managers were just as naïve about how to handle the avid new interest from vultures. Although managers had long ago shed their 60/40 strategy and were branching out into more risky instruments, they were accustomed to being the ones who did the buying, not the ones who were bought. And they certainly had no experience in having someone throw out the structure they'd spent their careers husbanding. They ran the very real risk of losing their jobs, being confronted with furious workers and retirees, or hurting their company's ability to recover. Higher-level corporate managers were better prepared for coping with buyout and acquisition offers, but they, too, had never had to include the pension fund in their calculations before.

After a spate of newspaper and magazine headlines in the early 2000s about retirees thrown out on the street, political pressure began to build. One key Republican senator hauled Kandarian of the PBGC into a hearing regarding the US Airways pilots' pension. Other politicians talked about tightening the laws. So did the AFL-CIO. At issue were billions of dollars in investor, corporate, union, and public money. Ironically, some of the investors themselves were big pension funds that had assets in hedge funds and private equity funds. Entire industrial sectors were facing bankruptcy, potentially dragging down tens of thousands of workers and retirees. Clearly, there was now more in play than pension plans like my grandfather's.

All the players—corporate management, investors, lawyers, money managers, politicians, workers, retirees, unions, customers, and the general public—had something at stake, and all needed to take a closer look at these new financial interactions. Now there was indeed a need for a book that could explain how both pensions and bankruptcy worked, how a pension fund is killed, and whether the skeleton that remains can thrive.

My old beat now offered a lot more to write about after all.

Pension Dumping

Part One

The Reasons

1 | The Dispensable Pension Plan

"It's become all too easy for companies to use the Chapter 11 process to rid themselves of so-called legacy costs, then go about their business."

—BRADLEY BELT, FORMER EXECUTIVE DIRECTOR, PBGC

JOHN A. CASESA probably knows General Motors as well as any outsider could. He started on the inside, working in marketing at GM headquarters in Detroit from 1986 to 1989 after earning his MBA from Dartmouth College's Amos Tuck School of Business Administration. From there he went to Wall Street for seventeen years as an industry analyst, ultimately heading the auto group at Merrill Lynch. For most of that time, Casesa ranked in *Institutional Investor*'s "All-America Research Team," the magazine's yearly list of most-respected analysts.

In early 2006, deciding to put his money where his analysis had been, Casesa established a small private partnership with a veteran car dealer to invest in the auto industry and provide advice to other investors. He began analyzing GM and the other auto companies to determine whether they would make good investments not just for other people's portfolios but also for his own. So when John Casesa talks car companies—and their pension funds—he's worth listening to.

And investors can certainly use any guidance they can get. The U.S. auto industry of the early twenty-first century is flooded with red ink and punctured with insecurity and unknowns. Almost every decision is shadowed by the big question: Will the company go bankrupt? But within that mass of doubts, investors can find one little bolt of security: If a car manufacturer—or, for that matter, a company in just about any traditional industry—files for bankruptcy, it can easily pick up a few hundred million dollars or more in savings by throwing out its pension plan. Never mind the union contract. Never mind the promises the company once made to its workers. In bankruptcy, all's fair. Coldhearted or not, the option to dump the pension may in fact

3

be what keeps the company alive. That's because for some investors, the deciding factor in making their investment is the confidence that the company can junk its pension costs. That leaves one problem: how to use the dumping maneuver to revive the company without slashing so drastically that there's nothing worth reviving.

An Industry on the Brink

Short and trim, with rimless eyeglasses and wavy, brown-gray hair, Casesa the investor-analyst outlined his view of the auto industry's future, the looming fear that the giant carmakers might file for bankruptcy, and the fate of their pension plans late in 2006 and again in spring of 2007 from the office space his fledgling company sublets, just west of Manhattan's prime midtown district. GM, Ford Motor, and Chrysler had to change virtually their entire operations models and dramatically rethink the way they worked with their suppliers, dealers, and unions, Casesa declared, in order to build more collaborative relationships and build the kinds of cars that would sell.

In considering whether to invest in a particular company, Casesa focused first on the relationship with parts suppliers. "The Big Three historically have been very powerful, very integrated, and very concentrated. The culture is 'we do things our way.' They demand the lowest price, they often change the deal after there's an agreement, and the volumes have been volatile." Although the Big Three generally won their price cuts over the years, the suppliers never had the money to invest in new technology, which ended up hurting everyone. The small parts makers had started fighting back, pushing for higher prices, but the only clout they seemed to have had was the threat of declaring bankruptcy. The automakers, Casesa warned, were "going to have to create some trust with the suppliers."

Labor relations, too, had to change: "The union gives concessions in tight times, then the union claws those concessions back in good times. That was when the business was cyclical. Now the problems are ongoing." For GM, Ford, and Chrysler, the biggest single problem by 2007 was the cost of health-care coverage that the automakers, in flusher days, had promised their retired workers, a cost that reached almost the triple-digit billions for all three companies combined. "These companies simply are not profitable enough to fulfill that obligation," said Casesa. The United Auto Workers (UAW) seemed to acknowledge that it had to make concessions, agreeing to painful cuts at the bankrupt parts maker Delphi and a new health-care arrangement at Goodyear Tire & Rubber. The UAW didn't even contest the sale of Chrysler to the kind of private equity firm—Cerberus Capital Management in New York—that unions usually hate. Nevertheless, the union struck GM for two days in late September 2007 and Chrysler for six hours in October. Health coverage was not the issue in either case; early on, the UAW had agreed to let GM shift the responsibility to a trust that the union would run, with a fixed amount of start-up funding from the company. Rather, what caused the walkout was a more traditional concern—job security. Clearly, the auto companies could neither buy off their workers with rich benefits nor bully them into concessions. They would have to learn to get along.

Good relations were just as essential on the production side of the equation. The companies were converting to flexible, modern facilities that could easily switch gears to make a variety of models, and such a dramatic change in operations could be achieved only with union cooperation. That would require giving the workforce some positive incentives. "The union needs to have a belief that in the future, there would be some growth, some new hires," said Casesa. How were the auto companies possibly going to conjure up that faith and cooperation with workers whose health benefits they'd just lopped off?

There were also problems associated with the products themselves—the big, gas-guzzling cars with a reputation for poor quality. The long development cycles required for introducing more appealing choices meant it would take years to regain market share, but at least the companies could—indeed, had to—try to stop any further slippage.

With such a heavy load of pressures, is there any hope for the American auto industry? Are the Big Three doomed to bankruptcy? Should investors shut the door and look elsewhere? During our first conversation, Casesa pegged the possibility of bankruptcy at GM as "a very real threat." Six months later, with Cerberus's acquisition of Chrysler, he was more optimistic, suggesting that investors might want to stick around and give the industry the fresh capital it would need to retool, design new models, and change its public image. Four months after that, as the credit markets dried up in panic, almost stymieing the Chrysler deal, he turned more cautious again. The UAW strike briefly brought the B-word (bankruptcy) to the fore, but the settlement revived Casesa's optimism.

In all of his analyses of the industry's woes and the potential for collapse, GM's $95 billion pension fund and Ford's $42 billion plan play almost no culpable role. "Very rarely is an underfunded pension plan the sole or even the main reason for a bankruptcy filing," according to Casesa. "The root cause is usually operational—the company is out of touch with its market, it hasn't adapted to changes in customers' preferences." For that matter, as of those conversations in 2007, GM actually had more than enough money to pay the pensions it had promised its retired workers, by the most commonly used calculations, although not by the method the government prefers.

Even so, Casesa didn't hesitate for a second when he predicted what would happen to the pension fund if one of the auto giants actually went bankrupt. "In the event that a GM or a Ford filed [for bankruptcy], I think termination of the pension plan would be at the top of the list of proposals because they are very expensive, uncompetitive plans. The plan wouldn't be the main issue, but it's an important issue. Also, it's a problem you can eliminate"—he snapped his fingers—"like that."

Promises to Break

It's not just the auto industry where pensions are at risk. If Casesa specialized in metals, airlines, textiles, auto parts, utilities, chemicals, or durable goods, he might make the same prediction. In those and other old-line, unionized, largely manufacturing or regulated industries, when a company hits a major financial bump, one of the first expenses to be jettisoned is the pension plan. It's become almost an automatic reflex, an easy choice.

Once upon a time, pensions were unbreakable promises, money that workers could count on until the day they died. Thanks to these steady checks, month after month, employees were supposed to have no nasty surprises in retirement. Nowadays, however, it's a surprise when a bankrupt company *doesn't* dump its plan.

Corporate managers may suffer occasional qualms of conscience over breaking those promises. But just about every financial, legal, business, social, and investor pressure pushes the bankrupt company toward this choice.

The key pressures are financial, and the solution seems obvious. Troubled companies may be losing tens or hundreds of millions of dollars, even billions, every year in their basic operations. At the same time, they put tens or hundreds of millions of dollars, even billions, into their pension plans to cover annual payments to retirees that stretch into infinity. If these companies haven't built up enough assets in their pension trusts to cover those payments, they will have to dig into the operating budget for those millions and billions. How can they possibly afford to do that? The pat answer is they can't. So they unload the problem. Bethlehem Steel in 2003 shed a pension plan that was $3.7 billion short of what it needed. US Airways Group was $2.8 billion in the hole (in two separate bankruptcies, in 2003 and 2005); Kemper Insurance Companies, nearly $570 million in 2005. The record setter—as of 2007—was United Airlines: more than $7 billion in 2005.

Aren't there any laws against breaking a contract? Actually, the bankruptcy, pension, and labor laws do not discourage the practice in any meaningful way. Pension claims rank among the lowest priorities in bankruptcies, and the government agency that's supposed to protect pensions lacks the authority to force companies to keep the plans going. Unions are generally too weak to argue. Besides, they have more important battles to fight.

Ordinary business pressures also push pensions onto the scrap heap. After all, who is getting all those tens of millions of dollars in pension payments? People who don't even work at the company any more. If these financially shaky businesses do have any spare cash, shouldn't it go into something that will actually help build a future, such as acquisitions, R&D, new facilities, or compensation packages to attract new employees rather than handouts to pacify retired ones? True, a company trying to climb back up from bankruptcy may well need a good benefits package to lure wary potential employees. But that package doesn't have to include a pension plan. Ever since the 1980s, even healthy companies have been shedding their traditional pension systems in favor of 401(k)-style plans that are generally less expensive and whose costs are more predictable. So there's probably no competitive reason to keep the old pension plan.

There really isn't a choice. If a financially weak company hopes to have a second chance at survival, it will require new capital. Most likely, that capital will have to come from large investors. And those investors usually expect to see the pension plan dumped. They may refuse to even look at a company that doesn't wield the ax. When Aloha Airlines was negotiating its reorganization from bankruptcy in 2005, it told the federal district court that no one was willing to provide financing as long as it was carrying a $155 million pension underfunding. Over the objections of the government's chief pension agency, the court allowed Aloha to terminate its plans, and a partnership headed by the reclusive California supermarket mogul (and friend of former president Bill Clinton) Ronald Burkle and former football star Willie Gault (of the Chicago Bears and Los Angeles Raiders) promptly invested roughly $100 million in cash and debt financing.

KPS Special Situations Funds in New York, which buys the assets of bankrupt companies at auction, is an even more striking example of how casually investors dismiss pension plans. KPS is considered so sympathetic to the employees' plight that unions try to persuade it to purchase their faltering companies. Cofounder Michael Psaros grew up in union country—Weirton, West Virginia—where his father, his great-grandfather, and "most of the male members of [his] extended family" of Greek immigrants worked in the local steel mills. Psaros was in eighth grade in 1982 when National Steel announced that it would no longer invest any capital in the Weirton plant, which employed nearly half the area residents. Financial adviser Eugene Keilin—who later became the K to Psaros's P in KPS—helped the plant's independent steel union arrange a $66 million employee buyout to save the company and its jobs. The buyout kept Weirton alive for twenty-two years, although the steelmaker ultimately went bankrupt again.

KPS, Psaros proudly insists, always tries to work closely with the unions of the companies the firm acquires and to offer retirement plans, such as 401(k) plans, and health benefits. At least one of its investors is a large pension fund, and unions sometimes co-own its holdings through employee stock-ownership plans. "To me it's inconceivable that any investor would go into a distressed or bankrupt company and try to achieve an investment return by being overtly hostile to a union," Psaros says. "We would never proceed with a purchase unless our purchase was supported by the national union and the local union, and the collective-bargaining agreements were ratified." As for offering employees a retirement plan, he adds, "I have never met a union leader who didn't believe providing some kind of pension benefit is absolutely critical to what the union stands for and what it tries to be."

And what if a company he acquires has an underfunded pension plan? As a buyer at auction, KPS can reject or assume any of the existing liabilities it wants. It could agree to maintain the pension plan, keep the promises to those union workers, and put more money in. But KPS never does.

If even a labor-friendly investor like Psaros won't retain an old pension plan, is there any reason for any company in the dire straits of bankruptcy to do so?

Commitment Redefined

The fact that companies see their pension payments as a burden is a sad and significant change in itself. From the first North American pension plan, established in 1874, through the golden age of U.S. industrialization in the 1940s and 1950s, and well into the 1970s, the defined benefit pension became solidified in business law, practice, and expectation. If workers stayed on the job a certain number of years, their employers made a promise to pay them a specific amount of money after they retired. The companies put millions of dollars each year into pension trust accounts to cover those promises and invested the money conservatively, with an eye toward long-term gains, typically in a mix of 60 percent bonds and 40 percent stocks. For their part, the workers agreed to take less cash in their paychecks up front, in return for the guarantee that they would essentially get that money later, when they could no longer work. In 1974, the process was codified in a federal law called the Employee Retirement Income Security Act (ERISA).

To the companies, their employees, and their actuaries, these promises—known as legacy costs—were sacrosanct, stronger perhaps than any other business contract. "There's a great sensitivity to dealing with a pension plan," says James Sprayregen, one of the bankruptcy world's preeminent lawyers during the sixteen years he spent as a partner at Kirkland & Ellis in Chicago before moving to Goldman Sachs in 2006 as a managing director. "There's a whole range of legal issues, there are social issues, there's keeping your employee base with their morale sufficiently high that they're showing up to work, there are sociopolitical issues. These programs are intended to help people live their lives relatively comfortably for an indefinite period." What company would want to be seen as a callous ogre who would throw white-haired Grandma out onto the street after a lifetime of faithful work?

During the decades following the passage of ERISA, however, the world changed. The American economy stumbled; foreign competitors began selling similar goods for a fraction of the domestic price; new technology made the industrial giants' products obsolete. For a variety of reasons, including those that Casesa, the auto analyst, described, some of the companies that had so optimistically promised to take care of their employees, forever, fell into financial trouble, filed for bankruptcy, and either liquidated or tried to reorganize under Chapter 11 of the Bankruptcy Code. As part of the reorganization process, firms have the right to abrogate or renegotiate most of the business obligations they accumulated before filing. Shareholders' equity is wiped out. Office and equipment leases can be canceled. Unions, under the gun, almost always make concessions.

And, as several thousand companies have discovered, under both ERISA and the Bankruptcy Code, a pension promise too can be broken. In bankruptcy, funding for a pension plan is merely another debt to be discarded, no more sacred than a contract to buy pencils. "It's a claim, no different than someone having additional debt," says Edward Shapiro, one of four partners in the hedge fund PAR Capital Management in Boston, which invests more than $1.5 billion in an eclectic mix of industries. Among his holdings: US Airways, after its second bankruptcy.

"It's become all too easy for companies to use the Chapter 11 process to rid themselves of so-called legacy costs and then go about their business. It's a backdoor industrial policy being carried out through the federal government," complains Bradley Belt, the former investment banker and consultant who headed the federal agency that backstops pensions, the Pension Benefit Guaranty Corporation (PBGC), from April 2004 through May 2006. Belt had a front-row seat at this phenomenon because it is the PBGC that takes over the retirement plans when companies dump them. During his tenure, Belt was handed nearly two hundred such underfunded pension plans, with a combined shortfall of more than $9.7 billion. Overall, between 1975 and 2007, more than 3,500 financially troubled or bankrupt companies took that escape route.

As was clear in Casesa's analysis of GM, it hardly matters whether the pension plan even plays a major role in the company's troubles. Steelmaker LTV had plenty of reasons to file for bankruptcy in 1986; its $2.3 billion pension underfunding was only one of them. Recession had chilled its markets, lower-priced competition was moving in from abroad, and the federal Environmental Protection Agency was getting tough about pollution throughout the industry. But there was no question what would happen to the pensions. Karen E. Wagner, an attorney with Davis Polk & Wardwell, who was one of the five main lawyers representing the steelmaker in the bankruptcy filing, says matter-of-factly: "It was assumed that the pension plans would have to be modified or terminated." Even attorney Sprayregen, for all his professed sensitivity to the special promise of the pension plan, advised United Airlines during its bankruptcy on how to terminate its plans.

After all, the results would seem to speak for themselves: Once LTV and Bethlehem Steel dumped their underfunded pension plans, financier Wilbur L. Ross Jr. bought them, kept them running, packaged them into a new company called International Steel Group, added three more foundering steelmakers, and sold the lot to Netherlands-based Mittal Steel barely three years later for a profit of about $2.5 billion. United Airlines and US Airways both recorded respectable stock jumps within a year and a half of emerging, pensionless, from bankruptcy; US Airways was strong enough to make a takeover bid—albeit unsuccessfully—for yet another carrier that dumped a pension plan in bankruptcy, Delta Air Lines.

What happened to the promise? It simply became too expensive to keep.

2 Last in Line: The Retiree

"You're paying pensions to retirees, who have nothing to do with the ongoing operations. From an investor's standpoint, you're looking for what gives you value."

—HARVEY R. MILLER, BANKRUPTCY LAWYER, WEIL, GOTSHAL & MANGES LLP

ETHICAL QUALMS don't stop a termination. Nor can the pension plan expect much support from the legal process of bankruptcy. As far as the bankruptcy laws go, pensions are simply another unsecured prepetition debt, one of the obligations a company incurred before the bankruptcy petition was filed, no different from an account payable for bubble wrap or the rent on an office lease. There is nothing special about pension obligations. Just like all the other unsecured debts, the pension debt is subject to negotiation during the reorganization process, and the bankruptcy judge must approve any outcome. If the pension was part of a union contract, a termination must be negotiated with the union, but that's no different from what happens with any collectively bargained benefit. And in any case, if the union won't agree to the termination, the company can bypass it and appeal straight to the judge, as United Airlines successfully did in 2005. The PBGC is just another creditor—like a landlord, a bubble wrap supplier, or a bank lender—all of them haggling over how many pennies on the dollar they will receive from the company's remaining assets.

True, the PBGC has to agree to the termination, and it doesn't welcome underfunded pension plans with milk and cookies. It will ask tough questions, hoping to find some unexplored sources of revenue within the firm that can keep the pension plan going, such as divestitures, help from a parent company, or more aggressive penny-pinching. The PBGC also gets assistance from outside experts in analyzing a bankrupt business's financials. "They would use standard industrial metrics—credit and cash-flow metrics," says Brad Belt, the agency's former executive director. The experts pose

13

questions like, "Where are they cutting costs in bankruptcy? What is the projected secured cash flow? What are the required contributions?" Managers might be grilled as to why they are putting millions of dollars into expansion instead of using that money to fund the pension plan and whether they might share the pain by giving up a bit of their compensation. When Pan American World Airways sought to terminate its plan in 1991, the PBGC even analyzed whether it could survive if it spun off its profitable New York–Boston–Washington, DC, shuttle, recalls William G. Beyer, who spent more than a quarter century at the agency, from 1976 to 2004, as a lawyer, assistant general counsel, and deputy general counsel. (Pan Am terminated the pension plan but eventually collapsed anyway.) If the company claims that only one investor is willing to provide ongoing financing and that investor insists on dumping the plan, as in the Aloha Airlines case, the PBGC will push hard to make sure the company really has tried to find other deep pockets.

In the end, however, if the company is in such bad shape that it has filed for bankruptcy protection, the PBGC will almost always agree to let its pension go under. Gary Pastorius, a spokesman for the agency, estimates that the PBGC asks the bankruptcy judge to reject a termination only about 10 percent of the time. "In a sense we oppose them all. We want to see defined benefit plans continue," he says. "But in a bankruptcy, it's usually clear enough that maintaining the plan is too big a burden." The only question then is pretty much the same one all the other creditors are asking: How much of the company's assets can the PBGC get in repayment for the obligations—the pensions—that it is assuming?

Bankruptcy Clout

The pension plan is thus no harder to get rid of than any other corporate debt. In fact, it's often easier. Officially, pension debt has lower priority than debts like taxes and lawyers' fees; in practice, it ranks even lower than the debts that are supposed to be equal in priority. Far from being the lead player—a fitting role for a sacrosanct promise—pensions are actually the extras in the bankruptcy case.

That's largely because dumping the pension obligation is one of the few ways these companies can find big savings in one shot, explains Deirdre A. Martini. Petite, blonde, and energetic, quick with a laugh or a hug, Martini spent two and a half years, until April 2006, as the U.S. Trustee—the Justice Department official overseeing bankruptcy cases—for the New York City region, one of the two most influential bankruptcy venues in the nation. Then she moved to CIT Group to become a managing director and senior restructuring adviser, helping to provide loans to companies in bankruptcy while they attempt to restructure. "You can get only so much from operations and cash flow," Martini says, laying out the alternatives. "You can only borrow so much from the banks and nontraditional lending sources. You have to retain competent management. That management [must be paid] at a market rate of compensation, but when you look at the whole balance sheet and focus on the liabilities, you'll find management's compensation is minuscule. This pool of sacrifice, where you can get this enormous cost savings, unfortunately, lies with the employees."

Clearly, the thought that employees might bear the brunt of the sacrifices troubles Martini. Moreover, just how much management needs to be paid is certainly a debatable issue. For instance, a hail of protest erupted over the multimillion-dollar pay, benefits, and stock-option packages given to management at United Airlines as it emerged from bankruptcy. Also, Congress in 2005 enacted changes to the bankruptcy law that supposedly forbade extra retention payments to key executives at companies in bankruptcy unless the executives had received other job offers. However, two years later most judges were still allowing lavish payments.

"Are the employees now the sacrificial lambs of the reemerged company? The Code allows for it," says Martini. "I do not believe it's a good thing, because they are the lambs who can probably least afford it. It's like reneging on a promise. Employees were given their benefits as part of their employment promise." She offered to rerun the numbers from some sample companies to see if, as she put it, "you could realign the percentages" to find another significant source of cash. A month and a half later, she returned, unsuccessful. "It's a lot more complicated than coming up with just a mathematical formula to move money from one bucket, meaning executive compensation, to another, meaning employee benefits," she explained. "Even if management were to take a drastic reduction in their compensation, it would not be enough to fund the deficit for a massive workforce.

When you look at all the players in a bankruptcy case, no one is incentivized, given existing law, to give up anything for the rank and file. Professionals do not want to fund the Chapter 11 by virtue of a substantial discount of their fees. As for trade creditors, if you shipped a thousand rolls of toilet paper to a manufacturing plant, you want to get paid for those goods."

Why do trade creditors or management have more clout than the pension fund? Consider LTV again. Both the steelmaker and its creditors naturally looked for savings wherever they could, such as in the company's contracts for shipping and for purchasing basic supplies like coke and iron ore, recalls Mark S. Wintner, an attorney with Stroock & Stroock & Lavan, one of literally dozens of law firms that represented LTV creditors during the seven-year bankruptcy negotiations. The problem is that if a manufacturer is going to emerge and continue making steel, it will need an ongoing source of coke and iron ore. That gives it a certain incentive to maintain good relations with those suppliers and to honor a high percentage of their claims. Sure, the steelmaker could have tried using other suppliers. But if word had spread in the coke industry that LTV stiffed its old suppliers, it might have been hard to find anyone else to provide the vital items on decent terms. By contrast, the pension funds made an easy target, Wintner says, because "[the pension benefit] is a historical liability that is somewhat separate from its corporate business."

Lynn M. LoPucki, a law professor at the University of California, Los Angeles, argues in his 2005 book *Courting Failure* that the need to appease these so-called critical vendors can overcome the Bankruptcy Code's requirement that all unsecured creditors in the same class are supposed to be treated equally:

> Consider the example of a reorganizing debtor that manufactures an appliance from purchased parts, some of which are made by Motorola. To continue in business after filing the bankruptcy case, this debtor may need to buy more parts from Motorola. If so, Motorola is, for this debtor, a critical vendor.
>
> What if Motorola refuses to sell more parts to the debtor until the debtor pays in full the debt owing for parts Motorola sold the debtor before bankruptcy? . . . [Bankruptcy courts traditionally held the following view:] Payment of a prepetition

debt, even to a critical vendor, violated the Bankruptcy Code because it enabled some unsecured creditors to recover a greater portion of the debts owing to them than others. Courts rarely approved them.

Maintaining this hard line against critical vendor payments required effort and risk on the part of reorganizing debtors. . . . For any particular debtor, the path of least resistance was to give in to the demands of its critical vendors, pay them with other creditors' money, and leave the line-holding duties to others.

By contrast, who gets stiffed when a company sheds its pension plan? Mainly, it's people the company doesn't need any more—those who have stopped working. "You're paying pensions to retirees, who have nothing to do with the ongoing operations. It's unfortunate, but retirees don't contribute any benefit to the company," Harvey R. Miller, the silver-haired, impeccably tailored, impeccably composed, veteran bankruptcy lawyer, says in his quiet, even voice. "From an investor's standpoint, you're looking for what gives you value."

In a long career, Miller built the bankruptcy practice at the law firm Weil, Gotshal & Manges in Manhattan, switched to the investment-banking firm Greenhill & Co. as vice chairman, and then returned to Weil, Gotshal. During that time, he worked pretty much every side of the pension-bankruptcy equation, representing Bethlehem Steel as the target when it was bought by Wilbur Ross, America West Airlines as the acquirer when it bought US Airways after Chapter 11, and even the PBGC in its fight with United Airlines over the size of the pension underfunding. His assessment of the value of retirees may sound heartless, but Miller is hardly the only one making this cold calculation. On the union side, his views are echoed—bitterly—by Sherwin S. Kaplan, an attorney with Thelen Reid Brown Raysman & Steiner, who spent twenty-three years doing pensions litigation at the Department of Labor and who later represented pilots and retired pilots in their pension fights in the bankruptcies of US Airways and Delta Air Lines. "The active pilots have a negotiating tool," he says: "'Without us, your planes sit on the ground.' The company has to listen to the active pilots. The retirees have already done their work and they're gone. They really have nobody on their side."

At Delta, the retirees were granted approximately $800 million worth of unsecured claims; the active pilots, more than $2 billion in claims, plus a $650 million secured note.

Ultimately, the retirees may not be hurt very much. When the PBGC takes over terminated plans, it continues to pay the pensions, up to a maximum amount that's adjusted each year for inflation. That covers the full pensions of about 84 percent of the workforce. The main exceptions are highly paid employees like airline pilots with proportionately richer pensions, employees who retire early, and those who had gotten a benefit increase within five years of the bankruptcy filing.

There are—theoretically—other ways to save money on the pension plan itself. For example, the company could keep its debt from getting worse by freezing the plan in place, so that new employees can't join and current employees can't build up more credits. However, that doesn't get rid of the existing debt; in fact, it makes things worse, at least temporarily, by shutting off the inflow of contributions from new hires. Another possibility is to fiddle with the investment mix, increasing the stock allocation in hopes of a big return. However, many financiers say that's exactly the wrong way to go because it exposes the pension fund to more risk. Best of all would be to find the money to pay the debt by cost-cutting elsewhere, but if money were that easy to come by, the company wouldn't be on the edge of bankruptcy to begin with.

When Unions Give In

The people who are still on the job are hardly immune to the crunch when a pension plan is dumped, of course. They probably hope to retire themselves some day and enjoy those nice guaranteed pensions. At old-line industries, such as autos and steel, working at the plant is often a family tradition, and current employees may have parents who have retired and face shrunken pensions.

But the terminations are far from the worst thing happening to these workers. In the midst of bankruptcy, "companies are doing so many other things that are unpleasant to employees at the same time, it's hard to tease out the effect" of the pension loss, says Peter Cappelli, director of the Center for Human Resources at the Wharton School of the University of Pennsylvania. Employees may have their wages cut or be forced to take on more responsibility with no hike in pay. Some of the fringe benefits that made the workplace more pleasant are probably gone. Most important, they're worried about losing their jobs in the next round of layoffs. Compared with unemployment, what's so bad about a theoretical pension loss? It won't pinch their current paychecks. Furthermore, if they look around at benefits elsewhere, they can see that fewer and fewer colleagues are getting guaranteed pensions even at companies that are not in bankruptcy. Throughout the United States, the traditional defined benefit plans are being replaced by less-generous defined contribution accounts (more on that trend in Chapter 3).

That is where the company usually draws a line—between those who are working now and those who are no longer working. If the company pays the full pensions it has promised to everyone as planned, management will say, it will go out of business entirely. If it can save money on the pensions, it will have enough to keep going. Even some unions have come to accept this trade-off. Losing the pensions but keeping most of the jobs is better than losing everything. And in the end, the employees may not have a choice. They lack the clout to stop the termination in bankruptcy court.

All they can do is negotiate the best terms possible. Take for example Unite Here, created in 2004 as the union of two unions, representing some 450,000 workers and 400,000 retirees in the textile, hotel, and restaurant industries. Its headquarters are in the heart of New York's fashion district, in an airy, modern office done in bright bursts of primary red, white, and blue, with red pillars, slate-blue couches, blue walls, and white walls. In stark contrast, an antique Singer treadle sewing machine stands on display in the lobby.

Among the members of Unite Here are one thousand people at Cone Mills, a manufacturer of denim and home-furnishing fabrics in Greensboro, North Carolina, that started operating back in 1891. Pummeled by low-cost imports from Asia, Cone Mills filed for bankruptcy in September 2003. At that point, the pension plan had only about $80 million in assets to cover some $139 million that it had promised in benefits. "Very few players were interested" in acquiring the faltering company, recalls Bruce Raynor, Unite Here's general president. After all, what smart entrepreneur would still be manufacturing textiles in the United States? "Ill-conceived global rules of trade continue to drive production to the lowest-cost countries with the least amount of rights and the lowest pay," Raynor snaps. "If it's simply left to pure economics, we drive production out of the First World into the Third World." Raynor, of course, vehemently disagrees with the "pure economics" rationale for shifting production to low-cost countries, contending that it's shortsighted. "The future is having some Western owners who believe in having a global platform that will protect some measure of Western manufacturing, as opposed to [setting up shop only in] the cheapest places." Cost is important, he argues, but how about "the technology, the service, fixing any problems?" He acknowledges, however, that not too many businesspeople share that view.

Wilbur Ross is one of the few who does, Raynor feels. After spending nearly a quarter century at Rothschild, running its bankruptcy-restructuring advisery practice and becoming one of Wall Street's go-to experts in that specialty, Ross had taken the leap to start his own fund for distressed investing—just as the tech bubble burst in 2000. He acquired LTV, then Bethlehem; more important, he kept them running in his International Steel Group. In 2003, he made a bid for textile manufacturer Burlington Industries, which was not represented by Unite Here. Even before the Burlington deal had closed, Raynor heard that Ross might be interested in buying Cone's assets at auction, hoping to create the same kind of conglomerate in textiles that he'd done in steel. "We were eager to bring in an owner who had respect for unions and a commitment to a global platform," Raynor says. "There were other players we did not consider committed to the facility, committed to working with the unions. We were hoping to save the plants and the jobs and the wage rates." The only other candidate Raynor will name is financier Carl Icahn, who indeed has a rougher reputation and who would later beat out Ross for control of another bankrupt textile company, WestPoint Stevens, in June 2005.

Ross paid $46 million in cash to acquire the Cone assets, and he and Unite Here worked out a deal. According to Raynor, the new owner recalled about two hundred union workers who had been laid off, to bring the Cone workforce back up to one thousand. Raynor said Ross did that by shifting work from nonunion plants he owned elsewhere in the state. The union's contracted pay levels were untouched. And the pension system was dumped.

Skeptics say that the reason unions often sign on to this sort of bargain with the devil is that unions generally represent active employees, not retirees. Their own members don't feel the impact. Kaplan, the retired-pilots' lawyer, is bitter about the Air Line Pilots Association's acceptance of a termination at US Airways that gave current pilots a replacement defined contribution plan but cost retirees as much as half of their pensions. "They had to make a decision between active workers and retirees, and they decided not to represent retirees at all," he argues.

Raynor, for his part, asserts that he would not agree to a Cone Mills–type deal in just any situation—not, for example, for his hotel, food service, or industrial cleaning members, which don't face competition from low-cost imports. At Cone, he says, "that was a deal we made as a consequence of saving a thousand union textile jobs in North Carolina. I was not happy with [giving up the pension]. I would rather have given up nothing. But that was worth the trade."

3 Pension-Free and Ready to Compete—Or Not?

"The easiest thing for any company to do is dump. They're going to be better off financially if they get rid of this thing."

—RANDOLF HURST HARDOCK, BENEFITS LAWYER, DAVIS & HARMAN LLP

SOON AFTER Wheeling-Pittsburgh Steel emerged from Chapter 11 in 1990, Ron Gebhardtsbauer, then the PBGC's chief actuary, was driving through Pittsburgh, Pennsylvania, the steel company's original headquarters. "I remember seeing those signs, 'We're Wheeling-Pittsburgh, a lean and mean company,'" he recalls. "And that was pretty frustrating. I thought, yeah, you can compete, because we've taken over the pension."

During a five-year bankruptcy battle involving three different sets of feuding investors, a ninety-eight-day strike by the United Steelworkers of America, and the ouster of Wheeling-Pittsburgh's CEO, the steel giant dumped its pension plan and its $500 million deficit in the lap of the PBGC. The company was then able to strike a deal with the Steelworkers for relatively small wage reductions, and it emerged under the aegis of a holding company created by investor Ronald LaBow. Journalist Hilary Rosenberg, in her 1992 book *The Vulture Investors*, calculated how the major investors came out. Oppenheimer & Co. and its customers, having put up about $66 million to purchase bank debt and unsecured debt, "more than doubled their investment, for a total profit of about $74 million—some spread over three years, some over two." LaBow's group, which provided $185 million in stages, "received $193.5 million in notes plus 54 percent of the stock . . . for a total value of about $270 million." That might not seem like much, especially since most of the investment was tied up for three and a half years of negotiations, Rosenberg writes. But considering that much of the stake was borrowed, the returns "appeared to

23

be impressive." Nevertheless, the third investor, Goldman Sachs, "recouped less than a third" of the $14 million it spent on Wheeling-Pittsburgh equity, not counting the $4 million in fees it reportedly paid. For its part, Wheeling-Pittsburgh lasted ten more years as part of LaBow's holding company, WHX Corporation, before filing for bankruptcy again and shedding a new set of pension plans with a $143 million deficit.

Winning Without a Plan

Although it's not a classic case of happily ever after, the story of Wheeling-Pittsburgh has a pretty happy ending as bankruptcies go, thanks in large part to the pension maneuver. The signs that annoyed Gebhardtsbauer in Pittsburgh sum up exactly what investors expect. Freed from the multimillion-dollar burden of paying for retirement promises, troubled companies have more money to devote to capital expenditures, R&D, marketing, salaries, and whatever else it takes to improve their business. Thus, they should be in better shape to square off against the competition.

Looking just at labor costs, the competition typically comes in three basic forms. One is the ultra-low-cost manufacturers in Asia, Eastern Europe, and Latin America—the kind Raynor of Unite Here worries about. Compared to those countries' labor costs, any pension savings will be essentially meaningless. The gap in labor costs, including wages, health care, vacations, overtime, and other employee benefits, as well as pensions, is just too wide. The minimum wage in the United States as of summer 2007 was $5.85 an hour; the average pay in China about that same time was $160 a month. That doesn't mean a company shouldn't try to achieve efficiencies wherever it can, including from pensions. The point is that those savings will have to be applied to broader corporate purposes, not to a one-on-one labor comparison. To compete against China without simply giving up and outsourcing, U.S. manufacturers have to focus more on Raynor's arguments about the convenience and technological sophistication of a U.S. supplier and the value of a global platform, rather than comparing wage and benefits rates.

A second group of competitors—and the arena where pension savings can really pay off—is the domestic rivals that continue to offer defined benefit plans. Yes, despite the bankruptcies and terminations, these plans still exist. Although the number has been sliding dramatically since the late 1980s, nearly twenty-nine thousand private-sector employers were offering traditional pensions as recently as 2005, according to the PBGC.

Companies in a given industry start out more or less even in the pensions scale. Every year their workers build up more credits toward their retirement pay, which the companies must provide for in their pension trusts. While factors like staff turnover, pay rates, the number of years the company has been in business, the size of the workforce, and the specific benefits offered will affect the exact value of the pension promises among the various companies, they will be within the same order of magnitude. This balance is thrown askew, however, once a major company, such as Wheeling-Pittsburgh, LTV, or US Airways, files for bankruptcy, transfers its pension plan to the PBGC, and no longer has to shell out hundreds of millions of dollars for all the old, built-up credits. Naturally, the rest of the field will try to get the same bargain for themselves. "There is a certain domino effect," says Brad Belt, the former PBGC executive director. "When you have companies in an intensely competitive industry and some of them are able to offload and have the federal government effectively subsidize their labor costs, that puts a lot of pressure on the rivals." US Airways and United terminated most of their pension plans in 2005; a year later, in August 2006, Delta shed its pilots' plan, and Northwest Airlines threatened to do likewise unless Congress eased the rules on pension funding. Congress finally did, but the Pension Protection Act of 2006 only gave the airlines more time to fund the pensions; it didn't eliminate the funding requirement altogether. The fact that so many competitors no longer have to pay pensions at all, Gebhardtsbauer, the former PBGC actuary, warns, "will make it tougher for American [Airlines] and Continental [Airlines]," two major carriers that still maintain comprehensive defined benefit programs.

The same domino effect occurred in the steel industry, although LTV tried to get an extra leg up on its competition. Almost as soon as it terminated its pension plans, the steelmaker turned around and started up a new "follow-on" program that the PBGC claimed violated the intent of ERISA. The LTV arrangement would have allowed the company essentially to keep offering its workforce the same pensions as before termination, while paying only for the value of benefits earned in the future. Who would pay for all the years' worth of benefits the workers had earned up until then, which was by far the most expensive part? The PBGC. In other words, LTV would be providing a benefit equivalent to its rivals' but not paying for it. The PBGC sued. Five other steelmakers filed a brief supporting the PBGC's position, arguing that the maneuver would give LTV a "sizable competitive edge" equivalent to $20 per ton. "They didn't say, 'What a great idea; we should be able to do this too,'" notes Mark Wintner, the attorney for the LTV creditors' committee. "They took the opposite position, that LTV should not be allowed to shed a liability that gives it an unfair competitive edge."

The 401(k) Advantage

The third—and most interesting—type of labor competition comes from domestic rivals that offer either no retirement plan or the relatively inexpensive defined contribution variety. Of these, the most widely used is the 401(k), named after the section of the tax code that inadvertently authorized it. In these retirement programs, the company does not guarantee any particular payments to its workers. Rather, while they're still working, employees put aside their own cash in special savings accounts set up under the company's aegis. As an incentive, savers pay no federal taxes on this money until they retire, and sometimes the employer will match a portion of what the workers contribute, typically 50 percent of the contribution up to 6 percent of salary. The company determines which investment options will be available, handles all the paperwork, and generally offers at least some basic financial education, but all the investment decisions are up to the employee. Thus, whether a person ultimately has any nest egg to retire on depends almost entirely on whether he or she put money into these accounts, how much was saved, the luck of the markets, and how savvy the investment choices were. The defined contribution plan has been spreading rapidly since the 1980s, apart from the phenomenon of bankruptcy and termination; and by the 1990s, it had become more common than defined benefit plans.

Companies that dump their traditional defined benefit plans and then face rivals with defined contribution programs don't pocket 100 percent of the savings from eliminating the pension obligation. As they do with any labor cost, the companies must match the competition. If the rest of the industry offers 401(k) plans, the pension dumpers will have to introduce this benefit, as well. So the key question becomes, how much does a company save by substituting a 401(k) for a traditional pension?

The answer may be disappointing. "The cost of a defined benefit plan depends tremendously on the worker mix. It's all over the place. You can even design a defined benefit plan to be cheaper" than a 401(k), says Olivia Mitchell, one of the country's top pension experts and the executive director of the half-century-old Pension Research Council, a think tank based at the Wharton School. As noted earlier, the generosity of the benefits, along with the ages, salaries, size, and staying power of the workforce, all influence the cost. To give just one example: In a traditional plan, people can't take out their money until they retire, and they generally have no vested right to any of it until they've been at a company for five years. With a 401(k), however, people can take their vested money with them any time they leave the company, for whatever reason, not just at retirement. So a company with a 401(k) that matches 50 percent of contributions, with most of the employees contributing a high percentage of their salary, could well end up paying out more than a company with a traditional pension and heavy turnover. What's more, the company with a 401(k) also fares worse in a bull market. The company with the defined benefit plan gets the windfall from the market returns, which may even cover the full cost of paying for that year's benefit accruals. At the company with the 401(k), the returns pile up in each employee's individual account, not in the company coffers; yet the company still has to pay the full match.

Beyond the financial pros and cons, traditional pensions have some hard-to-quantify bonuses in the human resources (HR) arena. Because the size of the pension rises exponentially with age and years of work, defined benefits serve as a way to retain experienced scientific researchers, middle managers, and other key professionals who might otherwise take their institutional know-how to the highest bidder. If they have to start accruing a pension from year one at a new job, they will never reach the level they could if they stayed thirty years at the old place. Also, by adjusting the payout formula, a company can somewhat manipulate its staffing flow. It can offer early retirement incentives that let people retire before age sixty-five with full benefits, or set a cutoff date after which benefits no longer rise, in order to nudge middle-aged workers out the door without the trauma of layoffs.

A company with a 401(k), by contrast, has no such control. "You have people staying and leaving at the wrong time," notes Steven A. Sass, associate director for research at another respected pension think tank, the Center for Retirement Research, tucked away on the dormer floor of an old red brick house just off the Boston College campus. "They leave in boom times as assets [in their 401(k) accounts] grow"—which, of course, is just when companies are expanding and need to retain staff. "And employees stay put in a recession," because their 401(k) portfolios have shrunk, which is exactly when companies need to contract. (Chapter 9 has more on the relative plusses and minuses of both types of retirement plans.)

Despite all these disadvantages, most companies are likely to achieve some of the savings they expect by replacing a pension with a defined contribution system. In large part, that's because they don't have to pay for actuaries, insurance premiums to the PBGC, and other administrative fees. Edwin C. Hustead, a former chief actuary for the federal government, calculates that a large defined benefit plan would spend about 0.23 percent of payroll for administration, and a small plan about 3.10 percent, compared with 0.16 percent and 1.44 percent, respectively, for defined contribution plans of similar sizes. Then there's the slippage inherent in a system in which it's up to the employees to save on their own initiative. When participation is voluntary, only about three-fourths of eligible employees typically contribute money to a 401(k), and very few put in the maximum allowed by law. If the company is matching just 50 percent of that—or zero—then almost by definition the plan will cost less than would contributing to every employee's defined benefit pension, unless the defined benefit is incredibly stingy.

"The reason most companies say defined contributions are cheaper than defined benefits is that they're consciously providing a lower benefit," says Dallas Salisbury, president and chief executive of the Washington, DC–based Employee Benefit Research Institute, or EBRI, a nonprofit center that provides a wealth of data on retirement issues. Overall, experts estimate that a traditional pension will cost a company something like 5 percent to 8 percent of payroll, whereas a defined contribution runs approximately 2 percent to 4 percent. Thus, as a general rule, a company with a traditional pension is spending maybe 3 percent or 4 percent of payroll more than its nonpension rivals. That would seem to be a significant competitive drag.

Another advantage of the 401(k) from the company's perspective—and probably more important, in the view of most pension experts—is that the outlay is predictable. By analyzing the number of eligible workers, their salaries, the percentage who historically participate, the salary percentages they historically have contributed, and the percentage of the corporate match, a company can get a good sense of what it will have to pay each year. In other words, the company's contribution is limited, or defined—hence the name. With a traditional pension, the amount of the company's expenditure depends on unknowable factors such as interest rates, market returns, employee turnover, and longevity. The company must pay whatever it takes to give retirees their promised monthly checks; yet it cannot control or predict the key factors that will influence that amount. That fuzzy math is also a reason investors generally want the pension plan dumped. How can they fit such uncertainty into their calculations?

Shedding a pension system offers one more competitive gain, although it's rarely mentioned. This one has to do with the concept of pensions as deferred wages, the arrangement in which workers agree to take lower pay today if the company will use that money to finance a pension for tomorrow. Indeed, that trade-off helps explain why the pension promise has been considered sacrosanct: The workers essentially paid for that promise with their deferred salaries. When the company ends its pension plan, however, it doesn't raise wages retroactively to the level they would have been had they not been deferred. What if a rival company never had a pension plan, and thus its staff never deferred their wages? Odds are the wages there would be higher than at the pension dumper's, although not as high as the full value of the pensions plus the wages. The pension dumper will undoubtedly have to raise pay a bit to be competitive, but probably not as much as the amount it would have had to pay in the intervening years if there had been no pension plan, notes Michael W. Peskin, a managing director at Morgan Stanley who specializes in benefits issues.

Corporate Qualms

Legally and practically, it's pretty easy for a financially tottering company to unburden itself of a pension plan. Most likely the company will gain a competitive edge and some much-needed savings.

Still, many managers and potential investors hesitate to do it. The echo of the pension promise lingers, and whether because of moral qualms or operational practicalities, they wish they could find a way to keep that promise. They know that while the company may not be paying in dollars for its pension underfunding, it will pay in other ways.

The biggest costs are in morale and public image. Even if the people still on the job aren't immediately hurt and the unions agree to the deal, even if the retired employees are made whole by the PBGC and the lost pensions are largely replaced with a generous 401(k), something has changed. The bond between employer and employee has weakened. The pension plan that was supposed to be an inviolate promise turns out to be no more than another cost center. Management's word can no longer be trusted.

Workers think, "I had this implicit contract that if I stayed here, I would have a good pension, and that has been violated," says Steve Sass of Boston College's Center for Retirement Research.

"What it's done is break the social compact, particularly in industries like steel and autos where there's a family history of commitment to the industry, generation after generation," says Phyllis Borzi, a professor of health policy at George Washington University and a benefits lawyer at the Washington, DC, firm O'Donoghue & O'Donoghue. "It was a source of great pride that they were part of this company. Now, it changes the view that people have of the company." Blunt, no-nonsense, and an easy talker, Borzi was the resident congressional expert on pensions as the ERISA counsel for the House Education and Labor Committee from 1979 to 1995. "There's a sense of betrayal."

Both sides of the morale issue played out at Delta Air Lines. First, the company tried to maintain morale by maintaining its pension plans; then, when it switched gears, it bungled the termination of its pilots' plan and squandered any goodwill it might have earned.

Although the carrier filed for bankruptcy in September 2005, it waited eleven months to end the pilots' plan and even continued the pension benefits for flight attendants and ground personnel, hoping that Congress would come through with some sort of funding relief. Delta actually had an extra incentive to terminate: The pilots' plan had an expensive trigger, a unique provision allowing pilots to get half their entire pension in one lump sum if they retired before the plan was shuttered. With the prospect of more than $400 million walking out the door, Delta had gotten temporary permission from the PBGC to halt the lump-sum payouts, but that freeze wouldn't last forever. "The easiest thing for any company to do is dump. The government will take it. They're going to be better off financially if they get rid of this thing," says Randolf Hurst Hardock, a onetime staffer for the Senate Finance Committee and the U.S. Department of Treasury in the 1980s and 1990s, who worked on benefits matters for Delta as a partner at the Washington, DC, law firm of Davis & Harman. As *BusinessWeek* magazine saw things in late 2006, not dumping right away showed poor business judgment:

Some rival carriers readily used Chapter 11 as a way to break unfavorable aircraft leases, dump pensions on the government, and renegotiate labor contracts that put them at a competitive disadvantage to the [low-cost airline] discounters. But Delta, which has long prided itself on its paternalism, held out until late 2005 in hopes of preserving its employee pensions. That put it a good year or two behind the restructuring efforts of rivals like US Airways and United, which are now reporting strong profits, and may have left Delta more vulnerable now that the industry's fortunes are improving. "They should have taken their medicine earlier," says Roger King, an analyst for CreditSights.

Congress finally passed the Pension Protection Act—the same one that rescued Northwest's pensions—barely in time to save the plans at Delta, except for that of the pilots, in August 2006. According to Hardock, Delta couldn't have waited much longer, because its reorganization plan was due to the bankruptcy judge.

So why didn't the company take the easy route and terminate everyone right away? "The Delta people did not want to dump those plans," Hardock says. "The clear sentiment of management was loyalty to employees. If you jerk people around, they won't be as good employees."

Ultimately, Delta did dump the pilots' plan, however, and the pilots were furious, for a variety of reasons. For one thing, a number of top executives managed to come out with their own rich pensions intact, or even enhanced, including CEO Leo Mullin, who raked in $16 million. Meanwhile, the pilots who hadn't yet gotten their lump sums, and whose benefits typically far exceeded the PBGC guaranteed amount, lost as much as half of their original entitlements. Moreover, the pilots had taken a 32 percent pay cut just a year earlier, supposedly to save the airline. They were also angry that they were the only employee group to suffer. And many of them felt a perennial resentment that management always seemed to have "an inbred hatred of the pilots," as one put it in a supposed morale-building meeting with chief operating officer Jim Whitehurst in July 2006. The employee anger and bad PR were undoubtedly among the reasons the new CEO, Gerald Grinstein, turned down any bonus, stock, or other extra compensation after Delta emerged from bankruptcy in spring 2007. "I wouldn't say that safety's ever been compromised, because if the guys in the cockpit didn't have the integrity and honesty, they never would have made it that far. But morale was horrible. They were less willing to fly extra trips," says David Villarrubia, a veteran Delta pilot who retired seven years earlier than he'd planned, just two months before the bankruptcy filing, in order to get his lump sum payment.

Growing up in New Orleans in the 1950s, watching the planes take off at New Orleans International Airport, Villarrubia had dreamed of being a pilot. "I was amazed that the planes could fly," he recalls. "I just dreamed of the freedom and wondered where they were going." The first time he actually set foot on an airplane was after high school, when he became an air traffic controller in the Navy and participated in its civilian Flying Club on his days off. But he didn't want to be a pilot at just any airline; he wanted Delta. After all, it was still the local airline—launched as Delta Air

Service in Monroe, Louisiana, in 1928, although it had moved its headquarters to Atlanta by the time Villarrubia was born. "Delta was the premier carrier in the world!" Villarrubia declares flatly. He even turned down a commission in the Navy to apply to Delta. The day he was hired, in 1978, "was the best day of my life." He stayed for twenty-seven years, moving up from engineer to captain, earning the choicest international routes to Paris and Rome. Yet by the time he took his early retirement, the thrill and the loyalty were both gone.

In the end, most financially distressed companies feel they have no other choice. If things are so shaky that they have to file for bankruptcy, the pension plan is probably a dead man walking, and everyone knows it. There are few other sources for achieving the big savings that are necessary if the firm is to emerge in any sort of competitive shape. The real issue is *how*, not whether, the pension plan will be killed—painfully or very painfully? How can the company break its pension promise in a way that offers the best deal for all sides—the company, its investors, its employees, its customers—and gives it the best chance to be a profitable enterprise again?

Part Two

The Laws

4 Writing the Rules

"When ERISA was passed, termination of defined benefit plans was supposed to be very difficult. The standards were very, very high."

—Sherwin Kaplan, labor attorney, Thelen Reid Brown Raysman & Steiner

On September 2, 1974, President Gerald Ford signed the Employee Retirement Income Security Act (ERISA), which established a national system for regulating pension plans and created the Pension Benefit Guaranty Corporation (PBGC) to make sure plans had enough money to meet their payout obligations.

Two days later, on September 4, 1974, the PBGC got its first call that a company was shutting down its pension system.

It was an abrupt but appropriate beginning to the drama of pension dumping still playing out more than thirty years later. At that time the PBGC consisted of fewer than a dozen staffers, on loan from the Departments of Labor and Treasury and camped out in abandoned government office space in suburban Maryland. "We didn't even have furniture. We had one telephone for the whole agency," recalls Henry Rose, the short, bespectacled, and soft-spoken lawyer who was then the PBGC's general counsel—and its sole attorney. "This call was the last thing we needed."

Of course, Rose and his colleagues knew they would be getting termination cases eventually. A key function of the new agency was to pick up the pieces after companies closed down their pensions and to ensure that retired workers continued to get paid. Nor did any of the staff doubt that they would be kept busy. Pension plans had been toppling since the 1920s, and the typical plan in 1974 had barely half the amount of money it should have had. In fact, it was generally acknowledged among the rarified group of consultants, money managers, lawyers, and lobbyists who followed pension issues that Senators Jacob K. Javits and

Harrison Williams Jr., the driving forces behind ERISA, were particularly worried about the shaky pensions of milliners and milk deliverers in their home states of New York and New Jersey, respectively. Williams, a Democrat and chairman of the Senate Labor Committee, inserted a provision into the new law ensuring that any plan terminated between June 30 and September 2 of that year would be covered, as long as the company notified the Department of Labor within a set time—specifically to include a particular New Jersey brewery, according to Rose. So Rose and his handful of colleagues were steeling themselves against what they expected would be a stream of pension dumpings. But not on day two. And not Franklin National Bank, one of the largest banks in the country.

Luckily, Franklin was a false alarm. "It turned out the bank had enough money to cover all the benefits," Rose says. That gave the agency a few weeks to scrounge up leftover furniture from a federal warehouse, issue its first regulations, and start collecting the premiums it would need in order to pay claims.

Over the next three decades, those premiums would be stretched thin. More than thirty-five hundred financially weak companies would eventually dump their underfunded pension plans on the PBGC's makeshift doorstep, with a total deficit of some $32.6 billion by the early 2000s. The immediate reasons, of course, were the companies' own troubles. But the underlying reason was that flaws in the new law encouraged the practice. Because ERISA left the requirements for paying for the pension promises unclear, companies let the red ink pile up year after year. Because ERISA made it logistically easy to shed a plan, the PBGC was deluged. Because ERISA set the premiums for the PBGC's pension insurance too low, the PBGC faced its own shortfall after a few years of big bankruptcy terminations. Most important, because the rules were so lax and everyone knew the PBGC would step in to take the political heat and keep retirees from starving, dumping the pension plan became an easy choice—the default option chosen as soon as a company was in trouble. Thus, the law that was supposed to preserve and protect pension plans in fact became one of the greatest tools for destroying those plans.

The Birth of the Pension Plan

The story of how ERISA came to be written, with all its loopholes and misconceptions, starts one hundred years before the doors opened at the PBGC. It could be argued that Americans have been enjoying retirement checks ever since the colonial era, when the British government handed out pensions to certain employees and some churches made payments to the widows and orphans of clergymen. After the Civil War, Union veterans also received stipends. By and large, however, for almost the first century of U.S. independence, no one entertained any concept of paying people once they or their family's breadwinner were too old to work. A typical American in the eighteenth and nineteenth centuries worked for himself or herself, most likely on a family farm or maybe in a small crafts shop, and when these typical Americans were too old to labor in the fields—if they didn't die first—they sat at home weaving, canning, doing piecework, and watching the grandkids.

The Industrial Revolution and its factories altered that labor paradigm, but it took a lot longer to change attitudes toward old age. "We had pensions to begin with because being 'an employee' was a whole new concept since the mid-nineteenth century. Now you're working for someone else. And suddenly, [once you get old], they don't want you anymore. It was a shock and a surprise," says Steven Sass of Boston College's Center for Retirement Research, amplifying an idea presented in his book *The Promise of Private Pensions: The First Hundred Years*.

Historians point out that the concept of retirement payments didn't start from any sense of charity or even loyalty to long-time workers. Rather, companies were spurred by a logistical problem: How could they get rid of people who were too old and incapacitated to do the job and create openings for rising—and cheaper—young talent? They could simply fire the older workers, of course, but with all the attention focused on big businesses like the railroads during the Populist era of the late 1800s, when farmers and other workers began organizing and staging mass protests, it would have been politically disastrous. So the answer was the carrot, rather than the stick: pensions as a bribe. If older workers could be guaranteed some income, maybe they would go quietly. That tactic had the secondary advantage of offering a lure to keep desirable new employees from jumping ship. (Stick around until you're sixty-five, and you, too, can get paid for not working.) "Managers believed they could reduce labor costs by replacing older, high-wage workers with younger employees who received lower pay. A pension plan allowed a firm to move older workers out of a firm when managers wanted them to go," writes James A. Wooten, a professor at the School of Law at the State University of New York at Buffalo, in his classic historical analysis *The Employee Retirement Income Security Act of 1974: A Political History*.

Not surprisingly, railroads led the way in North America. Relying heavily on physical labor, they needed to make room for a constant delivery of strong, young workers. "They had old people who couldn't operate the equipment anymore, and they became a public hazard," notes Sylvester Schieber, the director of North American benefits consulting at the consulting firm Watson Wyatt Worldwide until he retired in 2006. It wasn't just manual laborers who were needed; railroads and other businesses also wanted to make room for ambitious managerial talent. "Railroads were the first modern enterprises to require large bureaucratic organizations, and they likewise adopted the pension to develop a loyal, experienced, and permanent administrative staff" to run those bureaucracies, Sass writes. "Such associations encouraged longevity and loyal service by basing rights on years of service." The first corporate pension plan in North America was established in 1874 by Grand Trunk Railway of Canada, and the first in the United States the following year by American Express Company (which was then a railroad).

The concept spread slowly for three quarters of a century. Some leading universities set up a retirement system for professors in the 1890s, and Andrew Carnegie did the same in the early 1900s for disabled employees at his steel mills. By 1919, about 15 percent of the total work force—and 75 percent of railroad workers—were covered, according to Sass. The big jump came during and right after World War II, when a number of legal, economic, and political pressures merged to make pension plans suddenly irresistible to the corporate world. First, there was the federal Stabilization Act of 1942, which put strict caps on wages. With labor markets tight, businesses desperately needed some other sort of financial inducement to draw in recruits. As it happened, the Stabilization Act specifically exempted "pension benefits in a reasonable amount" from its controls. At the same time, several key unions, led by the United Mine Workers of America, the United Steelworkers, and the United Auto Workers, were pushing to make pensions a standard benefit. Wooten also notes in his book that changes in the federal tax laws in 1942 made more rank-and-file laborers subject to income tax, thus giving them an incentive to find ways of sheltering their income.

Perhaps the final turning point came in 1948, when a federal appeals court ruled in a case involving Inland Steel that pensions weren't merely acts of generosity by the employer but a condition of employment that could be included in labor negotiations. It took a strike threat by the steel union and intervention by President Harry S. Truman, but before 1949 was over, Ford and Bethlehem Steel had introduced defined benefit plans, and for the next decade the concept burgeoned. In 1945, according to Sass, just 19 percent of the workforce had a pension; in 1960, 41 percent did.

Next, a Pensions Law

Unfortunately, all these workers were relying on a jerry-rigged structure. The American pension system was cobbled together in bits and pieces over seventy-five years to fill a range of corporate and individual needs, from opening career paths to sheltering wages, without any overarching philosophy or plan. The whole foundation was voluntary; no company was obligated by law to have a pension plan. The standard age for retirement, sixty-five, was based on an arbitrary demographic from nineteenth-century Prussia. "The current arrangement requires an employee to work today with the faith that in twenty-five years the employer will make good on its promise," says Elizabeth Warren, a law professor at Harvard University and a bankruptcy expert, who was an adviser to a commission appointed by Congress in the mid-1990s to review the bankruptcy laws. "Anyone starting out to design a system would never design it like that."

Nor had anyone made any long-range financial projections for this haphazard concoction. The fundamental problem was that pensions almost always start out in deficit. That's because companies begin funding the pension trust only on the day they launch the plan, but they generally give their employees credit for all the years they worked before that date—before any money was being set aside. Although most companies even pre-ERISA would contribute a little extra to cover that past liability, there was no incentive to put in more than 10 percent beyond the credits workers were building up in the current year (known as benefit accruals), because that was all the companies could deduct from taxes. Still, didn't that mean the plan would be fully paid up after ten years? Nope. Every time a new labor contract came up for negotiation, employers inevitably increased the benefit—retroactively. They would never catch up. "Defined benefit plans just grew like Topsy. They were never seen as an expensive item. Companies never anticipated the size or the potential or the uncertainty that pensions would impose," says Olivia Mitchell, the director of the Pension Research Council at the Wharton School. A short, animated redhead, Mitchell seems to have a book to illustrate every point she makes, piled high on shelves in her small office on the third floor of the modern, brick Wharton School building.

For all the generosity of the pension benefits in theory, workers might never see a single dollar in hard cash. In many plans, employees were guaranteed to get their benefits, or became vested, only if they had already retired or were old enough to do so. Thus, they could work for a company for thirty years, and then quit or be laid off at age fifty, and they would be entitled to zero. Moreover, if the business started foundering and couldn't afford to pay the full pension, even workers with supposedly guaranteed benefits could get less than their guarantee. And that's exactly what happened.

Herman G. Nelson worked as a machinist and tool-and-die maker at the Hopkins, Minnesota, plant of Minneapolis-Moline Power Implement, a big farm equipment manufacturer, almost nonstop from 1942 until he retired in 1962 at age sixty-two. He and his wife, Ruth, then settled down with his $75-a-month pension. They didn't worry when White Motor bought Moline a year later. Moline seemed to be as solid as they come, with its famed Prairie Gold tractors and a history dating back to 1929. It even made the ranks of the Fortune 500 for three years in the mid-1950s. Nelson's pension, negotiated by the International Brotherhood of Electrical Workers, inched up to $103 per month. Then in May 1974 White abruptly ended the Moline pension plan, which covered about 1,300 employees and 1,100 retirees like Nelson.

White owed these people somewhere between $16 million and $19.15 million, but it claimed that it didn't have the money. Nelson's monthly pension was slashed by more than half, to just $48.

Over the next eight years, until Herman's death in 1982, Herman and Ruth Nelson got by on the shrunken pension, Social Security, assistance from their four children, penny-pinching, and some income from Herman's occasional electrical jobs. ("I don't know how he did it, because he was blind in his left eye," recalls the elder son, Don, himself retired from an eclectic collection of jobs as an oilfield pipe worker, hospital maintenance man, high school teacher, and roofing factory laborer.) Ruth Nelson lived twenty years after her husband died. Luckily, Don Nelson says, his parents' mortgage was fully paid, and they were frugal people. "I don't think they were angry with either company," he adds. "I think they were more hurt. Deeply hurt. He had been dealt with very badly by the company."

Stories like Nelson's were repeated throughout the United States, especially in the industrial heartland. Kaiser-Frazer closed its main auto plant in 1953. American Motors did away with two major assembly lines less than a year later. In December 1963 came the earthquake that would finally shake up Washington, DC: Studebaker-Packard, a nine-year-old merger of two small auto makers, announced that it was shutting down its big factory in South Bend, Indiana, $15 million short of what it needed to pay the pensions of nearly 4,400 employees—leaving everyone under age sixty, many of whom had spent decades making cars, without the pensions they thought they would get.

By then, a growing number of people in Washington were ready to listen. Pensions had been percolating as a political topic ever since the Senate had opened hearings on retirement fund corruption at the International Brotherhood of Teamsters and elsewhere in 1957. The legislators had a wide range of concerns, including financial conflicts of interest and tax breaks for the self-employed. In 1958 and again in 1962, Congress passed narrow measures dealing with pension plan disclosure, and in March 1962 President John F. Kennedy created the special Committee on Corporate Pension Funds and Other Private Retirement and Welfare Programs with a high-powered membership that included three cabinet secretaries, the director of the Bureau of the Budget, and the heads of the Council of Economic Advisors, the Securities and Exchange Commission, and the Federal

Reserve. Senator Javits introduced a wide-ranging pension reform bill in 1967 to be followed by many others. Retirees like Herman Nelson started talking with their old colleagues and writing to their representatives. Then Javits staged one of the most brilliant pieces of political theater in U.S. history. Instead of hauling corporate CEOs and union presidents to Capitol Hill to testify at hearings, the way Congress traditionally does, Javits and his cosponsor, Senate Labor Committee Chairman Williams, took their staffs, the Labor Committee—and the press—out to the communities where people had actually lost their pensions.

Frank Cummings, then the staff attorney for the committee Republicans led by Senator Javits, had been collecting letters from the retirees. Throughout a career that began in 1958, Cummings has represented players ranging from the iconic steel and auto companies like LTV and Studebaker to pilots at United Airlines. He explains how Javits' concept caught on: "If you're a congressional correspondent working on a Saturday, you need a story for the Sunday paper. But Washington shuts down on Saturday. Reporters would come in, so I would open my file cabinet, and I'd ask, 'What state are you from?' I had folders from every state. They would rummage around [for a heart-breaking story about a worker losing a pension]. Before we knew it, we had a local interest story. That story would generate another flood of mail. Then some congressman who had read about this story and had heard from his own constituency would call Williams and Javits and ask, 'Would you hold a field hearing in my state and let me sit on the dais with you in my town?' The hearings would present the stories," Cummings continues, "and Williams and Javits would say, 'If my bill were law, this wouldn't happen.'"

Things take time in Washington, however. During the eleven years from the Studebaker shock to 1974, various versions of pension bills from Javits, Williams, and other legislators inched their way through committees, stalled, changed, and merged, while presidents came and went, appointing new advisory panels. Congress debated whether it even had the right to intervene in what was seen as a private contract between workers and employers, beyond cracking down on basic financial malfeasance. Despite all the headlines and hard-luck stories, pension reform actually had a very weak institutional constituency. Big business opposed most of the measures, as it generally opposes any regulation, while the labor movement was split. The proposals were also caught up in power plays between the congressional barons of finance and labor. "For many years, I never thought it would pass," Cummings confesses three decades later. And most experts agree that in normal times, it probably wouldn't have.

But 1974 wasn't a normal time. It was the time of the Watergate scandal, and that's what saved ERISA. By the end of July 1974, the House Judiciary Committee had passed three articles of impeachment against President Richard Nixon because of his abuse of power. The warning spread throughout the corridors of Congress: If you have any legislation pending, get it done before September, because after that the Hill would be consumed with impeachment hearings. The committee chairmen who had been feuding over pensions quickly realized that they had to swallow their disagreements and shove something through. In fact, in the waning days of August 1974, ERISA passed unanimously in the Senate and with just two dissenting votes in the House.

ERISA: What's Included, What's Left Out

Although ERISA may have created a legal structure for pension plans, it wasn't as solid as it could have been. True, some provisions were strong enough. For starters, the law did not require any company to offer a pension plan, but if a company did, it had to be a real plan, with real cash behind it. Each year, employers had to put aside enough money to cover all the benefits that employees had earned that year, plus enough to fund the previous years' benefits—including any retroactive improvements—amortized over thirty or forty years (depending on when the benefits were earned). The law also imposed fiduciary and disclosure rules intended to prevent financial shenanigans. Furthermore, it established that anyone who worked full-time at a company for five years earned a vested right to at least a portion of the pension, which could not be taken away, even if the person was fired the next day. (The full vesting schedule in the law is a bit complicated, and it spells out three alternative procedures and timetables.) Nor could the company change its mind: Once a pension amount was promised, it could not be reduced retroactively.

Just in case all these provisions proved inadequate, the law created the PBGC as a kind of insurance agency, to take care of workers at a future Studebaker and provide a reduced pension if a plan fails. As with any insurance arrangement, the PBGC receives income from premiums—in this case, premiums paid by employers that sponsor pension plans. Although there's a cap on the size of the pension that the agency will pay, the cap is adjusted each year for inflation and historically has been generous enough to fully take care of about 85 to 95 percent of retirees.

All these safety mechanisms might seem sensible and reasonable enough. The problems start with the fact that the PBGC isn't an ordinary insurance company. "From the day Congress began in the early 1970s to consider a PBGC-type program, there was never a consensus on what this program ought to be—whether it's supposed to be a true insurance program or a social insurance program," recalls Phyllis Borzi, the benefits lawyer and former counsel for the House Education and Labor Committee.

In a true insurance program, customers who pose a bigger risk are charged bigger premiums. Auto insurance is a classic example. Drivers with a history of accidents pay higher rates than do safe drivers; so do younger drivers, even if they have never had an accident, because their age group is statistically more likely to smash up their cars. Social insurance, by contrast, is the kind of coverage found in traditional group health plans, in which everyone in the group pays the same deductibles and copayments. To keep rates down, social insurance tries to encompass a big pool of customers, so that healthier policyholders help subsidize the unhealthy. Another way this kind of insurance can lower costs is to offer incentives for members to engage in less risky behavior—to quit smoking, take exercise classes, or get annual checkups. "The point is to spread the cost across the greatest possible base. But you have to have rules to prevent behavior that will unreasonably add to risk," Borzi explains. Whatever the type of insurance, in other words, there is some effort to align premiums with payouts.

Congress tried on several solutions for the insurance issue. If ERISA went with traditional insurance, charging higher rates to companies that were more likely to default, the cost of the higher rates might be too expensive for these companies, which were, by definition, in tight straits. Moreover, who would determine which companies posed the biggest risks? "People were worried that the government would become another Standard & Poor's and would actually begin rating companies," Frank Cummings, the onetime Labor Committee lawyer, says. To avoid that quagmire, ERISA's authors opted for a social insurance structure, with all companies paying the same rate. Unfortunately, the law omitted any incentives and rules for good behavior. "It's not an insurable risk," protests Michael Peskin, the Morgan Stanley managing director who specializes in benefits. He and many others argue that pension funds that invest in riskier asset classes should pay higher premiums (more on this in Chapter 8). Compounding the problem is the long-term nature of the pension commitment, adds Elizabeth Warren, the Harvard bankruptcy expert: "A bank wouldn't make a loan stretching over twenty-five years without taking a mortgage. The PBGC needs all the tools an ordinary bank has, but they've only been given limited tools. They should have more tools to evaluate the creditworthiness of the company. They should be able to take a security interest." In the end, termination insurance was so problematic that it was one of the last concepts the business community signed on to and one of the last sections squeezed into the law, which meant there was less time to craft it correctly.

On top of the rate structure problem, ERISA initially set the premium much too low, at just $1 per participant per year. Where did the $1 rate come from? "Out of thin air," scoffs Cummings. "Nobody had the foggiest notion of what to charge. They knew this thing would have to get fine-tuned." Henry Rose, the original PBGC counsel, says the premium was based roughly on the annual number of terminations according to Internal Revenue Service records going back to 1942. "That obviously grossly underestimated the real need," he adds wryly.

Unforeseen Problems

The congressional sponsors back in 1974 could not have anticipated macroeconomic and political trends such as Web-based financial transactions, airline deregulation, the September 11, 2001, terrorist attacks, or the rise of China as an export powerhouse, all of which would shake the foundations of some of the key business sectors that offer pensions. Henry Rose, Frank Cummings, and legislators writing ERISA expected mainly to see just two types of terminations—and rarely: companies in liquidation and small fry. "When ERISA was passed, termination of defined benefit plans was supposed to be very difficult. The standards were very, very high; they were considered impossible to meet" unless the company was completely liquidating, recalls Sherwin Kaplan, the veteran Labor Department attorney who represented pilots and retired pilots at US Airways and Delta. The other main source of customers was expected to be small companies, particularly "fake plans," as Cummings puts it. "A fake plan might be in a closely held corporation owned by Mom and Pop and employing one clerk. There's high turnover and no vesting. It pays a pension only if you work there twenty-five years and you're working there on the day of retirement. We know who is going to be working there twenty-five years—Mom and Pop but none of the clerks. It's a huge tax shelter for the owners, and nobody else is going to get anything." Once ERISA kicked in, with strict requirements for vesting and funding, the PBGC figured plenty of these tiny plans would shut down.

"What nobody realized at the time they set it up," says Olivia Mitchell, "was that entire industries could go down the tube: autos, airlines, steel. Insurance only works when there is a risk pool to share the risk, and that risk pool was evaporating."

There were other problems. The bill's authors agreed that any future Studebakers should not be allowed to simply drop their pensions on the PBGC without sharing the cost in some way. Such an escape hatch would create a moral hazard: Spendthrift companies could recruit workers with sky-high pension promises, fail to fund these promises adequately, squander their corporate cash on lavish executive salaries or ill-conceived acquisitions, and then hand off the whole problem to Washington. The key question—how much of the cost should the failing companies have to pay?—was essentially a repeat of the debate over premiums: At what point did the fees for having a pension plan become so high that they pushed companies over the edge? Deluged by competing suggestions, Congress set what seemed to be a reasonable, if not stern, threshold. If a company wanted to terminate its plan, it had to pay 30 percent of its net worth toward the cost of the underfunding. Thirty percent of net worth may sound pretty stiff, but what Congress apparently didn't consider was the possibility that a bankrupt company with zero net worth might terminate its plan—in which case, it would owe nothing.

The requirement that companies put money behind their promises was supposed to make sure that people like Herman Nelson weren't abandoned, but it opened up more loopholes. To set aside the required funding for future payouts, a pension plan has to make assumptions about staff turnover, pay raises, employee longevity, interest rates, and market returns for decades ahead. Of course, there are standard actuarial and accounting formulas for all these items, but they leave a certain degree of wiggle room, especially when it comes to two vital assumptions: the discount rate (the rate used to estimate future benefit costs by translating the value of those payments into current dollars) and the plan's return on assets. The higher the assumptions, the less cold cash the company has to contribute to reach the same end total. That was an opening plenty of businesses were happy to drive right through. If a company relies on an overly optimistic assumption one time, it may not matter very much. So what if a $5 billion fund earns 8.6 percent one year, rather than the 9 percent it assumed? It's only $20 million less than expected; it can easily be recouped with a slight tick up in the stock market the next year, a minor shift toward equities in the asset allocation, or some faster-than-expected staff turnover. But pushing the envelope that way year after year for thirty years can leave a fund several hundred million dollars short. That becomes serious money.

Sure, companies could avoid a lot of these problems by putting more into the pension trust than they needed in flush times, as a kind of rainy day fund. However, ERISA discouraged that strategy because companies couldn't get a tax deduction for overfunding (based on a complicated formula). The rationale was to stop companies from using what was supposed to be an employee benefit as a plain old tax shelter. But the result was to push companies to do the complete opposite of what ERISA was supposed to accomplish—prudent long-term funding and planning.

In short, ERISA was written with sand under many of its pillars. Disaster was only waiting for the next strong wind.

5

Failure's Fallout: LTV and Other Precedents

"[LTV's pension termination] raised many companies' awareness that this might be a strategy."

—OLIVIA MITCHELL, EXECUTIVE DIRECTOR, PENSION RESEARCH COUNCIL AT WHARTON

MORE THAN twenty years after steel giant LTV filed for bankruptcy in 1986, its pension plans remain among the largest ever to be dumped on the PBGC. The case involved about two dozen banks, dozens of attorneys, and seven years of negotiations. Lawyers who worked on the deal—professionals who work on nothing but bankruptcy cases day in and day out—say it had the biggest creditors' committee they had ever seen. By the time the proceedings were finished, the case had also prompted at least four major judicial precedents and two new laws involving, among other issues, how much priority the PBGC was entitled to in bankruptcy court, how to calculate the underfunding, whether a company could dump other benefits, under what conditions a company could dump its pension, and what kind of plan a company could give its workers to replace the old pensions.

"These issues never had been tested," recalls Joel B. Zweibel, who represented the swarm of bank creditors as a senior partner at O'Melveny & Myers in Manhattan. "There were virtually no other significant cases that had these situations. If it had been a small company and if they could have negotiated something with the PBGC, things could have been resolved that way. But a $2 billion claim was not a claim that could easily be negotiated. This was the biggest [pension plan termination] the PBGC had ever faced, and they wanted the issues determined."

And that was only the beginning. LTV made it clear not only that ERISA had some serious flaws but also that the PBGC was fair game for tinkering. Swamped with terminations and buffeted by economic forces, the agency over the next two decades changed its practices, its requirements, and its financial standards. But pensions continued to tumble.

A Rush to the Courthouse

During the boom years of U.S. manufacturing, LTV had gobbled up three other large steelmakers: Republic Steel, Jones & Laughlin Steel, and Youngstown Sheet and Tube. The conglomerate also had a hugely successful aerospace division. But in the early 1980s, the steel industry was pounded by recession and competition from low-cost imports. (Chapter 8 discusses the industry's travails in more detail.) With more than $3 billion in red ink flowing like molten metal, LTV in July 1986 filed for protection under Chapter 11 of the Bankruptcy Code.

Anticipating this move, LTV's bank creditors had already hired Zweibel a couple of months earlier. On the day the company filed, Zweibel was in Florida for a different bankruptcy case. "At eight in the morning, when I was about to go into court, I got a call from one of my younger colleagues in New York, and he said, 'Guess what? At 7:30 LTV filed a Chapter 11,'" Zweibel recalls. "I made my argument to the [Florida] court that morning—I was first on the calendar. Then I flew back."

LTV's largest liability was four major pension plans covering more than one hundred thousand employees and retirees, underfunded by about $2.3 billion. In addition, the company announced that it would cease paying for the health care of seventy-eight thousand retirees and would halt operations at about a dozen facilities, which would trigger as much as $700 million in additional, special pension benefits. At that point, some delicate maneuverings began.

"It was assumed, and it was part of the LTV plan of action in Chapter 11, that it would terminate the pension plans and have them taken over by the PBGC," Zweibel says. But LTV couldn't just dump its plans, even if it followed all of ERISA's requirements and paid thirty percent of net worth. Separate from ERISA, as part of a new amendment to the federal Bankruptcy Code known as Section 1113, the company faced another hurdle: If it wanted to make changes in collectively bargained contracts, it had to negotiate with the

United Steelworkers (USW) and demonstrate that the changes were "necessary" and "essential" to its survival. Three of LTV's pension plans were collectively bargained. If they were terminated, about eight thousand union members would lose out on some $200 million in benefits, mainly because they had retired early or had pensions larger than the PBGC maximum. Although it wasn't clear how hard it would be for LTV to prove the "necessary" and "essential" standards, no one expected the Steelworkers union to agree to terminate its members' plans and give up $200 million without a tough fight.

Since the health care coverage did not fall under ERISA or the Bankruptcy Code, LTV was free to trash that. However, that move evoked such public outrage that Congress quickly passed a second bankruptcy amendment giving health plans and other nonpension retiree benefits the same protection as pensions.

Meanwhile, the PBGC was getting nervous about LTV's pending shutdowns of the twelve facilities. According to the agency's regulations, if the pension programs ended first, before the steel plants closed, the PBGC wouldn't have to cover the special shutdown benefits. But if the PBGC or LTV dallied on the pension terminations and the steel plants went dark first, the extra pension liability would be dumped on the government. Faced with these deadlines, the PBGC ordered the LTV plans terminated, effective January 1987. (Sixteen years later the PBGC would step in again to terminate Bethlehem Steel's pension plan and block at least $200 million in similar shutdown benefits. Steven A. Kandarian, who headed the PBGC at that time, flatly declares that "the shutdown-benefits rule is a bad regulation. It results in a race to the courthouse." Nevertheless, it's the law, it's big bucks, and Kandarian gave the order to lower the axe on Bethlehem.)

LTV didn't actually object to the terminations. The Steelworkers, however, were furious that they had now lost more than $900 million, including the early retirement payments, the pension amounts that exceeded the PBGC cap, the health care, and the special shutdown benefits. The terminations also weakened the union's credibility among its members. After all, pensions are supposed to be deferred wages; workers accept lower wages today for the promise of getting that money back in the future as a pension. If they cannot be sure that they will in fact receive those pensions, the workers would never agree to the lower wages. "We had what we believed was a contractual promise from the company to provide us pension benefits of a defined amount," says Paul Whitehead, who was then an assistant general counsel at the steel union and later its general counsel. "The fact that the company had missed its contribution obligations, which was the premise for the PBGC to terminate, didn't change the fact that we still had a contractual promise from the company. If you've taken action which makes one vehicle no longer sustainable, that doesn't relieve you from your obligation to find some mechanism to deliver on these benefits." Accordingly, the USW challenged the terminations in bankruptcy court and threatened to strike.

Even in this era of fading labor power, the Steelworkers have perhaps unique clout thanks to the intricacy of turning off a roaring furnace, which must be done if work is going to be halted—whether for a strike or bankruptcy. "At other industries, you try to settle these things [contract negotiations] at the last minute, at two in the morning. In steel, you've got to bank those furnaces days in advance of a threatened strike," explains Frank Cummings, the onetime aide to Senator Javits, who went on to become a labor lawyer for LTV during that termination. Then, once the strike or other problem is settled, the whole furnace system has to be put back on line.

Events from late 2001, when LTV was in bankruptcy a second time, provide a sense of the complexity of a steel mill closure: The union sent one hundred workers to three of its biggest plants to prepare for a shutdown by draining water and rotating lubrication systems, according to David McCall, director of a USW district in Ohio. (This time, the closure was because of the bankruptcy, not for any looming strike.) The cost, hassle, and delays have made brinkmanship basically impossible for a steel company, experts say. "That gave the union a tremendous hammer," Cummings concedes. Adds Karen Wagner of Davis Polk & Wardwell, another of LTV's lawyers back then: "We needed the union to run the steel mills."

Supreme Court Shocker

LTV gave in. It enacted the controversial "follow-on" retirement and disability plans, and the PBGC and other steel companies promptly cried foul. As the critics saw it, the new retirement program essentially replaced all the benefits lost in the termination while saddling the PBGC with the bulk of the cost. Adding to the PBGC's annoyance, the U.S. economy was on an upswing and the industry's fortunes were improving, meaning that LTV was probably in a better position to foot the bill than it was when the plans had been shuttered. Furthermore, the USW bragged a little too openly about how well it had made out, agency insiders say. Just eight months after ordering the terminations, the government took LTV to court, arguing that if the company was going to provide a pension plan that looked more or less like its old plans, it should just take back the original plans.

For the next three years, no one knew for sure whether the PBGC had the legal right to toss the liabilities back to LTV. The situation had never occurred before. Two lower courts upheld LTV's actions, saying the PBGC had gone beyond what ERISA intended. "We knew that [the follow-on plans] would be controversial," Karen Wagner, the LTV lawyer, acknowledges, "but we hoped that we had balanced everybody's objections and come up with an acceptable compromise." Finally, in June 1990, to the surprise of both the PBGC and the Steelworkers, the U.S. Supreme Court by an 8-to-1 vote overturned the lower courts to rule in favor of the PBGC. A precedent was established: If a plan was terminated, a company couldn't wriggle around that by creating a virtually identical successor plan while leaving the PBGC with the bill for the old one. At the PBGC, staffers went out for drinks to celebrate, and the phones hardly stopped ringing.

But that was not the story's final chapter. Despite the improved macroeconomic situation, LTV still couldn't afford to pay for all the pension liabilities that the PBGC was handing back. So it ended up with a reprieve anyway. The PBGC and the Internal Revenue Service set up an extraordinarily generous schedule for LTV to pay off its liabilities over thirty years.

The ruling on follow-on plans wasn't the only precedent that LTV established, and in fact the company won more than it lost against the government. For instance, the PBGC argued that its claim as a creditor in bankruptcy court should be treated like a tax claim and have priority over all other creditors' filings. The PBGC and LTV also disagreed about the size of the underfunding, which had to do with calculating the present value of pension payouts that could stretch out for decades. Naturally, the PBGC wanted to follow its own regulations, which assume immediate termination and essentially equate present value with the cost of buying an annuity today. That would have made the LTV underfunding look relatively large, giving the PBGC a bigger claim on the company's assets. The PBGC's reasoning is that, if a company is in bankruptcy, there's a good possibility it will not continue in business much longer, so no one should assume the pension fund will continue either. Just as naturally, LTV wanted to use a method of calculation that would reduce the size of the claim. So it argued for the "prudent investor" standard, which assumes that the plan is ongoing and the assets will grow over time. The reasoning behind this method is that, regardless of what happens to the company, the pension plan in fact will continue in operation, the PBGC will manage the assets if the company goes under, and the workers will collect their payments in the normal fashion month by month after they retire. The bankruptcy courts ruled against the PBGC in both the tax priority and liability cases at LTV, lowering the value of the underfunding to $1.5 billion. (In practical terms, the issue of calculating liability became moot after the Supreme Court bounced the plans back to the company.)

To Joel Zweibel, the ruling on priority was crucial. "If the PBGC had been given priority, there would have been no motivation for them to settle. This meant we [LTV and the creditors' committee he represented] now had leverage with the PBGC to negotiate." Indeed, no court has ever granted the PBGC tax-equivalent status. As for determining the size of the liability, it has become a regular point of dispute between the agency and companies, with the PBGC usually losing the legal contests. A dozen years later, US Airways would unsuccessfully try to use the LTV case to create one more precedent, claiming that if the PBGC could stretch out the funding schedule for LTV, it could do the same for any other company. (Chapter 10 has more about this effort.)

Ironically, none of these victories and negotiations could save LTV. In 2000 it filed for bankruptcy again. Although the cost of paying for the restored pensions didn't help, LTV's biggest problems were the same ones faced by all steel companies, including global competition and shrinking demand. This time the company was liquidated, and Wilbur Ross snapped up its plants, kept the residue operating while he combined it with the assets of four other feeble steelmakers, and sold the whole caboodle less than four years later to another steel company for a $2 billion profit. In short, just about every phase of the LTV saga set a precedent. LTV's first termination, says Olivia Mitchell of the Pension Research Council at Wharton, "was a learning experience for everybody. It raised many companies' awareness that this [pension termination] might be a strategy." Wilbur Ross's subsequent success did the same for investors. Suddenly, the finance world saw that big money could be made by sagely playing the PBGC.

Mending ERISA

In the first thirty years since the PBGC opened its doors, more than thirty-five hundred companies in financial distress have shut down their pension plans and saved themselves, in total, some $30 billion in pension costs. The PBGC also got real office space—a modern, twelve-floor brick building with Greek-style columns and a three-story atrium, in the heart of Washington's infamous K Street lobbying district.

To try to limit the corporate collapses as well as bolster the PBGC's bank account, Congress passed five laws making major alterations to ERISA during those thirty years. Premiums were hiked eight times, and a new risk-related premium was added for underfunded companies. Other reforms made it harder for companies with plans that had large funding deficiencies to increase their benefits, required them to catch up on funding more quickly, and set tighter limits on the actuarial assumptions they could use in calculating liability. Of course, most of those changes just revived the old debate that ERISA had never resolved: Since the companies that most need to put extra money into their pension plans are probably the ones that can least afford it, how far can the law push them, imposing higher premiums and other restrictions, before they buckle? The 2006 Pension Protection Act, by giving the airlines extra years to catch up, marked the first time Congress acknowledged that dilemma in legislation.

Probably the most important change passed during this time was the redefining of distress terminations. With this alteration, no longer could a company shutter its plan any time it wanted just by paying 30 percent of its net worth. Instead, spurred by the epic LTV fight, Congress established specific conditions under which an underfunded pension plan could be killed. (A healthy plan may be terminated at any time, through a totally different procedure, as long as the company sets enough money aside to pay all the benefits that have been earned, usually by purchasing annuities for the participants. In addition, the PBGC can demand that a plan be terminated, usually to prevent the underfunding from getting worse.) Thus, a plan is eligible for distress termination if the company is in liquidation, pension costs have become "unreasonably burdensome" solely because the workforce is shrinking, the company convinces the PBGC that it will not be able to stay in business if it has to pay the pension costs, or the company can convince a bankruptcy court that termination is necessary in order for it to reorganize.

Essentially, all four standards require a company to prove in some way that the funding requirement is so onerous, and its financial situation so dire, that it would collapse if it had to pay its obligation. The bankruptcy-reorganization route is the most popular simply because the requirements for the first two are particularly strict, and the third method ends up ceding a lot of control to the PBGC. Besides, says Sherwin Kaplan, the lawyer for the Delta pilots, companies soon realized that "having to prove [the financial burden] in a bankruptcy court is a lot easier than having to prove that anywhere else, because the bankruptcy court is biased in favor of the debtor." If the company can prove its case, the PBGC takes over, pays out the pensions from then on, and fights with all the other creditors in bankruptcy court for a claim on the company's assets.

During the 1980s the financial pendulum swung in the opposite direction. With pension funds fattened by the bull market of the time, companies tried to figure out ways to terminate their overstuffed plans—not to avoid paying contributions, but to get at the "excess" assets that would be left after buying annuities for all the employees who had vested benefits. The first prominent company to attempt this was Harper & Row in 1981, which took the $9.8 million "left over" after its pension plan was closed and used the money for a stock buyback to fend off a possible takeover. During the next seven years, the tactic was quickly copied by the A&P supermarket chain, AM International, Exxon, FMC, Union Carbide, GAF, Pacific Lumber,

Celanese, Occidental Petroleum, and more than 130 others, to the tune of over $5 billion. "We consider the pension fund assets to be as much of an asset of the corporation as anything else we have responsibility for," Vincent Blake, then the vice president and controller of the mining giant AMAX, flatly told me in 1983, as his company was trying to siphon off $100 million from its $313 million plan. Statements like that astounded pension experts, employees, and politicians, who thought ERISA made it clear that these assets actually belonged to the employees, not the corporation. In an attempt to halt this practice, Congress in 1986 clamped a 10 percent surtax on all these withdrawals unless the money was used for retiree health or other pension-type benefits. When that didn't do the trick, it upped the surtax two more times, to 50 percent in 1990.

Tweaking ERISA can't alleviate all the other pressures on pension plans. Economic downturns, for instance, can transform a plan into a major expense. The pension portfolio's returns tumble while the present value of the liabilities jumps up. Because companies can no longer assume that their pension trusts will keep earning high rates into the future, under actuarial rules, they need to increase their contributions. Of course, those very same economic conditions are hammering the companies' overall budgets and stock prices, making it harder to afford the increased contributions. That was exactly the situation in the first few years of the twenty-first century, as industries like steel, autos, and airlines reeled under recession, aggressive global competition, the rising price of oil, and plunging air travel after the terrorist attacks of September 11, 2001. No wonder the PBGC saw a slew of big-time terminations in just the five years from 2001 through 2005, including nine of the eleven largest in its history—United Airlines, Bethlehem Steel, US Airways, LTV's second, National Steel, Weirton Steel, Trans World Airlines (TWA), Kemper Insurance, and Kaiser Aluminum.

The pressures continue. The passage of ERISA roughly coincided with the weakening of the labor movement, so that just as the government was establishing parameters for protecting pensions, workers were losing the union clout that might have helped enforce those protections. Then there are the demographic pressures. The baby boomer generation moves inexorably closer to retirement every year, closer to the day when its members will stop letting money accumulate in retirement plans and start taking it out. But companies with defined benefit plans are generally not in growth sectors, so they are not hiring new employees to replenish the cash. Just the opposite: The companies with pension-funding troubles are also the ones most likely to offer early retirement incentives, which means that even more workers are taking money out sooner than the actuaries had calculated. And companies have their own individual reasons, from competition within their industry to the specific benefits or asset allocation they've chosen, that lead them to feel they can't afford their pension plans.

A major premise behind ERISA was that long-term pension programs needed government protection because it was impossible for companies, employees, and actuaries to predict the future when they set up the programs. As it turned out, the legislators who drafted ERISA had just as much trouble predicting the law's future.

6 The Bankruptcy Court Minuet

"You can work for a company for forty years, and in bankruptcy court you are equal to a creditor who showed up two days ago and sold them roof bolts."

—Micheal Buckner, trustee, United Mine Workers of America

The official story of how a pension plan gets dumped in a Chapter 11 bankruptcy reorganization goes something like this: First, the debtor company must persuade the Pension Benefit Guaranty Corporation (PBGC) that it is unlikely to survive unless it terminates the pension plan. Then, if the pension is part of a collectively bargained contract, the union must agree to any cutbacks. Finally, the debtor company must persuade the bankruptcy judge, just as it convinced the PBGC. The extra complications of getting approval from the union and the PBGC make it much harder to dump a pension plan than to break most other prebankruptcy agreements, such as building leases.

Here's the real story: If a company wants to get out of its pension obligation, it will.

For reasons grounded in history, law, and practical experience, a bankruptcy court judge will virtually always approve a termination. Largely, that's because bankruptcy judges have become the company's advocates, doing pretty much whatever a company says is necessary to get itself in strong enough shape to stay in business postbankruptcy, whether it's dumping the pension or reducing the payout to particular creditors, regardless of whether the PBGC or any other creditors object. "The bankruptcy judge's role is to help the company emerge. All the principles embedded in ERISA are secondary," snaps Bradley Belt, the former PBGC head. Pensions get no special treatment compared with other debt.

Nevertheless, although it's almost a foregone conclusion that the pension plan will be dumped, its existence can still complicate

61

the whole bankruptcy process. Bankruptcy is essentially a squabble among creditors over an insufficient pool of assets, so a pension deficit adds at least one more creditor, the PBGC, to the fight—and a big creditor at that. That means more people jumping into the fray and more claimants who have to be appeased. It also complicates negotiations with the unions by adding another benefit to argue over. Moreover, if a company has multiple plans and some are actually well funded while others are not, there may be competing sets of employees joining the fight on different sides. Those in the healthy plans will argue to keep their own programs going and minimize the others' claims; whereas those stuck with the underfunded plans will want to shutter everything and share the pain (and assets). To varying degrees, these players can slow down the proceedings, block certain asset sales, and demand a bigger cut of the pie. In short, a bankruptcy with a pension termination has quirks not found anywhere else.

The Creditors' Hierarchy

Throughout almost all of the nineteenth century, the United States had no national law regulating bankruptcy. Wavering back and forth between debt-ridden farmers and the commercial interests that provided loans, between financial crises and recoveries, Congress approved—and rescinded—three bankruptcy laws from 1800 to 1878 before finally passing one that lasted, the Bankruptcy Act of 1898. Some of that seesawing continued into the next century, as the 1898 law was drastically revised and then replaced. Was bankruptcy an indication of a flawed company that should be condemned or just a vagary of fortune to be mitigated? How easy should it be for debtor companies to get a second chance?

The Bankruptcy Code that governs the process today, passed by Congress in 1978, falls solidly on the "second chance" side. (The official name of that bill is the Bankruptcy Reform Act of 1978, but it's usually referred to as the Code to distinguish it from the 1898 bankruptcy act.) In other words, bankruptcy judges favor corporate management because the law in essence pushes them to. For instance, one of the most dramatic ways the new code changed previous laws was to give the existing corporate management—the management that probably got the company into trouble in the first place—more control over the bankruptcy process and a second chance to make the business work, including at least four months of exclusivity when no one else could offer a reorganization plan to the court. The new law also allowed companies to start the bankruptcy process before their assets were totally depleted, on the theory that the healthier they were when they went into bankruptcy, the more likely they would be to emerge.

This chapter looks only at the process in place when a company seeks to reorganize and continue in business under Chapter 11 of the code. When companies liquidate and go out of business entirely, their pension plans always disappear, and Chapter 7 will analyze how some investors explore the liquidation route. Under another alternative, known as a prepackaged bankruptcy, or "prepack," creditors, investors, and management cobble together a restructuring arrangement on their own, outside of court. Large companies started taking this pathway during the heyday of junk bond defaults in the 1980s, and its popularity increased after the bankruptcy laws were tightened somewhat in 2005. In theory, a prepack can be done faster and therefore more cheaply by avoiding the legal bureaucracy. However, getting a swarm of creditors to agree, without a judge to mediate, isn't easy, especially for big companies with a lot of creditors, each demanding its full payment in top-quality paper. And if a pension fund is involved and unions have to be included at the table too, experts say that a prepack becomes virtually impossible. In any case, most of the issues and processes discussed in this chapter would apply to a prepack.

Pensions have no official role in the basic bankruptcy legal process. The Bankruptcy Code establishes a strict, hierarchical order in which creditors are supposed to get paid, known as absolute priority. The PBGC, as the creditor representing the unsecured pension obligation, is almost at the bottom. The fact that it may be one of the largest creditors is irrelevant. First in line, the IRS gets its share. Next are secured creditors, including banks with collateralized loans and holders of equipment trust certificates and senior secured notes. Employees may also squeeze in here if they were due to be paid just as the company filed for Chapter 11 and their paychecks were frozen. Then come the bankruptcy lawyers and other postpetition professionals. *Then* it's the PBGC's turn, along with all the other unsecured creditors such as trade creditors and holders of unsecured notes. Last are the stockholders, who essentially have no rights whatsoever.

As soon as the bankruptcy is filed, the judge basically slams the door on these creditors by issuing an automatic stay, which protects the debtor company from all past obligations. Only outlays that are deemed essential to keep the company in operation, such as ongoing wages, basic administrative expenses, and payments to vendors for new supplies—plus the lawyers' bills—are allowed. At this point the court also arranges what's known as debtor-in-possession (DIP) financing, which includes any loans or credit to keep the company going; those new loans, too, get top priority for repayment. Those are the loans Deirdre Martini works on at CIT. This was also the reason Joel Zweibel had to rush from his bankruptcy case in Florida to LTV's hearing in New York, to negotiate his clients' stake in the DIP package.

Pension funding does not fall into any of the "essential" categories. After all, the people getting the pensions are no longer working at the company, by definition, and thus they can't be essential to the company's ongoing survival. True, the termination will undoubtedly deal a blow to morale, which in turn can lead to problems ranging from sloppy work and absenteeism, to strikes and a brain drain, as Chapter 3 points out (and as Chapter 9 will discuss in more detail). But those problems, though serious, are not imminently life threatening the way a total cutoff of raw materials would be. Besides, once a company is in bankruptcy, virtually anything that happens will hurt morale. Pensions aren't special.

With the company's immediate needs taken care of, the fight over its long-term prospects begins. Existing management starts with the upper hand because a key provision of the 1978 code gave it a four-month period of exclusivity in which to put together a reorganization plan. In one sign of the way judges tend to favor the debtor company, bankruptcy courts would regularly extend those exclusivity periods for years. The United Airlines management, for instance, took more than three years to produce its plan and pull out of Chapter 11. The code revisions in 2005 supposedly got tough on the endless extensions by setting a strict limit of eighteen months.

As the creditors join the fight, competing interests clash head on. Secured creditors may want to take their collateral and run, worried that those assets could be drained away in a fruitless effort to keep the company afloat. Meanwhile, unsecured creditors, along with management, employees, and stockholders, typically figure that their only hope of getting back any money is for the company to keep going and climb out of its troubles. Vulture hedge funds gather on the sidelines, ready to buy up the debt—cheaply—of any unsecured creditors who get cold feet. Their aim is to convert that debt into brand-new equity that would give them control of the company after it emerges. During this maneuvering, the PBGC shares some interests with the rest of the unsecured creditors and, theoretically, has as much—or as little—clout as anyone else in its class.

The PBGC does, in fact, have some potential muscle. For a reorganization plan to be confirmed by the court, it is supposed to be approved by creditors holding two-thirds of the dollar value in each creditor class and constituting a majority of all those voting in each class. That gives the one-third minority—which can include the PBGC—a certain amount of bargaining power to demand more than their absolute-priority share. Some investors, in fact, will buy up one-third of a subordinated class of debt on the cheap for just that reason. But life is never simple, and in this case, the added complexity is known as the "cramdown" exception: Even if the required numbers of creditors in each class don't approve, the judge can nevertheless "cram" the reorganization plan down their throats as long as it adheres to the absolute-priority structure and as long as each class will get at least as much as it likely would have gotten in an outright liquidation. In which case, whatever bargaining clout the PBGC or other creditors hoped to wield is out the window.

The one place where the PBGC truly has a chance to exert some influence is through the official creditors' committee, appointed by the regional U.S. Trustee. The PBGC is often named to the committee, and it is the only government agency that ever gets full voting privileges, according to Bill Beyer, the veteran PBGC lawyer. There's some debate among investors as to whether it's truly an advantage to be on the committee. On the negative side, members are banned from any further trading and their committee work can eat up twenty hours or more per week. Larger holders sometimes figure they have the clout to negotiate on their own. But most creditors consider it a plum to have a seat at the negotiating table as the reorganization is hammered out, especially since they also get access to the company's deepest financial secrets. And the PBGC at least has that plum in its pocket.

Bankruptcy Judge Bias

Short, almost elfin in appearance, with steel-gray Brillo hair, Joel Zweibel is one of the veterans of the bankruptcy scene. For forty-two years he represented banks and other creditors, playing a part in some of the biggest bankruptcy cases of the late twentieth century, including LTV, Eastern Air Lines, R.H. Macy & Co., Texaco, and Public Service Company of New Hampshire (owner of the Seabrook nuclear power plant).

Zweibel is usually as soft-spoken and courtly as a Victorian gentleman. But when he talks about bankruptcy court judges, the courtliness disappears. At times, he almost spits out his words. "I would break them down into two categories. One: just single-minded. The debtor gets the benefit of the doubt whatever we do. Two: more thoughtful, not knee-jerk. But overall, the goal of Chapter 11 is to reorganize a company, and they want to give the debtor the benefit of the doubt."

In the case of LTV, Zweibel continued, bankruptcy Judge Burton R. Lifland of the Southern District of New York had already granted the company seven extensions of its exclusivity period, and LTV's chief financial officer, James F. Powers, was on the stand arguing for an eighth. "I cross-examine him. I ask him several questions that are based upon allegations that the debtor made in its own motion papers. The debtor's counsel objects to one of my questions. The judge is about to say, 'Objection granted!' I interrupt to say, 'What is the objection based upon?' The debtor's counsel says, 'Irrelevancy.' I say, 'It can't be irrelevant; it's based on paragraph so-and-so in *his* filing.'" Zweibel grins at the rare memory of winning a point, but then the anger returns. "The judge said, 'I'll let you ask a couple more questions along this line, but keep it brief.'"

"Judge Lifland has blinders on as far as a debtor is concerned," says Zweibel. Lifland, who has a reputation for being prodebtor, would not agree to an interview because he was still a sitting judge, hearing cases. That was the response of most judges contacted for this book.

Ask anyone who has had any dealings in bankruptcy court if such bias exists, and the answer is almost unanimous: Bankruptcy judges favor the company that filed. After all, the basic intent of the 1978 law is to help the debtor company successfully reorganize. If the company says it no longer wants to buy the six new machines it had contracted for, the judge is likely to go along. And if the company says it will have to dump its pension plan, the judge is likely to go along with that, too.

Zweibel believes that bankruptcy judges are prejudiced against his bank clients, and others in the pension-termination universe, from unions to the PBGC, say the same about the way judges treat their clients. "When a union is going to bankruptcy court to save a labor agreement, the climate is less friendly than if you're going to the NLRB [National Labor Relations Board] or an arbitration hearing. Bankruptcy judges want to save the company. Some of the judges are perceived [by attorneys] as sort of the CEOs of the company," says Paul Whitehead, the lawyer who represented the United Steelworkers in the LTV case. And why should the PBGC be exempt? "The bankruptcy judge is the seven-hundred-pound gorilla," says Phyllis Borzi, the no-nonsense former congressional committee counsel. "Presumably, the goal of the judge is to give the company the tools that it needs when it emerges from bankruptcy, so it won't be in front of him again. If he or she thinks the way that is accomplished is to not give the PBGC everything it wants, so be it."

Henry Rose, the original PBGC counsel from the early days without furniture and phones, offers a typical example. In 2004, a group of US Airways executives hired him to argue that there was really no reason to shut down their $900 million pension plan, along with those of the machinists and flight attendants, as the company was requesting. By a quirk in the contracts, according to Rose, the airline was actually not required to fund the executives' plan. U.S. Bankruptcy Judge Stephen S. Mitchell "was very courteous and listened very carefully," says Rose. He asked Rose no questions. Then he ruled in favor of the company. "If there was any request US Airways made that [the judge] didn't go along with," Rose adds, "I don't recall it."

One veteran bankruptcy judge I spoke to, who asked not to be identified, and who has handled at least one major pension-termination case, insists that judges don't start out with any bias. "My aim is to do what the statute tells me to do. I am not trying to impose my personal beliefs." Yet the judge also agrees that the basic goal of bankruptcy court is to help the company survive. "Rejection of the union contract may be necessary to allow a reorganization. Everybody is worse off if there is a failure of the company."

The degree of bias—indeed, if there is any at all—depends on which judge is hearing the case. UCLA law professor Lynn LoPucki

has analyzed each judicial district to see which ones tend to favor
debtor corporations and their key lenders. His controversial thesis,
presented in his 2006 book *Courting Failure*, is that to attract big,
prestigious cases, some judges will try to establish a reputation for being sympathetic to the companies that file those cases. So they will
agree too easily to the companies' motions, even if those motions are
actually not in the companies' long-term interests. "Courts want these
cases for prestige," he explains. "You can do Enron and WorldCom
and Adelphia, or you can do Mom and Pop's Chapter 13 [personal
bankruptcy] and try and save their house." His research shows that
the Second Circuit Court in New York and the Third Circuit in
Delaware are the most generous to filers, although other courts are
scrambling hard to catch up.

Even skeptics who don't go along with LoPucki's conclusions
agree with the obvious observation that every judge comes in with
a unique personality and background. Some are better at getting
opposing sides to work out a compromise. Some just want to ram
through a reorganization plan. Some have more blatant agendas.
Jonathan Carson, an attorney who used to work with Jamie
Sprayregen at Kirkland & Ellis and who now runs a consulting firm
in Los Angeles that fulfills back-office bankruptcy functions, claims
that one Los Angeles bankruptcy judge, whom he wouldn't name,
favored secured creditors because she used to be a lawyer for that
type of creditor.

The Mostly Powerless PBGC

When the pressure to terminate bears down—whether it comes
from the judge, the debtor company, or elsewhere—the PBGC usually gives in.

The company in bankruptcy presents the PBGC with its arguments about why it must terminate its pension program, and the
PBGC pores over the numbers (see Chapter 2). In a chapter in the
book *Annual Survey of Bankruptcy Law*, Bill Beyer describes what
the agency looks for:

> The inquiry must go beyond evaluating the currently proposed
> reorganization plan to determine whether the pension plan is

unaffordable under any feasible reorganization plan. In addition, all alternatives to termination, including benefit freezes [in which current employees cannot earn any more benefits, and new employees aren't eligible to join the plan at all], IRS funding waivers [limited exemptions from funding], borrowing to cover unaffordable funding spikes, etc., must have been explored and found unavailing. Meaningful sacrifices must be made by other stakeholders (e.g., cutbacks in salaries, wages, and executive compensation) and all reasonable savings possibilities exhausted (favorable refinancing, onerous contract rejection, and capital expense reduction).

In rare instances, the PBGC has been able to force a company to scrounge up the money to continue its pension, most notably at TWA. Veteran raider Carl Icahn owned fully 90 percent of the stock at the time the airline filed for bankruptcy in January 1992. Maybe TWA had no money, but Icahn had plenty. *Forbes* magazine valued his holdings at around $660 million, including an estate in the upper-crust New York suburb of Bedford; the *International Herald Tribune* put the value at $900 million. So the PBGC, during lengthy negotiations, pressured Icahn to contribute $320 million in cash and loan guarantees toward the airline's roughly $1 billion underfunding.

Ultimately, the contribution did not save the pensions: The PBGC agreement gave Icahn the right to unilaterally terminate the plans after 1995, and in 2001 TWA in fact dumped nearly $700 million worth of claims on the government and then liquidated. But at least "we did get a few more years where people got their benefits," points out Randy Hardock, the Delta benefits lawyer and former Treasury and Senate staffer.

In a smaller case in the spring of 2006, the privately held industrial conglomerate the Renco Group agreed to continue administering the underfunded pension plan of a bankrupt steel subsidiary in Ohio, WCI Steel, which it was spinning off to a group of financiers who didn't want the pension plan. The financiers even agreed to chip in $20 million toward the underfunding of $100 million-plus. The PBGC had unusual leverage in this instance: It threatened to foreclose on the holdings of Renco and its owner, Ira L. Rennert, including Rennert's $185 million estate in the snazzy beachfront Hamptons community of Long Island, New York.

Generally, however, there isn't a majority owner with deep pockets and an expensive house to go after. Most times, the company truly is a financial goner. It simply doesn't have a hundred million dollars to spare for the pension plan. So the PBGC agrees, reluctantly, to let the pension go.

The argument then moves to the mathematics of how to calculate the size of the underfunding. This is where the mess hits the fan. It's an issue that has been argued in and out of court at least since the LTV bankruptcy. The PBGC prefers a more conservative approach—calculating the claim as though every pension had to be paid immediately—to make the underfunding look as big as possible, which in turn will give the agency a bigger claim on the remaining assets (see Chapter 5). The companies generally prefer an approach that assumes the payments will be spread out over time, which lowers the immediate size of the claim. Here, again, the PBGC usually loses. Most courts have agreed with the companies' preferred method of calculation. Only in one major case, US Airways' second bankruptcy, has a court ever sided with the PBGC's math. And if the company has been playing games with its actuarial assumptions, even the PBGC's claim may still understate the real funding shortfall.

"The PBGC is just like all of the other creditors," says Sherwin Kaplan, the pilots' lawyer at Delta and US Airways. "It will take over the underfunding of the plan and then file a claim in bankruptcy court for all of that underfunding. Then it will negotiate with the debtor and the creditors' committee to have a given amount of that claim approved." One difference is that the PBGC is probably one of the largest creditors, so it will get a hefty share of the assets at the end. At United, the agency came away with approximately 12.5 million shares, or about 20 percent, of the new common stock—the single largest holding—along with $500 million in notes and some 5 million convertible preferred shares. It took a 7 percent stake in US Airways in the second go-around.

For a typical investor, a share of that magnitude might bring clout. The problem for the PBGC is that it doesn't want any of these holdings. It would much rather that the companies stayed in business and kept their stock along with their pension funds. In fact, the PBGC tries to unload its new shares as quickly as it can, because as a matter of policy it doesn't believe government should be involved in corporate governance or management. Its stake in United was down to just 3 percent in less than a year. And of course such unwanted ownership comes at a steep price. Like all the unsecured creditors, the PBGC most likely ends up with less than a dime for each dollar of its claim.

Small Victories

All of this is not to say the PBGC is completely powerless. For one thing, every additional layer of approval and negotiation inherently slows down any process, and the PBGC is one more step in the bankruptcy march. "If all the airlines are filing at one time"—which seemed to happen between September 2004 and September 2005, as US Airways, Northwest, and Delta all tumbled within twelve months of each other—"the PBGC is much busier. They clog the system," says Shelley F. Greenhaus, one of the veterans of distressed investing, whose experience with pension dumping goes back to his investment in Wheeling-Pittsburgh in the 1980s, when he was a portfolio manager at Oppenheimer & Co. He left Oppenheimer in 1990 to cofound Whippoorwill Associates, a private equity manager and investment adviser in suburban New York.

Even in less busy times, the PBGC frequently moves more cautiously and slowly than the rest of the financial world would like, whether because the amounts of money at stake are so huge, or because it's carving out new terrain, or simply because it's a government bureaucracy. "Often, it doesn't want to set a precedent," Greenhaus suggests. Lisa G. Beckerman, an attorney with Akin Gump Strauss Hauer & Feld, who has worked with creditors of various sorts at Delta, Kaiser Aluminum, Weirton, National Steel, and LTV, says that the agency has been known to "sit on a case for a really long time," six months to a year. Meanwhile, the other players want to hurry things along because their money is tied up, the physical assets could deteriorate, and key employees could get impatient and leave.

But the agency's potential influence goes beyond delaying tactics. "The PBGC has leverage in acquisition and spinoff situations," says Dallas Salisbury of EBRI, the pension data resource center. "It has the ability to keep things from happening if it does not agree or approve of the financial terms relative to a defined benefit plan." This power harkens back to the way the PBGC scrutinizes a company's financial condition, looking for assets that could cover the pension liability. The agency doesn't have to wait until there's an actual Chapter 11 filing and termination request. Through its early warning program, the PBGC is continually on the prowl for corporate actions like divestitures, spinoffs, and leveraged buyouts (LBOs) that could jeopardize the pension funding of a company in shaky but not bankrupt condition and push the plan onto the government. When it spots such a situation, the PBGC has the right to demand that some of the proceeds be used for the pension plan. "Going back the fifteen years, give or take, that it has had that law on its side, it has been quite aggressive," Salisbury adds.

This early-warning provision came into play in the spring and summer of 2006, when General Motors was negotiating to sell a controlling share in its profitable consumer-finance unit, GMAC, to an investment group led by the private equity firm Cerberus Capital (the same Cerberus that later acquired Chrysler). At that point the giant automaker's bonds were rated as junk, and GM and the PBGC were caught up in the standard dispute about how to calculate the pension-funding level. GM claimed to be overfunded, after making a big catch-up contribution in 2003, but the PBGC considered it about $31 billion underfunded. The GMAC spinoff was delayed until the pension agency issued a letter promising that it would not terminate GM's pension plans as a result of the divestiture nor hold Cerberus liable for any underfundings.

Hovering behind every termination, as well, is the ghost of LTV—the threat that the PBGC might someday throw the pension plan right back at the company. The agency can try to do this not only if the company seeks to put in a virtually identical follow-on retirement benefit without paying the old accrued liabilities, as LTV did, but also in much less dramatic instances, merely if the company seems to have recovered its financial footing so soundly that it could probably afford to start paying those pensions again. The only time the PBGC has ever actually forced a restoration was at LTV. Nevertheless, "it's talked about a lot. The PBGC can just say, 'You're healthy enough now; we want to put your plan back in place,'" says Michael A. Kramer, a partner at the investment boutique Perella Weinberg Partners in New York, who has spent his career advising on restructurings from all sides of the battle. Before joining Perella Weinberg, Kramer represented debtors like Bethlehem Steel, as well as the PBGC in the Delta and United terminations, for Greenhill & Co., and for his own firm. Wising up to the threat, Delta and United got the PBGC to promise not to exercise the restoration option in their cases. According to Kramer, United in exchange let the PBGC have a bigger claim than it otherwise would have agreed to. But the threat never ends. A year and a half after US Airways had emerged from its second bankruptcy/termination, a bipartisan group of five senators asked the PBGC to restore the company's pension plans.

The PBGC's ultimate power is its ability to force a termination, as it did at LTV and Bethlehem. This generally happens in order to block the liability from getting bigger, such as just before a shutdown benefit would be triggered or in certain types of divestitures (see Chapter 5). Of course, the PBGC tries to avoid taking such a fateful step. It doesn't want more debts to oversee.

To have real clout, a PBGC claim would have to move up the absolute-priority ladder to the lofty status of a secured credit or even a tax payment. The agency has been seeking this status for its claims—without success—for years, starting with a case under the pre-1978 bankruptcy law soon after ERISA was passed and continuing through the LTV saga. Thwarted regularly in court, supporters began calling for Congress to change the law. David Walker, a former PBGC acting executive director, who in 1998 was appointed U.S. Comptroller General (essentially, the nation's chief auditor), proposed a trade-off: The PBGC would give funding relief to companies with severe liabilities, "but if they terminate, the PBGC gets a priority claim for what they would have had to pay if there had been no relief." As he explains, "We're going to provide additional flexibility in some circumstances. But if you terminate, we want a backstop." However, a month after he said that, in August 2006, Congress went ahead and passed the Pension Protection Act granting funding relief without any priority trade-off.

Trashing the Union Contract

The other major bulwark supposedly blocking a pension termination is organized labor. When the workforce is represented by a union, the pension plan is probably one of the benefits negotiated in the union contract, and under normal circumstances the employer cannot unilaterally cancel any provision in the contract. The company cannot suddenly declare that it will no longer pay retired workers' full pensions or no longer maintain the pension plan's funding.

But bankruptcy is not a normal circumstance. The 1978 code provides that companies in Chapter 11 *can* unilaterally abrogate executory contracts, or basic business contracts. Thus, bankrupt companies will, quite legally, break their leases on office space or fail to pay for pencils they have ordered, without a by-your-leave from the landlord or pencil vendor, as long as they can produce a sound business reason. Meanwhile, ERISA lays out its own procedures for a company in financial distress to break one particular contract, its pension funding promise.

Not surprisingly, the question quickly arose after the passage of both ERISA and the 1978 bankruptcy law as to whether a union contract, including the pension plan, is one of those easily trashed executory contracts. To the shock of the entire labor and benefits worlds, the Supreme Court in a 1984 case involving a small New Jersey building company, Bildisco Manufacturing, ruled that a company in bankruptcy could indeed reject a union contract outright "if the debtor can show that the collective bargaining agreement burdens the estate and that after careful scrutiny, the equities balance in favor of rejecting the labor contract." There was no question that this ruling applied to pensions, because Bildisco had unilaterally stopped paying pension benefits that were part of its contract with the Teamsters. So it would seem that pensions really were just like pencils. The last vestige of the supposed sacred bond between management and workers had been erased, and organized labor had no power to protect it.

Public outrage pushed Washington to promptly shore up workers' protection. Later that same year Congress passed Section 1113 as an amendment to the Bankruptcy Code. (That was the provision that required LTV to negotiate with the United Steelworkers. Four years after that, in 1988, in response to LTV's move to curtail retiree health coverage, Congress also approved Section 1114, to protect nonpension benefits.) Among other things, Section 1113 states that before a debtor company can reject a collectively bargained agreement, it must first negotiate in good faith with the union by giving complete information and offering proposals that "provide for those necessary modifications in the employees' benefits and protections that are necessary to permit the reorganization of the debtor." However, if the union refuses these proposals without good cause and if the company can show that the changes are "essential to the continuation of the debtor's business," then the company may unilaterally throw out the contract—including its pension provisions.

That hardly settled matters. Starting as early as 1985, different courts have interpreted the law differently, especially the significance of the key words *necessary* and *essential*. Do those words mean the same thing? Or does *necessary* imply a less urgent need? If the two words have different meanings, then it might be easier for a company to get a judge's approval by arguing that the changes it seeks are merely *necessary*; the company need not assert that it will collapse entirely without them. (The variation in interpretation is one reason bankruptcy experts like Lynn LoPucki say that the outcome of a bankruptcy filing depends on where the case is filed.)

The contrast is particularly sharp between New York and Delaware, the two most popular venues for filing corporate bankruptcy. The Delaware court, in a 1986 ruling on Wheeling-Pittsburgh's bankruptcy, basically declared the two words synonymous. What the words meant, the court said, was that a company should make only the most minimal modifications in its contracts with the "goal of preventing the debtor's liquidation." That set a fairly high bar of proof for a filer. Throwing out the pension plans for the entire work force probably wouldn't qualify as a minimal change, and even if it did, the company would have to show that without that move, it would most likely go out of business. But New York's Second Circuit lowered the bar in *Truck Drivers Local 807* v. *Carey Transportation, Inc.*, specifically rejecting the Wheeling-Pittsburgh premise. Instead, the Second Circuit said the debtor company had to prove only "that its proposal is made in good faith and that it contains necessary, but not absolutely minimal, changes that will enable the debtor to complete the reorganization process successfully." That ruling swung the door open again for companies to make changes in their union contracts more easily, because they could probably prove that saving tens of millions of dollars through a pension termination would help them reorganize.

Whichever interpretation was used, union power was being whittled away. Anyone who has ever participated in any sort of negotiation knows how malleable terms like *good faith* or *good cause*—let alone *necessary* and *essential*—can be. The one unambiguous right that Section 1113 gives unions is another bite at the apple. Pensions that are part of a union contract do have a bit more protection than pencils: After declaring that it wants to renege on the contract, the company must come back to the union in good faith and give negotiations one last chance. (Of course, employees who have defined benefit pensions but no union get no more protection than pencil vendors.) But if that last effort at negotiations fails, the pension plan can still be dumped without the union's consent. Indeed, that's exactly what happened with United Airlines. Its machinists, mechanics, and flight attendants unions all fought to keep their retirement plans, but in May 2005 Chief Bankruptcy Judge Eugene R. Wedoff of the Northern District of Illinois approved United's filing.

Weakened Unions

The provisions of Section 1113 follow a number of other trends that have pummeled organized labor, starting with the fact that fewer and fewer people with pension plans are even represented by a union. As of 2006, less than 8 percent of the private-sector workforce belonged to a union, a steep slide from the 35 percent level during the boom years of organized labor (and, not coincidentally, of defined benefit plans) in the 1950s, or even the 17 percent level of the 1980s. Plus, the labor movement itself is split by the different priorities of active and retired workers that were discussed in Chapter 2. With its declining influence, moreover, the union at a company in bankruptcy has to juggle which benefits to protect. Should it sacrifice jobs to save pensions, or kill pensions to save health benefits? In that popularity contest, pensions usually lose because their delivery is far into the future—and anyway, the PBGC will pay up.

Frank Cummings, the veteran lawyer who helped Senator Jacob Javits write ERISA, contends that unions have even less influence with the bankruptcy judge than other players do, because they are out of the loop. (Cummings usually works with corporate clients, although he did represent the United Airlines pilots.) Many unsecured creditors at least will be on the creditors' committee, where they get access to all the corporate financials. "Whose evidence does the judge listen to? No one in their right mind will bet on the union. It's the company's evidence. The company brings in an investment banker who says, 'We have analyzed the prospects, and you have to get blah blah blah if the stock is to be worth anything.' What can the union do to rebut that? The union's expert doesn't have access to the company's information."

Should a union resist the company's proposal under Section 1113, management can always brandish the nuclear threat: liquidation. Whenever a company says it will go out of business if it can't terminate the pension plan, most unions will settle (see Chapter 2). Better to have a job and a shrunken pension than no job at all—especially since liquidation and layoffs will probably mean a shrunken pension anyway.

There can be other alternatives, insists David Neigus, associate general counsel for the International Association of Machinists and Aerospace Workers, whose members have suffered through bankruptcies at US Airways, United, and other airlines. "That's kind of a false choice. That's the pressure they're trying to apply. The unions and the workers have to apply their own pressure [by saying to management], 'You promised these pensions; you have to keep them up. Look for ways to do the funding.'"

But what weapons does a labor leader have? Neigus tries to find allies among the other creditors, though he admits that's not easy. "There are a lot of forces that want to try to keep the airlines flying. The biggest creditors are your aircraft lessors and aircraft manufacturers, who want to keep the planes in the air. You make the pitch that it's a service industry and airlines can't fly without competent workers, and that they can't do it well with disgruntled workers." Another union lawyer, Paul Whitehead of the Steelworkers, suggests unions might have a shot at blocking a termination under Section 1113, despite the judge's inherent bias, "if we can show that labor costs are not the problem the company faces, if we can show that the company is overreaching. While maybe it needs a dollar an hour in relief, it is telling the judge that it needs five dollars an hour."

If the company's nuclear option is to threaten liquidation, the union's is to strike. In one of the first big fights over Section 1113, in July 1985, Wheeling-Pittsburgh demanded a staggering 30 percent cut in wages and benefits. The Steelworkers refused, Judge Warren Worthington Bentz gave the company permission to tear up its contracts, and the Steelworkers walked out. The strike lasted ninety-eight days. Ultimately, the union won some of its demands, including the ouster of CEO Dennis Carney, but the pension plan was terminated. At United, meanwhile, Joseph Tiberi, a spokesman for the Machinists union, says that the threat of a strike during bankruptcy negotiations helped persuade management to agree to a union proposal for another kind of pension, a multiemployer pension system (more on this in Chapter 9). And it was because LTV feared a strike by the Steelworkers that it put in the ill-fated follow-on plans.

Still, labor leaders know as well as anyone the limitations of the strike weapon. For one thing, it works best with hard-to-replace, highly skilled labor groups like pilots. It also runs the risk of destroying the company.

Do union leaders sometimes draw real weapons as well? Dave McCall, the Steelworkers' district leader in Ohio, says that if Wilbur Ross had simply tried to sell off the LTV plants for scrap and killed off the company, if he hadn't reached an agreement with the union on restarting the two most valuable blast furnaces (the Cleveland Works in Cleveland and the Indiana Harbor Works in East Chicago, Indiana), "we were prepared to take the plants over and block him and anybody else from coming." McCall, who is a fourth-generation steelworker himself, claims that his members would have surrounded the two plants, which together had the capacity to produce eight million tons per year of liquid steel, and "it would have been the police and National Guard [who would have had to force the workers out]. We were not going to allow those assets to be stolen from us. Our fathers and grandfathers and great-grandfathers built those plants; it was their blood and tears. We had as much stake in those plants as anybody who ever invested a nickel."

At the Cleveland plant in downtown Cleveland, McCall says, his union was winterizing and protecting the two continuous casting machines, each worth $300 million. "Management was prepared to allow it to freeze up. I sent a team of [about twenty-five] people on the four-to-twelve shift a few days before they were prepared to shut down. Several foremen and security guards tried to stop us. They eventually understood we were on a mission, and we were not about to be stopped.

"It's a good thing there was no violence," he continues. "It's a good thing they stepped down. I told our guys that if anybody tried to stop them, to whack them upside down with a pipe wrench. I think [the foremen and security] understood that those guys had those instructions."

Was McCall just posturing? Would union members really have wielded their pipe wrenches? "It's the only time in my experience of collective bargaining where I've said to somebody, 'If you have to protect this thing by forcibly pushing people away, I'm telling you to do it,' " says McCall. One former government official with pension-related experience doesn't dismiss such threats. The official pointed out that the Steelworkers' history is sprinkled with violence, including a long and bitter USW-led strike against Phelps Dodge in 1983–1984 during which a strikebreaker drew a gun on a crowd, some strikers pelted police with stones, and the National Guard was called in. "There were times I wondered if someone would come after me," the official says.

Rocks and pipe wrenches notwithstanding, the bankruptcy laws have rendered the unions largely powerless to block a termination if a company, its creditors, and its potential investors really want it. "We go in there making the best argument we can," says Joe Tiberi. "We cannot prevent the sponsored plan from being terminated. Ultimately, the judge makes the decision, but the judge's priority is the successful restructuring of the company, not the welfare of retirees."

"The bankruptcy laws are so stacked against workers and retirees that it is unconscionable," insists Micheal Buckner, trustee of the health and retirement funds for the United Mine Workers of America, which has had its own run-ins with bankrupt coal companies (see Chapter 9). "You can work for a company for forty years, and in bankruptcy you are equal to a creditor who showed up two days ago and sold them roof bolts."

Ganging Up on the Pension Plan

Actually, less than equal.

It's bad enough that in theory the PBGC is on the same level as all the other unsecured creditors, and the pension debt is no more sacrosanct than a bill for a roof bolt. In reality, the PBGC has even less clout than any of those creditors. Rather than gaining some extra moral authority from the broken promise of deferred wages and the headlines about Grandma thrown out on the streets, the pension plan has no allies when it comes to the fight for assets in Chapter 11.

From the beginning, recalls Henry Rose, the original PBGC counsel, "we found ourselves in a hostile situation in bankruptcy courts. Almost everybody is an enemy of the PBGC in bankruptcy court. There is a cadre of specialists who are local, and the judge has been chosen from among that group, so they're all friends. The PBGC is an outsider." As with any profession, the people who work together over and over—the same few top-notch lawyers specializing in corporate bankruptcy—develop a certain camaraderie. While their cases drag on, they negotiate together for years. Some of them become the judges who will try the other lawyers' cases. Perhaps, as Professor LoPucki of UCLA claims, the judges are trying to curry favor with the big-name lawyers so that their next headline-making clients will also file in this court. By contrast, the PBGC, with its in-house counsel paid at government rates, doesn't mingle on the bankruptcy circuit. It might go years without appearing in court about a sizable termination.

The PBGC is also the only creditor whose claim is not fixed at the start, a disadvantage that underscores its status as the odd man out. After all, if the debtor company has reneged on a lease for 300,000 square feet at $50 per square foot per month, with three years remaining, that's a claim of $540 million, plain and simple. But what's the size of the pension underfunding? Is it the bigger amount that the PBGC calculates or the smaller amount that the company usually asserts? Or could it be yet another amount altogether if the PBGC and the company work out a deal or the judge decides to split the difference? Even as the haggling begins over how much of their claims the unsecured creditors are going to end up with, no one knows what size claim the PBGC is going to start bargaining from. That makes all the other creditors uncomfortable and suspicious.

Another problem: The PBGC doesn't share other unsecured creditors' mutual interest in keeping the company going. The aircraft lessors and manufacturers that David Neigus mentioned want to continue leasing and selling airplanes to a reorganized US Airways or United; similarly, the "critical vendors" cited in Chapter 2 want to go on selling their goods. That is the judge's goal, as well. "Ultimately, the other creditors get a good return on their investment if the company survives," notes Phyllis Borzi, the former House Education and Labor Committee counsel. However, it doesn't really make any difference to the PBGC. Once the pension plan is terminated, it becomes the PBGC's responsibility, regardless of what happens to the company. Cases like LTV and perhaps US Airways, in which the emerged company grows so healthy that the agency might hope to send the plan back to the employer, are rare.

What's worse is that many creditors may look at the numbers and decide that the PBGC is trying to get more than its fair share. Say the pension plan is 60 percent funded. To the PBGC, the company, the actuaries, the retirees, and the workers, that's a pretty lousy deal. It means that the company has barely more than half the money it needs to pay its pension obligations. But to other creditors, 60 percent is enviable territory. "They're saying, 'You're starting out with sixty cents on the dollar; you're a secured creditor to some extent!'" says James J. Keightley, the PBGC's general counsel from 1995 to 2005. "The PBGC is not as sympathetic a creditor as might be expected, particularly to unsecured creditors."

In short, the bankruptcy process holds no special protections for the pension plan. Bankruptcy law won't save it. The union can't help. Nor can the PBGC. The other creditors won't cut it any slack. It's gone.

Part Three

The Investors

7 How Investors Play the Game

"We purchased certain assets of a company. To the extent that there were pension plans or liabilities associated with bankrupt predecessor entities, that's not our concern. We had nothing to do with it."

—MIKE PSAROS, COFOUNDER, KPS SPECIAL SITUATIONS FUNDS

How does an investor analyzing the value of a distressed company view a pension plan liability?

- "If the pension has to be continued, it may be a deal killer."
  —Harvey Miller, partner, Weil, Gotshal & Manges
- "It becomes a factor you price into the deal. It's not dissimilar to looking at an industry with asbestos claims."—Richard P. Schifter, a partner in the buyout giant TPG, which invested $3.6 billion in 2004 in a company with an asbestos liability
- "If you look at two companies that have the same cost structure, profit outlook, and balance sheet, and one has an underfunded pension plan, it factors into your thinking. That doesn't mean the deal can't work." —Ed Shapiro, partner, PAR Capital Management
- "It's all math. It's all analyzable. Investors can make some assumptions."—A senior manager at an investment-banking boutique specializing in restructuring

Clearly, there are almost as many ways of looking at a distressed company's pension liability as there are investors in distressed companies. Still, these investors do share some values and priorities. They start with one basic fact: Strong companies do not file for bankruptcy. If a company has reached this point, then it most likely has serious, long-term troubles, notwithstanding any pension underfunding, and recovery is far from guaranteed. The Chapter 11 process may be generous and forgiving, offering the filers a chance to shed some of the labor costs, leases, bank debts, and other expenses—including pension funding—that had dragged them down. But the Bankruptcy Code can't solve all the problems that brought the company to the brink. It can't turn a stubborn CEO into a brilliant leader or create gold out of the lead in the corporate labs. Investors still have to do their basic financial and business analysis, studying the company's reorganization proposal, its product line, its cash flow, its expected cost savings, its projected earnings, the type and maturity of its debt, its management, the broader market, how long it stayed in bankruptcy, its employee morale, and how other investors are likely to view its potential. (These topics, relating to bankruptcy in general, are beyond the scope of this book.)

Vultures also agree on what they don't know, and the biggest unknown is the size of the pension debt itself. No one can really be sure of the dollars involved until the company and the PBGC finish their inevitable rounds of negotiations, lawsuits, and judicial appeals, which can drag on for years. It may take a good year after the Chapter 11 filing just for the company to decide to terminate the plan, as was the case with Delta. If there is more than one pension program, the company may drop one, two, several, or all of them; or it may decide to keep them all (more on that situation in Chapter 9). If the unions mount a challenge under Section 1113 of the Bankruptcy Code, there's the possibility—slim though it may be—that they can block the termination. These complications, moreover, exacerbate all the standard problems in any bankruptcy, especially the issue of employee morale.

Whatever their specialty and style, all investors in companies with big pension deficits ultimately face the same short-term-versus-long-term dilemma that unions do. For unions, the issue is this: lose the pension to save the jobs. For investors, it's a question of taking perhaps a smaller return now for the promise of a stronger company and a bigger return down the road. "A [pension] termination increases the amount of claims that the company has got to pay back. It reduces the value of the estate. But at the same time, it ends up paving the way for when the company comes out of bankruptcy, because the company's got a cleaner balance sheet," says Marc Lasry, managing partner of Avenue Capital Group, a $12 billion hedge fund in New York that specializes in distressed properties and has invested in such pension dumpers as Delta. "It's absolutely worth doing long term. As to whether the short-term impact causes too many problems, that's the question." The pension factor, Lasry adds, makes an otherwise-standard deal "a lot more risky."

Beyond those common principles, however, the field is wide open. And a lot can be learned from the ways different investors have come to their decisions when a target company has a drastically underfunded pension plan.

Mike Psaros: Cherry Picking in an Asset Sale

In June 2005, when Jernberg Industries filed for bankruptcy, it had about seven hundred employees in Chicago making wheel hubs, transmission turbine hubs, and other parts for car manufacturers like Ford, General Motors, Chrysler, and Toyota Motor Sales. It also had approximately six hundred retirees, their dependents, and other former workers, and a million-dollar pension plan that wasn't even 50 percent funded. In the half year before filing, according to an article in the *Wall Street Journal* in December 2006, it had lost $3.4 million on sales of about $60 million. Mike Psaros's firm, KPS Special Situations Funds, offered to buy Jernberg's assets in a liquidation auction.

Psaros, the financier whose Greek-immigrant family worked in the West Virginia steel mills, is a short, quiet-spoken man with thick dark eyebrows that contrast starkly with his close-cropped, prematurely graying hair. In a tribute to his family's roots, his small office high up in the former Pan Am Building, just north of Grand Central Terminal, features two framed photos of Chios, the small Greek island that some of his grandparents came from. To invest in distressed companies, Psaros cofounded KPS in 1997 with Gene Keilin, the veteran Lazard Freres & Co. investment banker who had organized the employee buyout at Weirton Steel, where the Psaros family worked, and another banker, David Shapiro. The trio raised their first private equity fund of $210 million in 1998, with significant backing from GE Capital, then a second fund of $404 million in 2004 and a third of $1.2 billion in 2007. According to the firm's literature, "KPS targets manufacturing, transportation, and service businesses" with revenue of at least $100 million but "will consider all industries except for high technology, financial services, telecommunications, broadcast media, real estate, and natural resources." The literature also singles out for investment "businesses facing the threat of closure, liquidation, or with a history of operating losses" or operating in Chapter 11.

There were conditions to KPS's offer for Jernberg. Psaros may brag that "we would never proceed with a purchase unless our purchase was supported by the national union and the local union, and the collective bargaining agreements were ratified," but that support sometimes comes with the unions' backs to the wall. Even before the official bankruptcy filing, Psaros and his top management reportedly told Jernberg's United Steelworkers leaders that they needed to slash labor costs by 20 percent, by way of job cuts, a wage freeze, a reduction in overtime pay, and higher health care premiums paid by the workers. Plus, the old pension plan would have to go. If KPS didn't get these concessions, it threatened to walk. Within a week, the Steelworkers had accepted the terms, and in September a holding company created by KPS, called Hephaestus Holdings, bought Jernberg's plants and equipment for $54.5 million. The new owner brought in a new CEO, set up a 401(k) retirement plan, and invested $17 million in machinery, repairs, and other improvements. It also bargained hard—and semisuccessfully—to get its automaker customers to pay more for their parts, and faster. The plant, whittled down to about 575 workers, kept on churning out hubs, and the PBGC took over most of the $11.7 million pension underfunding.

Technically, KPS did not buy the company Jernberg; rather, it bought the assets of Jernberg through an auction conducted under Section 363 of the Bankruptcy Code and then established a new company to do what Jernberg had done for nearly seventy years. KPS prefers that method of investing because the purchases come with less baggage and more control. The buyer can cherry-pick which parts to accept. That also makes it the easiest way to dump a pension plan. There's no negotiating with the PBGC, no Section 1113 protection for the unions. "What [investors] buy," explains Stuart C. Gilson, a professor of business administration at Harvard Business School, "is generally just the assets but none of the liabilities that would otherwise deter anybody from buying those assets, like environmental claims or tort claims." Or pension claims.

"We create new companies to buy assets out of bankruptcy. These assets are sold free and clear of liabilities, other than the liabilities the buyer agrees to assume," Psaros emphasizes. But he also repeatedly says that he is concerned about his workers' welfare and believes that having a retirement plan is important: "I have never met a union leader who didn't believe providing some kind of pension benefit is absolutely critical to what the union stands for and what they try to be." In that case, why didn't he agree to assume Jernberg's pension liability? Psaros's answer is to stick to his mantra: "We did not purchase Jernberg. We purchased certain of its assets. We create companies de novo to buy assets, and we then set up new benefit plans. To the extent that there were pension plans or liabilities associated with bankrupt predecessor entities, that's not our concern. We had nothing to do with it." Okay, then why not set up a brand-new defined benefit plan in his "de novo" companies? Psaros admits that the question stumped him at first. All of KPS's holdings but one have either a 401(k) or a multiemployer plan, and Psaros doesn't even know if those are less expensive than a traditional defined benefit program would have been. (The one exception, Genesis Worldwide II, which makes metal coil processing and roll coating and electrostatic coiling equipment, actually kept its defined benefit plan because, Psaros says, it was fully funded at the time of purchase.) As for putting in a new defined benefit plan, he says, "It's just not done."

Because a 363 is such a relatively clean and simple process, it can be wrapped up quickly. That's certainly preferable to the years and years in which a Chapter 11 reorganization can drag on. "[A 363] works best in a company that is close to being marginal, where a continued stay in Chapter 11 would be erosive of value," says Harvey Miller of Weil, Gotshal. "The assets are sensitive, so the faster you get them away from the Chapter 11 arena, the more they have a chance to become solvent. If you're looking for a fast transaction, the fastest way is to do a 363."

Of course, buying a company without its pension liability through a 363 sale is hardly risk free. These companies are likely to be the weakest of the weak, businesses that aren't hardy enough to pull out of bankruptcy via Chapter 11. To sort out the most promising prospects, Psaros looks at three basic criteria: First comes the viability of the product line. "Does its product have a place in the marketplace? Does it have the technology, the brand, and the intellectual knowledge to compete?" Second is the feasibility of implementing significant cost reductions. "The wrong way to do a turnaround is to assume this company will be able to sell more widgets." Finally, he considers the potential for union cooperation.

Psaros also insists on bringing in new management. "We will never invest our capital behind a management team that created the train wreck," he says. KPS must have a controlling equity stake and, unlike many investors who trade in and out of distressed assets, it takes an active role in operating its investments. For instance, at Jernberg it chose the new CEO and directly negotiated with the Steelworkers. As the firm's official brochure puts it, "Our professionals work intensely with our management and employee partners at our portfolio companies." KPS aims for an annual return of 25 percent to 35 percent, with the goal of selling each holding to another company in the same industry or another investment firm in four to five years. Since KPS is privately held, Psaros won't reveal its actual returns, except to say that "we've exceeded our goals." The only publicly available number comes from the California Public Employees' Retirement System (CalPERS), which has a $20 million commitment to KPS's second fund. According to CalPERS's midyear 2006 report, that fund had a return of 54.9 percent. By 2007, ten years after it was founded, KPS had sold seven of the twelve companies in its portfolio.

Investor Wilbur Ross, too, has bid in 363 auctions—most notably, at LTV, where he acquired the physical assets but no labor contracts or pensions. He has also gone the Chapter 11 route, buying up bank debt and other debt in reorganization. A 363 purchase can cost 10 percent to 25 percent more, he says, when pressed. "But at least it's clean. You know exactly what liabilities you're taking, and you can leave behind whatever parts you don't care for." Besides, even with the 10 percent or 25 percent markup, the assets in a 363 auction are sold at bargain prices. In acquiring LTV's remains, Ross reportedly paid just $11 per ton of steel-making capacity, versus the going price of $200 per ton at most companies. Ultimately, of course, he sold LTV and the other steel companies for more than double what he paid for them and received more than ten times their price per share at the time of the sale.

Marc Lasry: Predicting Which Company Will Dump

Avenue Capital doesn't wait around for a bankrupt company to become a 363 corpse. Founded in 1995, Avenue is a hedge fund specializing in distressed investments, with about $12.3 billion under management as of early 2007. It is probably just as famous, however, for its political connections: Cofounder Marc Lasry is a big donor to Democratic politicians, and in autumn 2006 the firm hired Chelsea Clinton, daughter of former President Bill Clinton and Senator Hillary Rodham Clinton. Although Avenue refused to comment on her duties, Clinton could be seen, soon after she started the new job, in the small but airy main room of the firm's midtown Manhattan offices, just another headphone-wearing employee at another desk among a half-dozen rows of desks, facing the office's life-size statues of Batman and Superman.

To Lasry, the key to investing in a company that's likely to dump its pension is to guess when, whether, and how many plans might be terminated, and then try to scope out what the market is guessing at the same time. "It's not simple," he says. "There are all these separate decision trees that you're going down. The first tree is termination versus nontermination. If it's termination, is it all of the plans?" Each different tree changes the size of the unsecured creditors' total claim.

In deciding how much he's willing to pay for this risk, Lasry says, "I back into it, based on the return I want to generate." The thought process Lasry outlines turns out to involve some fairly straightforward addition, subtraction, and fractions. He gives a hypothetical case: Take a company with a general unsecured claims pool, before any pension terminations, of $1 billion. Assume that Avenue values the company at $500 million. "You expect to get fifty cents on the dollar"—that is, the debt minus the $500 million inherent value. "So you buy debt at thirty-five, forty cents, expecting to take two years to work it out." But what if the company has pension plans that are underfunded to the tune of $500 million? If it terminates the plans, the entire unsecured claims pool is now one-third bigger: the original $1 billion plus the new $500 million from the pensions. So Avenue will lower its purchase price ceiling by one-third. Now throw in another complication. "It depends when you invested in the cycle. If the plans never get terminated, that's even better for you, because then you end up buying at what you think is a pretty low price."

The variety of pension trees and branches was apparent at Delta. Lasry would not discuss individual investments in detail, but Avenue's holdings of at least $200 million worth of Delta unsecured bonds became a matter of public record in December 2006, when it helped set up an informal creditors' committee. The firm first considered buying Delta paper soon after the carrier filed for bankruptcy in September 2005. Although Delta had said it hoped to maintain all of its pension plans, Avenue certainly couldn't take that wish to the bank. If Delta terminated only the pilots' plan, it would be adding a claim of $3 billion to the unsecured creditors' pool. Terminate all the plans, and the claim would shoot up to nearly $6.4 billion.

As it happened, if Avenue in fact bought when it first was looking at Delta, it would have come in at a pretty good price, with the airline's unsecured claims trading in the high teens. During the next year, as the carrier restructured and terminated its pilots' plan, the claims moved up into the midthirties. When US Airways made its unsolicited bid in November 2006—the point at which Avenue is known to have held at least $200 million—the claims shot into the midsixties and even low seventies; then, as the bid collapsed, the claims fell back a bit into the midfifties, still far ahead of the opening mark. Overall, Avenue would seem to have enjoyed a comfortable profit, thanks to the lucky break of the US Airways bid, good progress in Delta's reorganization, a general upswing in the airline industry, and—presumably—the pilots' plan termination.

Shelley Greenhaus: Paying for Protection

Thirty miles north of New York, in suburban White Plains, Shelley Greenhaus of Whippoorwill Associates looks at the pension risk in a different way. Because a pension underfunding increases the level of insecurity in a deal, he wants more security wherever he can get it. That typically means buying debt high up in the priority chain. "Until there's more clarification as to how the pension fund will be dealt with, we as a firm will invest in debt that's senior to the pension fund, trying to invest ahead of the fray," he explains. "With the pension fund, there's a much greater uncertainty of whether there will be business interruptions, whether chaos will happen: more strikes, unions saying, 'We're not going to work for the new buyer unless they assume X, Y, and Z.' There's a different dynamic. The whole field is evolving, and it's better to be safe than sorry." Once it's clear whether or not the pension plans will be terminated and how large the claim will be, the firm will buy debt that has a lower priority. "We have bought subordinate paper after the pension is resolved. The risk-reward is more certain at that point."

Greenhaus still shows traces of his New York roots and his days as a long-haired, self-described "typical 1960s radical" at the City University of New York. He talks fast, with a hint of a Brooklyn accent, and, as of the early 2000s, had a bushy mustache and salt-and-pepper hair worn in the style of the Sergeant Pepper–era Beatles (collar length and parted in the middle). Abandoning his original goal of a career in urban government, Greenhaus was among the first to find gold in bankruptcy, according to Hilary Rosenberg's book *The Vulture Investors*. He started in the bankruptcy arena in 1981 doing investments with the family of Julius Rosenwald, who had built Sears, Roebuck and Co., and then moved to Oppenheimer two years later. In 1987 he launched a distressed-investing fund at Oppenheimer with Jon Bauer, another up-and-coming vulture. One of their first deals—Wheeling-Pittsburgh—was also one of the earliest pension-termination trendsetters. The deal brought Greenhaus in contact with Marc Lasry, who at that point was at a small trading firm called Cowen and Co. In the process of buying up claims from Wheeling-Pittsburgh vendors, Cowen had come upon a $75 million coal contract that was far bigger than the firm was accustomed to handling. Lasry and his partner passed it over to Greenhaus's partner at Oppenheimer for a finder's fee.

Some twenty years after their Wheeling-Pittsburgh dealings, Greenhaus and Lasry would intersect again in Delta's bankruptcy, with Lasry now at Avenue and Greenhaus at Whippoorwill, where he managed $1.3 billion in assets. Whippoorwill had started investing in Delta back in December 2004, even before the bankruptcy filing. Greenhaus was interested in the industry, but he wanted to pick his flights carefully, choosing carriers whose route structures seemed to make sense. "The airline business is an interesting one. They really have—I'm not going to say broken the unions—by going into bankruptcy, but they have been able to rationalize their cost structure, which includes the unions." Nevertheless, back in late 2004 it wasn't at all clear what would happen with Delta's pilots and their lump-sum pension bonanza. So Greenhaus bought $46 million of secured paper, collateralized by Delta airplanes, paying eighty cents on the dollar or almost the face value.

That close to face value might seem high, but it turned out to be smart. Delta bought the whole lot back from Greenhaus less than two years later—after the bankruptcy filing and the pilots' plan termination—at 114, or an 18 percent rate of return. "For being senior secured paper, to get an 18 percent rate of return, for the risk factor, I thought that was very good," says Greenhaus. "This is sleep-at-night, senior secured paper. We had multiple layers of security. We didn't have to worry about volatility. We owned the airplanes. The worst case, Delta would give us back the airplanes, and we could sell them."

According to David Hamilton, director of corporate default research at Moody's Investors Service, Greenhaus's approach is one of the two most common vulture strategies. It has a couple of advantages. First—and not surprisingly, considering its priority status and collateral—senior secured debt tends to enjoy the highest expected recovery. In June 2005, Moody's published a study of 303 U.S. companies in industries other than finance that had filed for bankruptcy, looking at their bond prices at default and then again just before the resolution of their bankruptcy. Senior secured debt like the kind Greenhaus buys had the best undiscounted average ratio, at 1.31. The second advantage is particularly important for activist investors who want to play a controlling role in running their target companies. Because they will be assured of having an equity holding if any equity is paid out, buying this kind of debt "puts them in the driver's seat for managing the recovery," Hamilton notes.

By the way, the second-most popular approach, Hamilton says, is the other extreme: buying the lowest subordinated debt, "debt that's trading really cheap and has the most upside, swinging for the fences, hoping that it's misvalued because of a fire sale." That type of debt had an undiscounted average ratio just below the senior debt in Moody's survey.

Uncalculated Risk

Regardless of their strategies, investors face a special risk at companies with a pension overhang: It's almost impossible to predict just how big their risk will ultimately be.

Of course, going into bankruptcy, no creditors of any sort know for sure how big a payment they will end up with, but at least they can put a dollar figure on the size of their claim to begin with. They can even make an educated guess as to what they will finally get, probably around seven to ten cents on the dollar. Similarly, investors may not know in advance what the total number and amount of claims will be: How many accounts payable will the company honor before filing? Will it pay this month's tab for its equipment leases? But, again, soon after the bankruptcy is filed, the creditors will make themselves known and their opening claims can be added up. "Normally, you look at the balance sheet and you see $400 million in public debt, $500 million in bank debt. You know exactly how much the debt is," says Greenhaus. Ed Shapiro of PAR Capital points out that with a typical corporate bond, "If a company has a $2 billion bond, it knows it's going to pay 7 percent a year, twice a year for seven years. You know what the cash flows are."

"Pensions," Greenhaus adds, "are much more of a black hole." The defined benefit plan is actually a long-term debt of an unlimited, unknown, and unknowable amount, owed to a large number of people: the employees who are already retired, those still on the job with vested rights to their future pensions, and those who have left the company but have not yet retired, also with vested rights. The PBGC is merely their stand-in. "With pensions, there are assumptions about how long the employees are going to live, how long they're going to work for the company, what their pay raises are going to be, what interest rates do, and what the stock market does," Shapiro says. Thus, it could take years to determine the size of the pension claim. The answer will depend on—among other factors—how aggressive the company's assumptions were, how far off those are from the PBGC's assumptions, how willing the two sides are to compromise, how tough the judge is in imposing a decision, and how sympathetic the judge is to one side or the other.

The lack of clarity need not prevent investors from putting money into a company with a pension liability. It just means they must make a unique kind of calculation. When Deirdre Martini's firm CIT figures out the size of the debtor-in-possession loan that it's willing to grant a company in bankruptcy, Martini assumes that the PBGC will take over only part of the claim, with the rest wiped out. "There is something special about it, because you don't know the extent to which it's going to be modified. There's a likelihood that the obligations will decrease. If you make your financial decision based on a worst-case scenario, you're in a better position." Bottom line? "I can ballpark a 10 to 15 percent reduction" in the size of the claim.

One hedge fund investor who generally eschews companies with big pension liabilities uses a similar discount when calculating his target return. "My gut says ten points additional for the pension situation," this investor explains. "It adds incremental risk to the situation, and volatility. You need an even higher return because you're changing the environment people are working in. People who are unhappy don't make as good a company."

Wilbur Ross: Finding the Tipping Point

In his forays into the world of auto parts, Wilbur Ross didn't always bid via a 363 auction the way he did with steel. Instead, he sometimes took an approach popular with vultures who want to exercise control and stay with the acquired company for the long term: seeking out the fulcrum paper. This paper—typically senior unsecured bonds—is "the most senior class that will be impaired, that won't get one hundred cents on the dollar," Ross explains. Because the ultimate goal for this kind of investor is a controlling equity stake in the new company, Ross and other vultures will simply swap the debt out for equity. Professor Gilson of Harvard puts it another way: "The fulcrum is the point in the old capital structure at which the money runs out. If you buy just above that point, you receive a significant share of stock in the new company."

The trick is figuring out exactly which paper meets that definition. If Ross were to take an approach more like Greenhaus's, that is, "if we buy [too-senior debt] at ninety cents and it goes to par, that's nice but it won't get us equity," Ross explains. It will probably be repaid in cash, notes, or new debt. By the same token, he continues, "if you go too low, you may get nothing," or at any rate, less equity. Finding the fulcrum point "requires skill in valuing the business," says Gilson. "It's a little bit like the waterfall that you see at weddings. You pour the champagne into the top glass; it spills into the next one and the next one until it runs out." The investor must try to determine the total value of the company, how much the most senior creditors are likely to get, and at what point the cash-and-notes payout is likely to peter out and the equity begin.

Ross admits that back in 2005 he might not have found that perfect point with Collins & Aikman, an auto-parts maker in bankruptcy. The entire sector was becoming a prime arena for pension-sensitive vultures, with such big-name investors as Carl Icahn; Avenue Capital; and the private equity firms Cerberus Capital Management, which later bought Chrysler, and Appaloosa Management taking and maneuvering for positions. And no wonder. The sector presented a classic Rust Belt scenario: an old and shrinking manufacturing base facing huge legacy costs, high oil prices, and growing competition from China, in desperate need of cost cutting and consolidation. Ross has publicly said that his grand plan was to essentially repeat in auto parts what he had done in steel, coal, and textiles: acquire a number of distressed companies; reduce labor costs, including pensions; reduce capacity; and merge the acquisitions into one conglomerate that could then enjoy economies of scale and flex its muscle on pricing. This time there would be the added twist of creating two or three conglomerates, one focusing on metal parts, one on plastics, and perhaps a third, smaller one focusing on auto safety products. But the risk, as Ross notes, was that the sector's very popularity would drive up prices and drive out bargains. "Lately, with so many people who are not professionals buying the debt, it's often the case that the debt is higher than the enterprise value, at least in our opinion."

According to an article in *Fortune* magazine in late 2006, it took Ross two years of research into the parts industry before he made his first move. He decided to home in on plastic parts for a couple of reasons, the article said. First, plastic scratches easily. Therefore, carmakers pretty much have to buy from local suppliers, so as to limit the amount of handling and the time spent in shipping. Furthermore, raw materials prices for plastic had recently risen dramatically. That would probably mean an abrupt financial squeeze for a company whose product line was otherwise solid, which meshed with one of Ross's publicly proclaimed criteria for investment: companies that were basically sound but simply lacked the deep pockets to adapt to global competition. He was also looking for niches that were fragmented and had high return potential, he told *Fortune*.

Collins & Aikman (C&A), based in Troy, Michigan, would seem to fit the bill. It specialized in plastic interior parts such as instrument panels and floor mats. Furthermore, an earlier buyout led by David Stockman, the U.S. budget director under President Ronald Reagan in the 1980s, had collapsed in May 2005. Stockman was forced out as CEO, and the firm filed for bankruptcy. After missing its required 2005 pension contribution of $5.5 million, C&A was in negotiations with the PBGC.

In October 2005, Ross bought some of the firm's bank debt. The *Wall Street Journal* in a November 2005 article put it at "about half," but Ross insists that his purchase was "not a lot, thank goodness," although he won't specify how much. He also won't reveal the exact price he paid, noting only that the debt started trading in the high nineties before the bankruptcy filing, which was almost at par (or the dollar-for-dollar face value), then dropped to the seventies, and then fell to the thirties at the time of his interview for this book, a year after his purchase. "We bought it relatively low, but not as low as where it's trading now," is all he would say. Even while he was buying the debt, Ross was also investigating a Section 363–like approach to Collins & Aikman's European and South American properties, which he purchased six months later.

Why did Ross's magic touch fail on the C&A debt? Ross himself says that problems in the industry in general and at the company in particular got worse than predicted. "The erosion of perceived value has been so severe," he says. He told *Fortune*, as well, that "we may have been a year too early." It didn't help that in October 2006, Collins & Aikman riled one of its biggest customers, Ford, by cutting off deliveries in a pricing dispute. Ford temporarily had to suspend production of one of its best-selling products, the Fusion sedan, at a Mexican plant, and it ultimately agreed to pay C&A more for its parts. The mutual tension was hardly unique; throughout the industry, parts makers were rebelling as the big car manufacturers were increasingly squeezing them on price. But no other firms had gone as far in their rebellion. C&A took a bad hit as Ford publicly threatened never to sign any new contract with the supplier. To add more trouble to the mix, Stockman, the former CEO of C&A, was indicted in March 2007 on charges of fraud, conspiracy, and obstruction of justice in connection with the firm's finances.

Ross also notes that timing can be particularly tricky in the auto-parts field. "Generally, contracts are awarded a couple years ahead of production," he says. "But original equipment [auto] manufacturers don't give you new contracts when you're in bankruptcy." So a parts maker that goes into bankruptcy in 2005 and emerges in 2007 will have missed out on all the orders that were signed in 2005 and 2006 for production through 2008. "If you're in bankruptcy too long, you don't have a backlog. That's very, very hard to recoup when you come out." Ideally, Ross says, a company should come out of bankruptcy within a year. At the time he made that statement, he had owned C&A for about a year, with no emergence in sight.

Still, Ross is far from ready to give up on his auto-parts empire. "The book is still out" on his investments, he says. "Those are still works in progress. It takes longer than one or two years to turn a company around. We'll see if we got it right."

Psaros, Lasry, Greenhaus, and Ross are only a few of the players in the pension-bankruptcy field. Distressed investing in general has been getting a lot more crowded since Max Heine pretty much invented it in the 1930s. It was his insight that value could be found in the rubble of the Great Depression, in the hidden difference between the price that the market was placing on a distressed company's securities and the true worth of its business. This philosophy went out of fashion in the Go-Go Sixties, but the passage of the 1978 Bankruptcy Code slowly reversed Wall Street's attitude toward bankruptcy. Filing for bankruptcy no longer had to mean utter liquidation; quite the contrary, the new law did everything it could to help distressed companies polish those hidden nuggets of value. By the 1980s, the vultures were starting to flock, ready to take advantage of the opportunities spawned by the recessions early in that decade. The phenomenon only grew in the 1990s, refueled by the 1987 stock market crash and the collapse of the junk bond market soon afterward. As stock prices, the bond markets, and shaky companies tumbled, the amount of defaulted debt doubled and then doubled again, between 1987 and 1989, and a secondary market developed for trading this debt. It became increasingly common for vultures to swap their cheaply bought debt for an equity stake—and control—in the new common stock, rather than holding on and waiting for the value of the bonds to return to the face amount.

At that point, the big Wall Street houses started paying attention. Distressed investing in the 1990s "matured into a much more efficient machine," journalist Hilary Rosenberg notes in her book *The Vulture Investors.* Even that was barely the toddler stage. The tech-stock debacle of 2000 gave these investors yet more buying opportunities. The number of institutional investors specializing in distressed debt jumped from fifty in 1990 to more than 160 fifteen years later, according to Edward I. Altman, a professor of finance at New York University's Leonard N. Stern School of Business and one of the nation's foremost authorities on debt financing. Altman maintains a database that is a standard reference tool for Wall Street.

The investors were mainly small private equity firms and hedge funds, such as Lasry's Avenue Capital and Greenhaus's Whippoorwill, although bigger institutions were also interested. Ironically, even a lot of pension funds have invested in companies that dump their pensions. That's because these pension funds frequently invest in hedge funds and the funds of private equity firms like TPG and KPS, which then buy the pension dumpers. For instance, CalPERS, the California public employees' plan, put money into KPS's second fund, which included Jernberg, the auto-parts maker. Amazingly, the Congressional Research Service in June 2007 estimated that nearly one-fourth of all corporate pension plans had put some of their money in hedge funds.

And the distressed investors were part of a rapidly expanding universe of firms playing in new, high-risk, often highly leveraged niches. By 2007, private buyout firms, on the prowl for turnarounds, were waving around upwards of $1.2 trillion. Hedge funds had roughly the same amount under management. Both sets of players were slammed later that year by a credit squeeze that began in the subprime housing market. As banks and other lenders toughened their terms, buyout firms became more cautious in choosing their targets and some particularly leveraged edge funds were wiped out. In the short term, at least, less money was available for investing in distressed property. Yet even the credit disaster didn't change these investors' basic philosophy. If anything, it promised to provide more fodder, in the form of more companies going bankrupt without access to liquidity.

Rarely, if ever, did these investors specifically seek out companies with pension trouble. But when they're playing on bankruptcy turf, they can hardly avoid it.

8 The Signs of Failure

IF THERE'S a single industry where an investor might expect every company to shut down its pension plans, the steel industry is probably it. Every factor that typically leads a company to shed its pension plan—an old-line, dying industry; recession; low-cost competition; hidebound management slow to adapt to technological innovation; comprehensive benefits; alternative products cutting into the market—pummeled the steel business in the late twentieth century. The imagery that comes to mind is all too apt: rusted girders, a blast furnace gone cold.

It's ironic that steel companies epitomize the decline of pensions, because these companies virtually created the modern American pension plan. Their union, the United Steelworkers, was one of the major forces pushing for this benefit after World War II. The 1948 federal court decision on Inland Steel established pensions as a legitimate item for collective bargaining, and Bethlehem Steel's retirement program in 1949 helped set the standards for corporate America.

In the decades since, the collapse of the industry played out according to a script perfect for pension dumping. In the recessions of 1980 and 1981–1982, demand for steel products declined just as imports were starting to pour in. Every big U.S. player in the industry lost money, and at least five collapsed into bankruptcy, including giants Wheeling-Pittsburgh and LTV. Business picked up again toward the end of the decade, but that lasted only for about a dozen years. Competition from Russia and Japan had entered the picture, even as the auto and construction sectors—two key customers—began deserting steel for lighter-weight or less-expensive substitutes like aluminum, concrete, and plastic. That wasn't the only competition. Nonunion mini-mills, which used cheap, easy-to-melt scrap metal instead of freshly mined iron ore, were becoming a threat. These mills had started out making inexpensive specialty parts like reinforcing bars that the large steel companies didn't care about. But the mini-mills were inexorably moving into the major companies' main product lines, churning out big-ticket items like steel plates and structural steel. Meanwhile, the older companies were still running mills the same sluggish, bureaucratic way they had in the 1930s, with dozens or even hundreds of job classifications at each plant and separate classifications for each step of a simple procedure.

To cope with the cost pressures, the big steelmakers modernized some furnaces, closed down others, and laid off tens of thousands of workers. These moves just worsened the pension problem, however, because the changes left fewer workers supporting each retiree. Moreover, special early retirement sweeteners like the ones offered at LTV gave some retirees pensions that were bigger and earlier than expected. Bethlehem's numbers track the decline: A decade after its pension plan began, it had about 167,000 workers on the job and only a few collecting pensions. By the mid- to late 1980s, there were only 35,000 active workers, with 70,000 retirees and dependents. By the time the company filed for bankruptcy in 2001, it had 12,000 workers, and 90,000 retirees and dependents.

Bethlehem wasn't the only company in trouble. Between 2000 and 2004, more than forty U.S. steelmakers filed for bankruptcy, leading to four of the biggest pension terminations in the PBGC's history: Bethlehem, with more than $3.6 billion in claims; LTV (in its second bankruptcy), with nearly $2 billion; National Steel, nearly $1.2 billion; and Weirton Steel, $690 million.

Just as steel companies had set the standard for creating pension plans, they also set the standard for ending them. That was largely because of their size and central role in American industry. LTV's termination was the first big claim ever faced by the PBGC, and the seven years of negotiations led to changes in the bankruptcy and pension laws and at least four significant court precedents. The size of the steel industry made its terminations far more significant even than those at Studebaker and the other failing auto companies', which stranded their workers without pensions in the 1950s and 1960s, producing the headlines that spurred Congress. "Studebaker was a small-potatoes company," says Steven Sass, the Boston College pension expert. "When the steel industry collapsed, that was not a small-potatoes industry. That shocked the PBGC. The liabilities were enormous." It was probably inevitable that the old steel giants would tumble and shed their underfunded pensions.

But if so, why didn't U.S. Steel, the biggest giant of them all, also go under and dump its pensions? It fit all the criteria. It faced the same problems.

The main difference was that U.S. Steel enjoyed an independent source of revenue through its 1982 acquisition of Marathon Oil and, in 1986, through the acquisition of Texas Oil and Gas. Not only did the nonsteel revenue give Big Steel (as it was historically known) protection against the elements that were hurting the rest of its industry; it also provided cash for the pension plans.

The saga of U.S. Steel shows that there is no simple formula that potential investors can use to predict which companies will take advantage of the ERISA bankruptcy loophole and shed their pension plans. That's because companies file for bankruptcy for a range of reasons, and pension woes may be just a small part of the mix. The mere existence of an underfunded plan doesn't proclaim that a bankruptcy and dumping are imminent. The company may stay afloat if it has plenty of other resources to cover the underfunding. At the other extreme, a company like GM with a supposedly healthy pension plan might file for Chapter 11 because so many other things are going wrong and then use the bankruptcy to get rid of the pension obligation.

So investors who want to get in ahead of the game will have to do the hard work of digging for clues. Luckily, the rules and peculiarities that make pension financing so complex also provide some guidelines. Investors can garner clues from a plan's financial ratios and assumptions, the demographics of the workforce, the pension trust's investment allocations, the generosity of the benefits, and the degree of competition in the sector in which the company is operating.

What Not to Look For

The first thing to remember, as John Casesa, the auto analyst, makes clear, is that a pension underfunding by itself virtually never brings down a business. Lynn LoPucki, the UCLA law professor, who has been tracking bankruptcies since the early 1980s, says that only six companies out of the seven hundred or so in his bankruptcy database as of late 2006 had filed purely because of pension issues. "The [pension] plan is not why they survive or fail. Certainly, legacy costs play a role, but they're not the only reason the company gets into trouble," says Judy Schub, managing director of the Committee on Investment of Employee Benefit Assets, a trade group for senior investment officials who manage pensions and other benefits money at 120 large companies. (Schub was the PBGC's assistant executive director for legislative affairs throughout most of the 1990s.) Adds Dallas Salisbury of EBRI, the pensions and benefits research center: "The fundamental issue being faced by these companies is not their employee benefits, but their basic business—little things like oil prices."

Not only oil prices: Companies also face recession and changing customer tastes, and more. The airline industry had to adjust to deregulation and widespread fear of flying after the September 11 terrorist attacks. American automakers relied too much on expensive customer incentives and weren't quick enough to start making fuel-efficient cars. Add to that the cyclical impact of falling stock markets and interest rates, the macroeconomic pressure from low-cost foreign competition and an overvalued dollar, zooming health insurance payments, rigid work rules, product liability lawsuits, plus plain old bad management. *Then* factor in pensions. "Why didn't a company contribute to its pension all these years? Because it was having some sort of other corporate trouble," points out Olivia Mitchell of the Wharton School's Pension Research Council.

It's true that older manufacturing companies are more likely to go bankrupt and dump. They are the ones with products that are becoming obsolete, aging plants and equipment that need repairs and environmental upgrades, and work rules and pay levels that were established long before the era of cheap foreign competition. They are also the ones more likely to have defined benefit plans. Steven Kandarian, who headed the PBGC from December 2001 until April 2004, cites Joseph Schumpeter's classic economic theory of creative destruction—dying industries, processes, and products giving way to new ones. "It's a natural evolution in a market-based economy,"

Kandarian says. "The creative destruction occurring in the economy disproportionately impacts the defined benefit world because it's the older companies that have these plans."

But that's hardly a reliable strategy for investing. Not every company that's more than forty years old and has a pension plan will go bankrupt.

Then how significant is the size of the pension deficit as an indicator? Companies with bigger deficits are more likely to bail out, right? Actually, size alone is pretty meaningless. The PBGC has taken over plans with underfundings as small as $23.5 million (Levitz Home Furnishings of Long Island, New York) and as gigantic as United Airlines' $7.1 billion. "The fact that you have a pension liability doesn't tell you anything about the health of the company," says Nell Hennessy, the PBGC's deputy executive director in the mid-1990s, who went on to run the Washington, DC-based pension consulting firm Fiduciary Counselors. Indeed, the PBGC in 1994 stopped issuing its annual list of the fifty plans with the biggest shortfalls in dollars—a roster that had become known as the "iffy fifty"—because "there was no calibration, there was no nuance in the list," says Bradley Belt, who succeeded Kandarian at the agency. (Critics claimed the list was pulled back because of pressure from companies that didn't want to be publicly identified as deadbeats.)

If not the age of a company nor the size of its deficit, then are there any signs that might predict an impending pension dump? Yes. But they're subtle.

The Relative Deficit

Steven J. Kerstein, a managing director at Towers Perrin in Stamford, Connecticut, one of a handful of benefits consulting firms that dominate the pension world, describes a plausible scenario: "Say I'm a billion-dollar company with a $100 million plan. I have $100 million in assets and $100 million in liabilities. Then the stock market goes down 10 percent, and interest rates go down 1 percent. Now I have a $90 million plan with $110 million in liabilities, a $20 million deficit. Can I afford [to fund] $20 million? I probably can. But what if I'm just a $100 million company with a $20 million deficit? Or a $10 million company?"

"When the plan isn't all that large relative to the company, usually there are financial management techniques the company can apply," Kerstein continues. The HR department can reduce benefits for new employees, while the money managers can juice up the equity exposure in the plan's asset allocation—although some experts would say the latter is exactly the wrong way to go (more on that later in this chapter). "But when the plan gets large relative to the size of the company, then the usual financial-management approach is too risky," says Kerstein.

Solutia, for example, a chemical company based in St. Louis, Missouri, which was spun off from Monsanto in 1997, filed for bankruptcy protection in December 2003. According to Michael Kramer, the Perella Weinberg partner and veteran of restructurings, Solutia had been hurt mainly by environmental and tort liabilities plus a debt overhang. As of early 2007, the company had what Kramer thinks was a pension underfunding of $300 million—insignificant to his mind compared to its $2 billion in revenue.

In other words, although the absolute size of the pension plan or its underfunding may not say much about a company's potential woes, the size of the deficit in relation to other corporate yardsticks can tell quite a story. Thus, Kerstein, Kramer, and other experts look at key ratios such as these: pension assets to corporate assets or to market capitalization, pension contributions to cash flow or to revenue, pension liability to market capitalization or to corporate assets, pension underfunding to the size of the plan, and the size of the workforce to net profit. They also consider nonpension factors, including the amount of other debt and the company's credit rating.

However, not all ratios are equal. Towers Perrin over the years has amassed a database of several hundred large companies, which its consultants analyze according to about two dozen different ratios. They also break down the database by industry and do a separate run of the very largest companies. Although Kerstein wouldn't say unequivocally what he considers a risky ratio for any of the categories, he will show clients where they stand in relation to their industry average. One particularly important number for him is pension deficit or surplus as a percent of market capitalization. For the big Fortune 100 American companies in 2005, the median deficit came to 1.1 percent of market cap, whereas for a broader set of three hundred companies it was 2.6 percent. Kerstein also places heavy emphasis on pension contributions as a percentage of operating cash flow; the medians in 2005 were 3.8 percent and 6.8 percent, respectively.

Taking another approach, Gordon Latter, a senior pensions and endowments strategist at Merrill Lynch, starts by looking at the size of the underfunding in relation to net corporate assets. If the underfunding comes to less than 10 percent of assets, fine. If it's between 10 percent and 50 percent, he considers it "iffy." If it's more than 50 percent, "it could be trouble," he says. The ratio of plan assets to corporate assets is also important, says Latter, because if a plan's assets overwhelm those of the sponsoring company, the pension plan's investment returns essentially drive the company. Even more crucial, in Latter's view, is the ratio of liability to net cash flow. But he emphasizes that any pension ratios are only part of the total corporate picture. "You could be a triple-A-rated company investing [the pension trust] in duration-matched bonds. I could be a junk company with a high equity component. The risk to the PBGC is very different," he notes. (For more on duration-matched bonds versus equities, see page 113.)

Latter developed some charts in the fall of 2006 that he writes for Merrill Lynch and its clients as part of the regular series of "Pensions and Endowments" reports, which dramatically show how different ratios can produce different winners and losers. He used the 360 companies in the Standard & Poor's 500 Index that have defined benefit plans. Based purely on the size of the underfunding in dollars, ExxonMobil was in the worst shape of the 360 at the time Latter did his calculations, with a deficit of more than $8 billion. But once he factored in criteria such as funded status, the ratio of promised benefits to market capitalization, the ratio of deficit to net cash, the ratio of debt to total capital, and credit rating, ExxonMobil disappeared entirely from his list of the thirty companies with the worst performance. Latter's preferred ratio was deficit to cash, which put Raytheon on top. However, drawing on all of Latter's criteria, I would give that dubious honor to Goodyear Tire & Rubber, which Latter agrees is a reasonable conclusion. Goodyear's plan was only 70 percent funded, its future benefit obligation was a whopping 328 percent of its entire market cap, it had a sizable $2.34 billion liability, its ratio of debt to total capitalization was 95 percent, and Standard & Poor's rated it just B+. Goodyear faced some competition from Ball Corporation, with the following statistics: 66 percent funded, 77 percent debt to total capitalization, and a BB+ rating. Meanwhile,

Goodyear's financial prospects improved in late 2006, after Latter had compiled the list, when it won big concessions on health care costs from the Steelworkers following a three-month strike.

The ratios for pension funding to corporate balance sheet have to be seen in a broader corporate context, experts say. Whether a ratio is risky or not may depend on the type of industry. Harvey Miller, the veteran bankruptcy lawyer from Weil, Gotshal, first shies away from discussing any specific ratios but then offers an example. "If more than 20 percent of a company's revenue is going to fund the pension plan, and if it's in an industry in which capital investment is important, it's risking its ability to really invest in recovery," he says. On the other hand, "if it's not in a capital-intensive industry," the pension percentage "might go higher than 20 percent."

And Sass of the Boston College Center for Retirement Research differentiates between stable and volatile industries. The more volatile the underlying business, he suggests, the harder it can be to cope when a sudden market drop pulls the rug out from under a plan's funding. He uses several yardsticks, all of which tend to be more macro. To give one example: Since companies traditionally are supposed to spend 8 percent of payroll on their defined benefit plans, and payroll is only one demand on corporate cash flow, the pension liability should certainly be well below 8 percent of net cash flow.

One solid sign of trouble might be found by comparing a target company's ratios with those of a company that just filed for bankruptcy or is on the verge of doing so. Delta Air Lines provides a convenient example because the 2006 ranking of the funding status of the nation's largest defined benefit plans, compiled annually by *Pensions & Investments (P&I)* newspaper and the Watson Wyatt Worldwide benefits consulting firm, was published less than two months before Delta dumped its pilots' plan. Not surprisingly, Delta led the chart, with the highest dollar value of underfunding (nearly $6.4 billion) and the worst funding ratio (just 50.6 percent funded). The *P&I/* Wyatt report also listed another ratio—pension assets to corporate assets—which is considered key by experts like Olivia Mitchell and Gordon Latter. Where did Delta stand? Its plan assets were a whopping 145.56 percent of corporate assets—at which point, as a common quip in the benefits world goes, Delta became a pension plan with a few airplanes.

Demography Is Destiny

Throughout the industrialized world, demographers are fretting over the aging of the population. The good news is that people are living longer. A baby born in 1960 could expect to live seventy years; someone born in 2000 has an average life expectancy of seventy-seven. The bad news is that there are not as many of those babies. Starting in the early 1960s, women in Europe, the United States, Japan, and other developed areas have been having fewer children, on average, as career opportunities and birth control both became more widely available. For the United States, the baby boom officially ended in 1964. Fewer children born in 1965 or 1975 means fewer adults entering the workforce in 1985 and 1995 and, more significantly, fewer adults still in the workforce in 2001, just as the first baby boomers hit the standard age for early retirement. Whereas in 2000 there were more than five American workers supporting each retiree, by 2025 there will be fewer than four, according to United Nations projections.

This demographic decline is a problem, because it basically means that debits are fast catching up to assets. Active workers are the assets; the company is putting money into the pension plan for them, and that money stays in the plan earning interest and compounding until they retire. Retirees are the debits; they're taking money out. Soon the boomer pool will swell the ranks of the debits. In fact, demography is a double problem, because those debits are also living longer, so that fewer assets now have to support more debits for a longer period of time. Bethlehem Steel circa 2001, with nearly eight times as many retirees as workers, has become the prototype.

But before a company gets to that dire point, financial pros look for some demographic warning signs. For one thing, the pension fund deficit can't really get too big if there aren't many employees to begin with, regardless of how old they are. Depending on the industry, payroll can constitute anywhere from 25 percent of total expenses in a highly automated field like oil services, to 70 percent in a more labor-intensive area, according to Anna Rappaport, a former partner with the Mercer benefits consulting firm and onetime president of the Society of Actuaries, who set up an independent consultancy in Chicago in early 2005. Mike Johnston, head of the retirement business at another major benefits consulting firm,

Hewitt Associates, says that pharmaceutical companies also tend to have relatively low staffing ratios, spending more of their money on expensive lab equipment and clinical trials. Thus, Eli Lilly and Co. enjoyed one of the best funding situations on the *P&I*/Wyatt list, with a shortfall of just $146 million on $14.65 billion in annual sales in 2005. Other drug companies were clustered around the midway level in funding, both that year and the next. On the negative side, demography could work against pension solvency if the average age of the workforce is rising.

Rose-Colored Glasses

As Chapter 4 explained, pension plans enjoy a certain amount of legal leeway in projecting how much their assets and liabilities will grow over the next few decades. The higher the projected earnings and the lower the projected liabilities, the less a company will have to contribute today. It doesn't take an actuary to realize how tempting it can be to make those projections more and more bullish. Nor does it take an actuary to calculate that the more bullish the projections and the skimpier the funding, the more likely a company is to be hit with an unpleasant shock later when the economy or the markets don't meet those projections. Then, when the company can least afford to pay, it may have to come up with extra funding.

Although no one can predict how accurate a plan's future estimates will turn out to be, investors can gauge where a company's numbers stand in relation to the average and to those of companies with some of the worst-funded plans. For instance, the average projected long-range rate of return on plan assets was 8.5 percent in the 2006 *P&I*/Wyatt chart and 8.4 percent the following year. Delta, which had the worst-funded plan in both lists, aggressively pushed up its assumption to 9 percent in 2006. Northwest Airlines, the second worst both times and also in bankruptcy, was way up at 9.5 percent. The obvious interpretation was that the two carriers had been relying on overly optimistic projections for a while, hadn't contributed much to their plans, hadn't achieved their projections, and were therefore faced with severe cash shortages. And by continuing to keep their projections so high, they were probably setting themselves up for even more problems down the runway.

(Apparently the two airlines realized that, too, because by the time of the 2007 list both had lowered their expectations to 8.5 percent.) General Motors, which was actually well-funded by the *P&I*/Wyatt standards (though not by the PBGC's measuring), also showed a 9 percent rate-of-return assumption, which it maintained for both years. Perhaps GM could afford a little optimism, but Olivia Mitchell, for one, isn't buying it. "I think they're dreaming," she scoffs.

Plans can also play with the numbers on the expenses side. Pension payments are usually based on the individual's earnings, either throughout his or her career or else during the final years at the company. In either case, that requires making predictions about pay raises into the future. The higher the raises, the bigger the benefit. When Watson Wyatt surveyed nearly four hundred companies with pension plans in 2005, it found pay-raise assumptions ranging from 1.7 percent to 9.5 percent.

The wild variations in the assumptions that companies choose finally caught the eye of the government. In the early 2000s, the SEC launched investigations of the pension assumptions at General Motors, DaimlerChrysler, and other big companies. Corporate boards, too, began taking a closer look at their own plans, especially in light of the Sarbanes-Oxley Act of 2002, which tightened the rules on business accounting; boards were also spurred by all the publicity over failing pension plans like Delta's. In the June 2006 issue of the monthly magazine *Directorship*, whose readership includes board members, CEOs, and other top executives, Karen Wiltsie, a partner at Deloitte & Touche, and John Stokesbury, a pension actuary official at the accounting giant, warn that members of a board audit committee "should show particular vigilance regarding [pension plan] assumptions. Why did management pick their particular assumptions? Certain responses to this question should raise red flags, including blind reliance on actuary recommendations; choosing assumptions identical to those of competitors; or using the same figures as last year."

Liability Matchmaking

When the age of defined benefits began, right after World War II, most pension trust money was safely, cautiously invested in bonds.

This was Grandma and Grandpa's money, and no one wanted to endanger it for even a minute. Some plan managers tried what was called horizon matching, or immunization, which meant buying bonds whose maturities matched the date—way out on the horizon—at which the company would have to start paying out the pensions.

With time, plan managers began to feel more confident of their investment smarts, and they rethought their strategies. Recognizing that pensions are long-term commitments and that equities generally outperform all other investments over the long term, they concluded that a pension fund should be heavily into equities to capture the upside market potential. Thus, the 60/40 golden rule of pension-fund management developed in the 1970s: Invest roughly 60 percent of the assets in stocks and 40 percent in bonds.

Of course, the standard has been tweaked over the years. The equally venerated principle of diversification counsels spreading the risk, so a pension fund might temper the 60/40 mix with a smattering of real estate and alternative investments. The concept of the "prudent person" began to replace the hoary 60/40 formula: Pension funds could invest in assets that a rational, prudent investor would deem appropriate. Some pension managers, seeking that extra little *frisson* of return, branched out into ever riskier asset classes, including aggressive growth stocks, international stocks, leveraged buyouts, and hedge funds. The Congressional Research Office study in 2007 found that the average pension plan allocated more than 5 percent of its assets to hedge funds, and some pension officials pushed far higher—fully 39 percent at Weyerhaeuser in late 2005, for instance, and 20 percent at Lilly. Another incentive for investing in equities came from the way pension costs are listed on the corporate income statement. Companies are allowed to subtract from their pension costs an item called "expected return on pension assets," and stocks give the plans a lot of flexibility in determining that return. As the Boston University management professor Zvi Bodie points out, "If they're investing in bonds earning a known interest rate of 5 percent, all they can justify is 5 percent. If they're investing 60 percent in stocks, they can pretty much assume any return they want."

The new millennium brought yet another round of strategic rethinking. As more and more pension plans tumbled into the PBGC's lap, people in the investment world began fretting over the role that equities and risk might have played in the terminations.

It seemed that by investing in stocks, pension funds were gambling with the taxpayers' money, and that stacked the deck in favor of everyone but the taxpayer. If pension plan stocks went up, the plans won by earning high returns. If their stocks went down, they still won, because they could always dump their liability on the PBGC. "If you're a weak company, it pays you to take a lot of risk on equities because of the existence of the PBGC," says Michael Peskin, the gentlemanly, South African–born Morgan Stanley Dean Witter managing director who is one of the most outspoken skeptics of traditional asset allocation. Companies that followed the old golden rule were almost compelled to dump their pensions.

Thus, a small but influential minority of financial and pension experts in Europe as well as the United States, including Peskin, Bodie, and Olivia Mitchell, started advocating that pension funds return to something akin to the old-fashioned immunization. This is the kind of duration matching that Gordon Latter of Merrill Lynch talks about and which he partially subscribes to. A related technique is known as liability-driven investing. The basic theory behind all of these approaches is that the pension funds try to match their assets to their liabilities, usually by investing heavily—or even entirely—in fixed income with maturity schedules that track their pension payment schedules. Although the funds lose the chance of gaining from big market upswings, they also lose the risk of big losses. "The nature of the pension promise in a defined benefit plan," Mitchell says, "is that you have to pay retirees every year until they die. It's a fairly predictable cash flow; some people characterize it like a bond. If you take that perspective, you would buy laddered bonds that would pay off in the same pattern as the pension obligation." International Paper began moving that way in 2003, and American Airlines did it back in 1987.

In theory, if a company that matched liabilities to assets were underfunded at all, it would be by only a small amount. It would regularly have bonds maturing just as it needed the cash. By contrast, Gordon Latter found that the thirty companies with the biggest underfundings in dollars in 2006 had an average equity allocation of 68 percent, with one (General Dynamics) as high as 97 percent. Is it just a coincidence that American Airlines, with its asset allocation so heavily in liability-matched bonds, is the only old-line carrier never to have filed for bankruptcy? Those who believe in liability-driven investing might therefore use asset allocation as another clue: The more stocks in the portfolio, the more likely the PBGC is to become the proud owner of the pension plan.

Payout Time

Income is only one side of the pension-funding story, of course. The other side is the outgo—the amounts the plan pays out in benefits. It may seem obvious that plans with the most generous benefits will need more funding and, therefore, be more susceptible to funding problems. However, it's not always so obvious exactly what kinds of benefit plans are the most generous or the best funded. To begin the comparison, some definitions are needed.

Usually, pension benefits are calculated in one of three basic ways: final-average, career-average, or flat-dollar (also known as step-rate or unit-benefit) pay. A *final-average* system is the most popular, used in 59 percent of plans, according to Watson Wyatt. As the name implies, the pension is based on the average of the retiree's last few years' pay (typically the last three or five years). A *career-average* plan is found in 27 percent of plans, according to Wyatt, and works much like the final-average, except that the pension is based on the person's pay throughout his or her entire tenure at the company. Finally, a *flat-dollar* system pays according to a straight formula, the same for everyone, regardless of salary: Everyone gets X dollars multiplied by years of service. About 14 percent of companies use this system, including most unionized and big industrial companies, such as the airlines, steel, and auto and tire makers, says Sylvester Schieber, the consulting veteran who retired from Wyatt in 2006.

Since most people's salaries are highest in their last years, the final-average system would seem to provide the richest payout. The lower-earning early years ought to drag down the average in the career-average calculation. To some degree that's true: EBRI has calculated that if a plan were frozen—in other words, if employees could no longer earn any more benefits, but the plan was not actually terminated—it would need to set aside 8 percent of the median employee's pay to cover future promises in a final-average system, compared with 7 percent in career-average.

In the real world, however, neither the career-average nor flat-dollar system stays static. Because the flat-dollar system is common in unionized industries, the dollar multiplier is usually increased with every contract negotiation. Similarly, the career-average formulas "get updated to take into account what's going on in an inflationary environment," Schieber says. Net result: All three tend to end up with roughly similar benefits, according to Schieber.

The catch is that only the final-average-pay type is actually funded appropriately in advance. That's because it's the only one whose formula acknowledges from the start the fact that the benefit will inevitably increase. Over time, Schieber says, actuaries can pretty safely assume that people's pay will go up 3 percent to 4 percent per year. (In the Wyatt survey of some four hundred companies in 2005, where the pay-raise assumptions ranged from 1.7 to 9.5 percent, the average was 4.6 percent.) By contrast, although the flat-dollar increases that are hammered out in labor negotiations may be equally predictable, they legally do not exist until the new contract is signed. "You cannot anticipate those benefit increases in the funding," Schieber says. "The law says you cannot fund for something you're not contractually obligated to provide." And the company is not contractually obligated, of course, until there is a new contract. Thus, when a twenty-year-old joins a final-average-pay plan, his or her company can immediately start putting away money to pay the pension, assuming salary increases of 4 percent a year for the next forty-five years. But for a twenty-year-old with a flat-rate plan, the company can only fund as though the benefits were never going to rise. Little wonder that Watson Wyatt's figures show that the flat-dollar systems—the ones likely to be found in airlines, autos, and other troubled industries—were the worst funded. The median final-average-pay plan was 98 percent funded in 2005; the figure for flat-dollar plans was just 87 percent.

Flat-dollar plans have kept up with the benefit levels of the other plans for the obvious reason that they have tended to be found at unionized companies, and unions have had the clout to demand better benefits. And the correlation between unions and rich pensions may go beyond that. Many people believe that over years and years of labor negotiations, starting as far back as the 1950s, ghost funding of the pension became the easiest way for a company to cut costs without seeming to hurt the workforce—and, the theory goes, the unions went along. A company couldn't reimburse its parts suppliers with IOUs, nor would any labor leader have accepted a vague promise to pay today's wages twenty years from now. However, pension payments, as deferred wages, are put off into the future by definition. So a fiscally strained company might have offered sky-high pensions, payable in thirty years, that it knew it might not be able to pay. Why not? It was so easy to manipulate the actuarial assumptions. The company might luck out in its investment returns. There was nothing to lose. "Employers liked it because it didn't cost them anything today. It became the problem of the CEO five CEOs down the road," shrugs Elizabeth Warren, the Harvard bankruptcy expert and congressional advisor. Even if everything went wrong and the company never managed to fund the plan properly, there was always the PBGC. "Employers still have the opportunity to exercise a put option on the PBGC with regard to their pension plans. You've got major underfunding? You can give that to the PBGC, and you can settle it for cents on the dollar," says David Walker, the U.S. Comptroller General.

If ordinary pensions were easy to fob off, it was doubly easy to promise and jettison the special shutdown benefits that spurred the PBGC to step in at LTV. After all, when is a company going to shut down a plant? Most likely, when it's in financial trouble. Which means that there's a good chance the company will eventually be sending the whole plan to the PBGC and never have to pay either the regular or the extra benefits. "If the union demands shutdown benefits as part of a contract negotiation," says Steven Kandarian, the ex-PBGC chief, "those who may end up paying for it—other plan sponsors or, ultimately, the taxpayer—are not at the table." Other plan sponsors would pay through their premiums to the PBGC, and taxpayers could end up footing the bill if the PBGC ran out of money, Kandarian explains.

Some see an even more conspiratorial twist. Richard A. Ippolito, a former pensions official at the U.S. Department of Labor, in his 1986 book *Pensions, Economics and Public Policy*, suggests that "firms deliberately underfund their pension plans . . . as a way of bonding an organized workforce. . . . By exposing workers to long-term unsecured debt in the form of underfunded pensions, the firm gives unionized workers a stake in the long-term viability of the firm." In theory, if workers realized that their pensions depended on the company's long-term health, they would be willing to work harder and demand less at the bargaining table.

Whatever management's motivation, why did the unions agree to this charade? Why didn't they insist on immediate pay raises or full funding of the pensions? Experts offer several answers:

Elizabeth Warren: "They knew they couldn't get it."

Olivia Mitchell: "Just like politicians, [union leaders] focus on the short term. They want to get reelected."

Michael Peskin: "Because of the existence of the PBGC."

Labor officials insist that they never played games with their members' pensions. "Unions are not in the business of negotiating benefits that are not going to be there for their members. Period," snaps Beth Almeida, assistant director for strategic resources for the Machinists union. Dave McCall, the United Steelworkers regional director in Ohio, points out that when his union was negotiating its last prebankruptcy contract with LTV in 1999, the stock market was booming, the company had $1 billion in spare cash, and the funding contribution to the pension trust that year was only $200 million. So why not push for some improvements in benefits and wages? Sure, everyone knew the market couldn't keep soaring forever, but LTV could have put a little extra into the pension fund, beyond the required $200 million, to hedge against bad times. And if it couldn't get a tax deduction for the excess contribution, that wasn't the union's fault. Punching out the words like Hollywood's version of a blue-collar worker, McCall insists, "They made a promise to give us a dollar, and they never set that dollar aside."

Another argument in the union's defense is that, while exercising the PBGC "put option" might be a no-lose proposition for management, employees could lose real cash. That's because of the 10 percent gap in the PBGC's coverage. Although most people will get their full benefit, a significant number will suffer a shortfall. If workers retire early—a common practice in physically demanding or shrinking industries like steel—the PBGC chops off about 7 percent for each year short of age sixty-five. The agency may not pay the shutdown benefits that figured in the LTV case. It reduces, on a sliding scale, benefit increases that were granted within five years of a termination; that provision cost machinists at United Airlines about 40 percent of the benefit improvement they had won in 2002. Finally, there's the cap on the total payable benefit, which is adjusted for inflation. "I've got people at LTV for thirty years who are entitled to $2,000 a month, but they're getting only $1,000," McCall grumbles. "We never wanted our pensions to go to the PBGC."

"I don't know of any union," Almeida says, "that is interested in having its members go through the kinds of things our members went through with those terminations."

Brain Drain

Whether a company keeps its pension plan intact is not just a question of money. Morale is always a concern when something is taken away from workers, be it salaries, benefits, jobs, or perks— or, in the case of pension promises, trust. Would employees be so demoralized that they wouldn't be able to work properly? Would they sabotage the company? Would so many key employees flee that the company would be crippled? In light of those possibilities, would the company decide that terminating the plan is just not worth the cost and instead find the cash somehow to keep the pension plan going?

Those are some of the questions Michael Kramer of Perella Weinberg asks when he analyzes the potential for restructuring a troubled company. He looks at the company's labor relations history, the employee benefits that would remain after a plan termination, what types of retirement benefits competitors offer, and how many retirees would be fully covered by the PBGC. "Is there another factory in town that people can go to? Do [the workers] all run out the door if you terminate their pension plan?" asks Kramer, a burly, outgoing man who may be the only person on Wall Street with a crew cut.

The employees everyone worries most about are the airline pilots. Although most workers get a certain amount of training, airlines put a lot more time and money into their pilots. The pool of people qualified to fly a jumbo jet is pretty small. As labor attorney Sherwin Kaplan notes, pilots have the unique ability to threaten that "without us, your planes sit on the ground." At Delta, that dim prospect was intensified by the lump-sum payment option. If it looked like the plan was going to terminate, how many pilots, like Dave Villarrubia, the New Orleans boy who had always dreamed of being a Delta pilot, would fly the coop?

What makes the pilots' situation even dicier is that they are also the ones who tend to lose the most in a termination. Because of their high skill level, they get paid at higher rates, which push their pensions far above the PBGC maximum. Plus, until the laws were changed in 2007, pilots had to retire by age sixty. Under the PBGC's definition, that meant they were taking early retirement, cutting their pensions even further.

Termination PBGC-Style

The PBGC doesn't like to be surprised. Through its early warning program, it monitors companies, looking for "any transaction that may pose an increased risk of long-term loss to the pension insurance program," according to the warning program's definition of its mission. Among the transactions that might worry the PBGC are a spinoff, a leveraged buyout, a major divestiture, payment of extraordinary dividends, and an exchange offer that involves trading a "significant amount" of unsecured for secured debt. Agency rules dictate that the warnings focus on companies whose bond rating is below investment grade and that have a plan that's underfunded by at least $25 million, or companies that have a bond rating of any quality but an underfunding of at least $5 million.

In rare circumstances, the PBGC will actually force a company to drop a pension plan that the company wanted to keep afloat, a procedure known as an involuntary termination. It's essentially a defensive measure, to prevent a funding hole from getting even deeper. LTV and Bethlehem Steel were classic examples, because the PBGC could have been stuck with several hundred million dollars in extra shutdown benefits if the plans had stayed alive. Another typical instance would be one in which the PBGC feared that a company was about to sell off a profitable business that happened legally to be an independent entity. Because of the laws of joint and several liability, the PBGC could not demand that proceeds of the asset sale help pay for any pension underfunding if the entity were sold before the plan terminated.

"These tend to be situations where something dramatic is going to happen very soon, and if the PBGC doesn't act promptly, it's going to lose money," explains Harold J. Ashner, who spent more than twenty years as a lawyer and assistant general counsel at the PBGC before leaving in 2005 to cofound Keightley & Ashner, a law firm in Washington, DC, specializing in PBGC matters. Ashner's cofounder was Jim Keightley, the PBGC's general counsel from 1995 to 2005; a third ex-PBGC colleague, Bill Beyer, joined them.

The PBGC actually initiates about 90 percent of all terminations, but that's a technicality. Gary Pastorius, the agency spokesman, explains that having the PBGC officially do the chopping can cut down on duplicate actuarial work. Unfortunately, the agency lumps these technical "involuntary terminations" together with the real ones, so there is no definitive record of how often the PBGC genuinely forces a termination.

Although the PBGC no longer publishes its "iffy fifty" list of companies with huge funding gaps, investors might be able to create their own early warning rosters by looking for the same clues that the PBGC watches for.

Fallback Strategy

In some cases, all this analysis on the part of investors may be futile. Companies aren't filing for bankruptcy and shedding their pension plans for any of the standard, somewhat predictable reasons. It's not because they face global competition in a shrinking manufacturing industry, or because the ratio of their pension underfunding to market capitalization has gotten out of whack, or because their fund's asset allocation is tilted too heavily toward equities, or because they've bargained themselves into escalating flat-dollar benefits. In fact, their pension plans may be quite decently funded, and they may have plenty of cash for the moment.

They are filing for bankruptcy deliberately, as a business tactic, for strategic and competitive reasons rather than financial reasons—and taking the pension plans down with them. As Kevin J. Delaney, an associate professor of sociology at Temple University, puts it in his book *Strategic Bankruptcy*, "The firm declares bankruptcy to pursue a limited organizational or political goal that it had unsuccessfully pursued outside of the bankruptcy arena." Similarly, another book on bankruptcy—*Debt's Dominion*, by University of Pennsylvania law professor David A. Skeel Jr.—asserts that "large debtors have used Chapter 11 to address a wide variety of economic problems."

In one of the most famous examples of this phenomenon, it is generally accepted that Texaco's rationale in filing for bankruptcy in 1987 was to avoid paying a $10.53 billion judgment to Pennzoil stemming from a botched takeover battle for a third oil business, Getty Oil. Pennzoil and Getty had agreed on a merger in early 1984, but before the papers were actually signed, Texaco stepped in with a higher offer, which the Getty board accepted. Pennzoil then sued for breach of contract and won, after fighting all the way to the U.S. Supreme Court. At that point, Texaco technically had enough in net assets to pay the humungous judgment. Although it would have had to sell off significant chunks of its business to raise the cash, it was hardly the classic picture of a bankrupt failure. And the oil patch is not exactly a suffering Rust Belt industry saddled with a shrinking customer base, a horde of retirees, and foreign rivals flooding the market with cheaper knock-offs. By filing for Chapter 11, however, Texaco forced Pennzoil to wait in line with all the other creditors, giving Pennzoil a big incentive to bargain for a quicker, albeit smaller, settlement. As part of Texaco's reorganization plan, they finally settled at $3 billion.

Professor Delaney contends that the bankruptcy filings of Manville Corporation in 1982 and Continental Airlines in 1983 were similarly driven by strategic rather than financial imperatives: in Manville's case, to avoid paying what was estimated at that time to be $2 billion in potential asbestos-injury claims, and in Continental's case, to impose the $100 million-plus in wage, benefit, and work-rule concessions that it had been unable to negotiate in the normal way with its unions. Both companies, Delaney writes, had assets into the hundreds of millions, if not billions, of dollars.

For other firms, the words "pension plan" can be substituted for "Pennzoil judgment" or "asbestos claims" or "labor costs." "All those years, the companies were taking money that should have been earmarked for their employees' futures and handing them out to shareholders and payments to other creditors," sums up Elizabeth Warren of Harvard. "Now that the money is gone, they go into bankruptcy and say, 'Pension costs are too high.' For some it's a straightforward strategic move: It's the fastest way to get rid of the pension obligations and any other promises left on the table. It's a way to wipe the slate clean."

A company might also use bankruptcy as an excuse to shift to a cheaper 401(k) plan, points out Steve Kerstein of the Towers Perrin consulting firm. Sure, the company could make the switch without being bankrupt, simply by closing its defined benefit program to new hires and not letting existing employees accrue more benefit credits. Hundreds of companies have done it that way. Employees remain entitled to the pensions they have already earned, and the company must still fund them. But that method "can be a nightmare. When employees see change, they are skeptical," Kerstein says. By contrast, he continues, if a company has filed for bankruptcy, it can tell its workers, " 'We can't survive with the defined benefit plan. But we do want you to have a pension. Here's a new one.' It's a much easier communication." In another variation of this approach, a pension underfunding "is used [in bankruptcy] as a bargaining chip to get the employees to agree on a reduced health care plan, a reduced pension amount, and a change to another type of plan," says Professor Edward Altman, the NYU expert on debt financing.

Arguably, the financial pressures in all these situations *could* eventually put the companies into bankruptcy if they didn't stanch the pension (or asbestos or whatever) bleeding promptly. In fact, that sort of early intervention—stopping the bleeding before it proves fatal—was exactly the reasoning behind the passage of the 1978 Bankruptcy Code described in Chapter 6. The 1978 law "led to bankruptcy being used much more strategically, because it made it more available to being used prior to a company being so far gone that all that could be done was an orderly liquidation," says James Sprayregen, the veteran bankruptcy lawyer at Goldman Sachs.

Yet many politicians say that companies, in filing Chapter 11 and terminating their pensions, have gone way beyond what either the 1978 bankruptcy changes or ERISA ever intended. "They're not using [the Bankruptcy Code] in the traditional sense of a company that's in trouble trying to work out a payment plan with creditors," protests Senator Benjamin L. Cardin, a Maryland Democrat who was one of the top pension experts in the House of Representatives for years before being elected to the Senate with the new Democratic majority in 2006. "They're putting their pension responsibility in the same position as a creditor. It's not what the law intended. It's your workforce. Wages have always been treated differently [from creditors] in bankruptcy. We are talking about a company that is planning to come out of bankruptcy, negotiating for less than 100 percent on its debt, and using the employees as part of that negotiation."

Bankruptcy carries its own costs, of course, and they're not insignificant. Shareholders are wiped out. Customers may flee. So might key employees. Creditors will set tougher terms for any future loans or purchases of raw material, and they might even demand that management be replaced. But bankruptcy has simply gotten a lot cheaper, easier, and more socially acceptable than it used to be.

David Walker, the tall, balding, quiet-voiced U.S. Comptroller General, views the rush to bankruptcy and pension dumping as part of a larger decline in society's moral values. "We've seen an increase in a 'me' society versus a 'we' society, an increased focus on short-term results. Before, there was a taint to going into bankruptcy. It used to be that people didn't terminate their pension plans unless it was absolutely necessary. It also used to be that people didn't go into bankruptcy unless it was absolutely necessary. When you see that employers have been able to terminate their plans and have to pay only cents on the dollar, and with the realization that the taint associated with declaring bankruptcy is gone—well," he concludes sadly, "it's not surprising that more people would be considering this as a viable restructuring option."

9 | Pensionless Restructuring

"You've got to get employees on board; you've got to end up convincing them that the short-term pain is beneficial. A lot of it is trust—whether they trust management."

—MARC LASRY, MANAGING PARTNER, AVENUE CAPITAL

THE ULTIMATE test of whether a company is a good investment is whether it survives and makes money. Shedding the pension plan, in itself, doesn't guarantee a passing grade on that test. In financial terms, it should help, but handled poorly a pension termination can actually decrease the company's odds of thriving. In any case, the strategy works only when it's part of a larger survival package. Thus, investors need to analyze what role the dumping might play in bringing the lucky survivors out of bankruptcy.

In particular, they might ask this: How is the company handling the inevitable blow to morale? Is it offering the demoralized workforce any replacement benefits, and if so, how generous are these benefits? What is the new management's reputation in terms of labor relations, and did it gorge on its own compensation? What is it doing to counteract any tarnishing of its public image?

But before investors consider any of these factors, they must define what constitutes survival.

The Test of Time

It's not as hard as it seems for a company to pull itself out of Chapter 11—at least, not the first time. Academics who study bankruptcy have found that in general nearly two-thirds of first-time filers manage to emerge. For instance, as of late 2006, 65 percent of the roughly seven hundred companies in Professor LoPucki's bankruptcy database had emerged (not counting the ones that were still unresolved at that point). The results were similar for Diane K. Denis of

125

Purdue University and Kimberly J. Rodgers of the College of William and Mary, who studied 224 businesses that filed for Chapter 11 from 1985 to 1994, based on reports from the Securities and Exchange Commission. They found that 141, or about 63 percent, were able to reorganize "as public going concerns." Furthermore, thirty-two other firms in that study were acquired while in Chapter 11, which could also produce gains for investors. The rest were liquidated.

So emerging from bankruptcy isn't the hard part. The challenge is staying afloat. Studies show that about one-third to three-fifths of these apparent success stories file for bankruptcy a second time. There are even a few cases of third and fourth filings. LTV survived seven years after emerging from bankruptcy number one in 1993 before succumbing in 2000; US Airways lasted just one and a half years between bankruptcies; Wheeling-Pittsburgh went through three bankruptcies, either on its own or as part of a bigger conglomerate. Of the 65 percent of the companies in Professor LoPucki's database that managed to climb out of bankruptcy, nearly 20 percent fell back within five years and another 10 percent refiled later. And those figures probably underestimate the actual failure rate, because LoPucki calculated the refilings only for the 280 companies that had been out of bankruptcy for at least five years at the time of those calculations. Presumably, some of the others didn't make it to their fifth anniversary.

Another study—this one by Edith Hotchkiss, an associate professor of finance at Boston College—found that 32 percent of Chapter 11 survivors refiled or restructured privately. The Denis-Rodgers report, using a fairly strict definition, had the worst statistics of all: Three years after filing, barely 43 percent of the companies that reorganized were still "independent, publicly traded firms" with no distressed restructuring, no subsequent reorganization, and "at least two years of positive operating performance."

Blurring the success rate even further is that experts can't agree on how long a company needs to stay in business after bankruptcy to qualify as "a success." According to LoPucki's research, the bulk of refilings take place within five years, so he figures that if a company manages to make it past the five-year mark, it has a better chance of surviving. However, Sylvester Schieber, the retired Watson Wyatt consultant, believes that three or four years is enough time to judge. Both the Denis-Rodgers and Hotchkiss studies use three-year benchmarks. Hotchkiss calls that "a long enough horizon to be able to see if firms are 'successful' after the restructuring" but short enough so that they haven't yet significantly altered the nature of their business from what was projected coming out of bankruptcy. At the other extreme, Lisa Beckerman, the Akin Gump attorney who worked on Delta, Kaiser, and three big steel bankruptcies, argues that steel and airline companies need more time to pull themselves together—seven and ten years, respectively—because their industries are so cyclical. Karen Wagner, the former lawyer for LTV, concurs that seven years is the usual cycle for the steel business, although "the reorganization might be judged a success on many grounds before then."

Then again, LTV proves how meaningless a guideline can be. By just about any of the experts' standards, lasting seven years would be deemed a success the first time out. Yet the company refiled and liquidated, and the independent company LTV has disappeared.

Veteran bankruptcy lawyer Jamie Sprayregen would not even estimate a specific time frame. His definition: "Does the entity still exist and provide a means by which tens of thousands of people can earn a living and still get retirement benefits? If yes, then that's successful."

Dumping's Mixed Record

By any logic, companies that shed their pension plans as part of their bankruptcy ought to be among the ones that survive longer. After all, the more obligations a company can get rid of, the more cash it can devote to the rest of the business. In the case of a pension commitment, that's tens of millions of dollars worth of cash. Yet the results don't always bear this out.

LoPucki's research seems to indicate that pension dumping actually *hurts* a company's chances of long-term survival. When he and a colleague, Joseph Doherty, ran a special analysis of his database for this book, they found sixty-four companies that had terminated their plans and gone through the full bankruptcy process. Of that group, only thirty—fewer than half—managed to emerge even the first time, and just twenty-three of those, or about one-third of the original total, lasted more than five years. Both figures are significantly lower than the percentages for the total database, including companies that never shed their plans, which were 65 percent and 81 percent, respectively.

The PBGC's records are more encouraging but still ambiguous. Consider the agency's ten largest cases, as of early 2007:

The all-time biggest claim came from United Airlines—four pension plans and a total tab of more than $7 billion, dumped in May 2005. Nine months later, in February 2006, United and its parent company, UAL, emerged from bankruptcy. The brand-new UAL stock took off briefly to a high of $43 in late March—far exceeding what the company itself had predicted and overpriced by most outside accounts—and then dove almost nonstop for five months to the low $20s before climbing steadily for the next five months to almost $52, including a little hop after the airline beat out three competitors for coveted new routes to China. But when fourth-quarter 2006 revenue came in lower than expected, the stock price dropped again, ending the twelve-month ride a few dollars above where it had begun.

Although the industry as a whole enjoyed strong profits, UAL—the second-largest carrier in the United States—took a loss of more than $50 million in the fourth quarter. And although its peers also suffered that winter from storms, cancellations, delays, rising fuel costs, and passenger fury, United went through some of the worst scheduling and consumer problems, ranking near the bottom in on-time arrivals. Wall Street had other concerns about it as well. Even though it had shed 20 percent of its fleet and nearly thirty thousand jobs, along with the pension plans, analysts complained that the carrier didn't close enough routes, cut enough costs, streamline services sufficiently, or reorganize its classic hub-and-spoke system of feeding flights to major hub airports. Then United blew its public image—and employee morale—with the extravagant bonuses, pay, stock options, and pension deals it handed to CEO Glenn F. Tilton and other top executives (more on that later in this chapter). Less than two years after the bankruptcy ended, employees sought to reopen contract negotiations to push for better salaries. Analysts' recommendations, upgrades, and downgrades were all over the lot. North Dakota Democratic Congressman Earl Pomeroy, one of Congress's reigning experts on pensions, angrily declares, "United is the poster child for creative use of bankruptcy." Within six months of the carrier's emergence, rumors of a merger with another airline began, and the rumors continued for two more years. Is that a success story?

Continuing through the rest of the PBGC's top ten: number two, Bethlehem Steel (a $3.65 billion claim); number four, LTV (about $2 billion from its second bankruptcy; the first bankruptcy claim was wiped off the books because it was ultimately sent back to LTV after the follow-on pension plan was ruled illegal); and number eight, Weirton Steel ($690 million), were among the five steel companies whose assets Wilbur Ross bought at fire sale prices starting in 2002, combined into International Steel Group, and sold for $4.5 billion to Mittal Steel less than four years later. That was a profit of about a $2.5 billion for Ross and his firm, although the names LTV, Bethlehem, and Weirton, have disappeared from the corporate universe. (So much for Weirton the company that Mike Psaros's family worked at for three generations, and the employee buyout that his future partner, Gene Keilin, arranged.)

Number three, US Airways ($2.86 billion), filed for bankruptcy in 2002, emerged, fell back into bankruptcy after one and a half years, reemerged, and then put in a strong performance in its first year and a half out of the second bankruptcy. However, it recovered the second time only because it merged with America West (find more on the US Airways story in Chapters 10 and 11). Number six, Delta ($920 million), managed to save all but its pilots' pensions, thanks largely to the federal Pension Protection Act of 2006, emerging from Chapter 11 in spring 2007. While it fended off a hostile takeover bid from the revived US Airways, industry watchers continued to speculate about possible mergers, and the pilots' morale was still a problem. Delta, United, and US Airways also benefited from lucky timing, as their volatile industry was going through an upswing when they all emerged, although Delta may have caught only the tail end of it. The tenth-largest, Kaiser Aluminum Corporation ($568.5 million), took more than four years to emerge from bankruptcy in July 2006, after a saga that included a struggle with the PBGC, a fight with the Steelworkers union over retention payments for top executives, and the sell-off of hundreds of millions of dollars worth of assets, including stakes in an Australian refinery. But the trimmed-down company seemed to shine. Its stock rose steadily, and it announced a profit in the second quarter after emerging.

Meanwhile, number five, National Steel ($1.16 billion); number seven, Pan American World Airways ($841 million); and number nine, TWA ($668 million), were thoroughly liquidated, with other companies picking up scattered pieces—their headquarters, steel mills, air routes, and even the Pan Am name.

Overall, is that a 70 percent success rate, counting only National, Pan Am, and TWA as outright failures? What about Bethlehem, LTV, and Weirton? Although jettisoning their pension plans didn't save them as independent businesses, Wilbur Ross made good money by investing in them postpension. US Airways crashed the first time despite dumping its pilots' plan; but in its second filing it shed the rest of its plans, and investors did pretty well. United, too, seemed poised to survive. As of this book's publication in 2008, it was too soon to judge the outcome for Delta and Kaiser.

Clearly, terminating a pension plan is not by itself a reliable predictor of a company's ultimate fate and certainly no assurance of success. There are several reasons for that. First, the pension dumper may start out with more disadvantages than the average bankrupt company, so that even after dumping, it's still in the hole. LoPucki, in analyzing his own data, notes that generally companies with pensions "are in a lot more trouble than other companies," more likely to be in ailing industries threatened by low-cost foreign competition, to rely on obsolete technology, and to be hampered by bureaucratic work rules, as described in Chapter 8. And as noted in Chapter 6, when a pension plan is involved, there's an extra creditor—the PBGC—fighting with all the other creditors for whatever assets remain. Moreover, just as a pension underfunding is never the sole cause of a bankruptcy, and probably not even the main one, shedding a pension plan cannot be the sole or main solution. Just as there are no simple formulas for predicting which companies will dump their pensions, the dumping itself is not a simple predictor of whether the company will survive. "It isn't that you can say, 'Aha, the pension—zap! That solves all my problems,'" Wilbur Ross says. "That's usually not enough to solve all my problems."

So investors have to turn to indicators other than the obvious. Among the most telling are employee morale, the type of replacement benefits, management attitudes, and the company's public image.

Rebuilding Trust

Morale may seem like one of those squishy, touchy-feely concepts that belong on the HR department's agenda, but managers and investors alike know how crucial it is to the bottom line of even a healthy company. Angry, resentful, scared, or depressed employees might do a halfhearted job, alienate customers, go out on strike, or sabotage production. If things get bad enough, a significant number of people may quit, forcing the company to find and train their replacements all at once.

In bankruptcy, all of these problems are compounded. Employees are worried that they'll lose their jobs and exhausted and resentful at doing the extra work of those who have already been laid off.

Terminating the pension plan while in bankruptcy adds yet another layer of pressure. If the impact on morale sometimes provides a clue in advance as to whether a company will drop its plan, as discussed in Chapter 8, it's even more important in predicting whether a company will succeed in reorganizing. That's why LTV fought the PBGC all the way to the Supreme Court to essentially reinstate its old pension plan and keep the Steelworkers union happy. But when the pension is dumped, workers don't lose just a benefit. They lose their trust in the company. No other provision in a typical employment or union contract carries such a supposedly rock-solid guarantee: Under ERISA, the benefits a person has earned for retirement cannot be reduced retroactively, even through collective bargaining. A company can alter the pension plan for the future: It can block employees from accruing credit for any potential earnings (known as freezing the plan), reduce the formula that's used to calculate benefits, or even eliminate the plan entirely for new hires (closing the plan). But it cannot take away what an employee has already earned. Nor can it demand or even negotiate givebacks as it can with wages. If someone has worked enough years at a salary high enough to be eligible for a pension of $200 per month, that person must get that $200. This unique treatment is grounded on the concept of pensions as deferred wages. Instead of getting $100 an hour today, which is the going rate, workers agree to take $90 today in order to apply the extra $10 to a pension. Thus, the company has no right to pull back that $10.

The employer reinforces those promises with the annual benefit reports it's required to provide its workforce. "Anybody who's joined the company and been there any extended period of time has been getting literature year in and year out, saying, 'This is what you'll be getting when you retire,'" points out Sylvester Schieber of Watson Wyatt. "People develop expectations that relate to the relationship that exists. If you change that relationship, it affects how you look at the people you're associated with."

What if a company dumps its pension fund and ignores its morale morass? Employee attitudes will eventually revive, says Peter Cappelli of the Wharton School's Center for Human Resources. "The workforce kind of readjusts their expectations. They get used to what they have," he says. However, that readjustment typically takes five years. "It [employee morale] will come back quicker," Cappelli adds, "if you do something to help them readjust."

And the single most effective thing a company can do for its workforce after terminating its pension plan is to put in another. Termination "has a significant adverse effect on the morale of the employees. You need to couple it with some other retirement plan, maybe of lesser value," warns Rick Schifter of TPG (formerly Texas Pacific Group), which almost invested in US Airways during the first reorganization.

"The company saw good reason to establish the plan in the first place, and in most cases those reasons still exist," says Christian Weller, a senior economist at the Center for American Progress, a liberal think tank in Washington, DC.

In fact, the biggest critics of replacement plans probably aren't bean-counting corporate managers; they're government officials. "Wait a minute. Before you put in a new promise, you must use that money for existing obligations," contends Brad Belt, the former PBGC director. That same point came up during the congressional negotiations over the 2006 Pension Protection Act, recalls Randy Hardock of Davis & Harman, the Delta benefits attorney and former lawyer for the Senate Finance Committee. "Some Hill Labor [Committee] staffers argued that if you have any money, it shouldn't go into a new retirement plan. Shouldn't that money instead go into the existing plan to fund it?" As Belt and those staffers see it, why should the PBGC be saddled with a company's old pension bills, just so that the company can then start a new plan and be in a better competitive position against rivals?

The answer comes back to the same basic argument that firms use to justify pension dumping: If they don't dump, they go out of business. If they dump and don't offer competitive replacement benefits, they also go out of business, or at least they have difficulty recruiting a quality workforce. Hardock rhetorically replies to the questions he says Hill staff members posed, as if he were a corporate manager: "No! I've got to run a business. If I can't contribute to a 401(k) plan for my employees, they're not going to work for me. Our competitors give their employees generous 401(k) plans." Any bankruptcy judge will allow a company in Chapter 11 to use some cash for ongoing business expenses, rather than turning every penny over to the PBGC and other creditors. The new retirement plan is simply one of those expenses.

Some critics said that in his first post-PBGC venture, Belt himself was adding to the problem of pension dumping. In 2007, he cofounded a financial services firm, Palisades Capital Advisors, to pioneer a new Wall Street niche: buying out pension plans that were frozen to new accruals and new employees. The theory was that Palisades and the handful of other firms in this arena, as professional money managers, would handle the investments better than the original companies. However, these new firms would have less reason to care about employee morale and keep the pension plans going. And of course, if Palisades and its colleagues stumbled, where would the pension plans go? Right to the PBGC.

To Wilbur Ross, morale certainly isn't a trivial issue. "Even though the bankruptcy court has a pretty clear path on how you can resolve these problems" relating to the logistics of terminating a pension, he says, "you have the other issue of the morale of the people on the other side of the bankruptcy. Because we're not just trading things. We're really trying to rehabilitate the company. We have to be concerned with that." What does he do to ease that problem? "I don't think we've ever acquired a company where we didn't make sure to have some kind of new retirement plan."

Will a 401(k) Suffice?

Although no one tracks how many companies put in a replacement plan or what kind they established, the obvious choice for a stand-in is the plan that is becoming the most widespread in corporate America: the 401(k). This choice probably saves money for the company (even with the caveats described in Chapter 3). And most employees will probably accept the new plan because 401(k)s are now so widespread. Even many financially shaky companies that come just short of pension termination by freezing their pension plan—covering only current employees and closing it to new ones—introduce a 401(k) for future benefits.

But a shiny new 401(k) plan won't solve the morale problem in all cases. That's because traditional pension plans and 401(k)s appeal to different types of people, in different industries, for different reasons. While younger, career-hopping employees usually like the flexibility of a 401(k), which they can carry from job to job, older workers tend to prefer traditional pensions, because the payout formulas are so heavily skewed to long tenure. And there are plenty of reasons companies might want to attract the kind of long-term employees, such as scientists and midlevel managers, who want defined benefits. "If it takes a company ten years to train a good employee, you don't want him to leave after twelve," says Mike Johnston of the Hewitt Associates consulting firm. "Having a very stable, very long-service workforce can be a real competitive advantage." Compounding that are the concerns that workers of all ages have about 401(k)s. They can do the math; they can tell when the 401(k) benefit is skimpier than their old one. And many people who aren't financial experts are scared of the responsibility of managing their own accounts. Replacing a defined benefit with a 401(k) in the midst of bankruptcy is only going to depress these employees' morale even further.

Thus, to really make the 401(k) plan work as a replacement, successful companies make it a super-401(k), with generous provisions. "For the most part, they usually have a sweetened 401(k), maybe for a short period of time. Workers do believe that something's being taken away from them when a company terminates, and therefore it has to do something or other to retain its workforce," says David John, a senior research fellow at the Heritage Foundation, a conservative think tank in Washington, DC. Sylvester Schieber of Watson Wyatt cites a more hard-nosed reason for generosity. Harking back to the pension's origin as a management tool for pushing older workers out the door, he says, "You can put together a cheap [replacement] plan, but if people can't afford to retire, you've created a new problem for yourself. Do you really want an eighty-five-year-old stewardess?"

The easiest way for a company to improve a 401(k) plan is to contribute a higher-than-average amount to the employees' individual accounts. After Wilbur Ross took over Cone Mills and merged it into his International Textile Group (ITG), a defined contribution plan replaced the defunct traditional pension. Under the new plan's formula, for every dollar that workers put in, ITG adds an equal dollar, up to 3 percent of salary; for the next 2 percent of salary, the company matches half the worker's contribution. By contrast, the most common formula for a 401(k) is to match only half of an employee's contribution from the start, according to regular biennial surveys by Hewitt Associates. The ITG plan also lets people enroll in the 401(k) plan from their first day on the job, whereas most of the companies surveyed by Hewitt make the staff wait anywhere from a month to a year. Another frill a plan sponsor might add is personalized investment advice.

In fact, when companies that aren't in bankruptcy decide to freeze their healthy pension plans in order to save money, they usually beef up their 401(k) plans, and for similar reasons—to maintain morale and bring the new benefits closer to the value of the old ones. Some examples: Stride Rite in 2007 increased its match to the same dollar-for-dollar level as ITG's, up to the first 6 percent of pay. IBM topped that in 2006, promising to contribute even if the employee did not.

A Reprieve for Some

Perhaps there are other ways to appease the workforce. If the company has more than one pension plan, it might dump the biggest but save the rest. It might offer nonpension benefit improvements.

Only the pilots at Delta lost their coverage, and the same thing happened in US Airways' first bankruptcy. For a lot of reasons, different plans at a company may well have different levels of solvency. Trying to gauge which and how many might go under is at the heart of Marc Lasry's investment strategy at Avenue Capital. Unions representing separate sectors of the workforce might negotiate varying levels of benefits and their separate contracts might expire at varying times. Some plans may have been picked up in a merger and have funding and benefits totally out of line with the rest of the company's plans. Even if all the plans are underfunded, the gap could be narrow at those with the fewest members.

Partial termination would, presumably, mollify the employees who are able to keep their plans. However, whether it helps or hurts morale overall is debatable. If some plans are shut down and not others, there's a risk that the targeted employees, like the Delta pilots, will feel bitter at being singled out. When Kaiser Aluminum sought to shutter six defined benefit plans after filing for bankruptcy in 2002, the PBGC asserted that the aluminum giant could afford to continue the four smallest, which were less than $10 million short in total. By contrast, the larger two (plus a third that the PBGC itself took over after Kaiser missed millions of dollars in required contributions) had a combined underfunding of $565.8 million. "Kaiser argued that you have to look at it on a global basis, not plan by plan. They wanted to treat all their workforce the same," says Lisa Beckerman, the Akin Gump attorney, who was counsel to the Kaiser creditors' committee. The bankruptcy, district, and appellate courts all upheld the Kaiser view.

An alternative approach some companies use is to try to make up for the pension loss—and make up with their unions—with other goodies. Wilbur Ross likes to brag that in taking over the pensionless steel companies, with union backing, he put in a defined contribution plan, a profit-sharing plan, and a retiree health plan called a VEBA (voluntary employee beneficiary association) that, combined, probably cost 25 percent to 30 percent of profits. He also added productivity bonuses and used voluntary buyouts, rather than layoffs, to shrink Bethlehem's ranks by several thousand. At as much as $50,000 per person, depending on years of service, the buyouts totaled $150 million.

And of course any parties in the bankruptcy can try to negotiate any side deals they want, as long as the bankruptcy judge approves. Delta pilots were in a prime position to bargain for particularly nice replacement benefits—in addition to the bonuses, profit sharing, and 4 percent raises the company tendered across the board when it emerged. Not only did the pilots enjoy the usual clout of hard-to-replace, skilled employees, but they could additionally threaten to take their lump-sum payouts and go. Ultimately, Delta and the pilots' union worked out a deal. The union agreed not to challenge the bankruptcy and termination and also acceded to wage and work-rule concessions in return for a $650 million note plus $2.1 billion in unsecured claims. Other players in the airline's bankruptcy negotiations, including the

PBGC, were not exactly pleased at this amount of cash being siphoned out of the claims pool. "Unsecured creditors didn't like the fact that they were probably going to have to pay [pension-related costs] twice—pay the PBGC and the pilots," notes Beckerman, who was also counsel to the unsecured creditors' committee at Delta. The PBGC argued that if there was any extra compensation for employees' lost benefits, it ought to go to the PBGC, as the employees' representative. The agency had suffered a similar setback with United Airlines a couple of years earlier, when the bankruptcy judge, for the first time in ERISA's history, ruled that the PBGC had to share a significant part of its claim with the airline's pilots to compensate them for losses in their wages, health benefits, and other contract givebacks. The Delta settlement was also about $1 billion higher than Wall Street had expected. "But at that point," Beckerman says, "the pilots had leverage. We needed the plan terminated."

Resurrecting Defined Benefits

Employers looking to mend fences have one more benefits option: They can offer a new defined benefit plan.

The plan would not be identical to the old one, of course. The PBGC would object quite strenuously, as it did with LTV, if companies seemed to be trying to circumvent their past liabilities. As part of the termination process, companies must tell the PBGC about any employee benefits they intend to provide in the future, whether a 401(k) or another plan. A team of agency attorneys, actuaries, and financial analysts scrutinizes the proposals, looking especially for follow-on or wrap plans that, in the words of PBGC spokesman Gary Pastorius, are "designed to wrap around the insurance benefits provided by the PBGC in such a way as to provide both retirees and active participants substantially the same benefits as they would have received had no termination occurred."

However, a company can combine its unionized workforce with those at other companies in a multiemployer pension program, also known as a Taft-Hartley plan, because of the 1947 federal law that established the system. These are essentially pension pools run jointly by union and management trustees. As part of the regular collective bargaining over wages and other working conditions, each company negotiates with its own employees how much it will contribute—perhaps fifty cents or a dollar per hour worked. Then, the employees earn benefits based on the size of the contribution. As in a traditional pension plan, the benefits are fixed and guaranteed by the PBGC. According to the PBGC, as of 2005 there were about 1,570 of these plans with nearly 10 million participants.

This may not be an option that investors immediately think of when analyzing a company's prospects, for two reasons. First, the program has to be arranged through a labor union, but less than 8 percent of the private sector workforce is unionized. Second, these plans are found mainly in industries with a lot of small companies and in which people switch jobs frequently, such as construction, trucking, mining, entertainment, health care, and retail. "If you're a construction laborer, you can work for thirty different companies over your career. Most are small employers. It really wouldn't be feasible [for each company] to maintain a defined benefit plan indefinitely," explains Randy G. DeFrehn, executive director of the trade group for these programs, the National Coordinating Committee for Multiemployer Plans. For a while, it looked like bankrupt companies might be required to include that option in their business plans after the U.S. District Court for Northern California in 2005 ordered Crown Paper, then in Chapter 11, to consider merging its seventeen pension plans for hourly workers into a multiemployer fund sponsored by the PACE International Union as an alternative to outright termination. However, with untold numbers of pension officers wiping their brows in relief, the U.S. Supreme Court in 2007 overturned the district court ruling.

Nevertheless, there's no reason a large company can't sign up, and several have, including US Airways, United, Aloha Airlines, and Northwest Airlines, all of which filed for bankruptcy in the early 2000s. And all of them except Northwest terminated traditional pension plans. Together, the four carriers brought a total of 45,000 machinists to the International Association of Machinists' multiemployer plan.

Nor is there a time limit for starting a Taft-Hartley plan. A company can join even after filing for Chapter 11. Joe Tiberi, the Machinists' spokesman, says his union persuaded United to set up its multiemployer plan as part of its bankruptcy negotiations. Ditto at US Airways during its first bankruptcy, in exchange for union concessions. According to DeFrehn, some steelmakers have considered these plans postbankruptcy as well.

For a company in financial trouble, it may seem tempting to share the burden. As Rick Schifter of the buyout firm TPG puts it, "The solvency of the plan is not dependent on the solvency of a single company." Not only is the risk shared, but so are the expenses. "Administrative costs are going to be much lower. You need only one actuary, one accountant, one administrator. There's an economy of scale," DeFrehn of the coordinating committee says. The pooled setup is exactly what United Auto Workers president Walter Reuther had in mind when his union pioneered the concept of retirement benefits after World War II, according to writer Malcolm Gladwell. In an article in *The New Yorker* in August 2006, Gladwell states, "In most countries the government, or large groups of companies, provides pensions and health insurance. . . . if you pooled the obligations of every employer in the country, no company would go bankrupt just because it happened to employ older people, or it happened to have been around for a while, or it happened to have made the transformation from open-hearth furnaces and ingot-making to basic oxygen furnaces and continuous casting."

The bankruptcy saga of Horizon Natural Resources in the early 2000s shows the power of pooling. After a long and bitter battle, Horizon's contracts with the United Mine Workers were thrown out, one small pension plan went to the PBGC, and Wilbur Ross picked up the company's remains to create a coal conglomerate. The only contractual benefits that were left standing were the multiemployer pension plan and health benefits that covered most of the miners.

That "we're-in-it-together" philosophy creates a new set of problems, however. If one company can no longer pay its share into the pool, the others must pick up the slack. For instance, Horizon owed $200 million in withdrawal liabilities to the multiemployer fund after its bankruptcy, and the Mine Workers sued. "That spills over to the other employers in the industry. It's hard enough to get an employer to be happy about providing benefits to its own employees. No employer is happy to be paying money for somebody else's employees," says Micheal Buckner, the Mine Workers' retirement fund trustee. Judy Schub of CIEBA, the trade group for corporate investment officers, agrees. "There is always a fear, particularly in some of the smaller [companies], of being the last man standing," she says. "You end up with the liability for everyone." In self-protection, a multiemployer plan could refuse to allow a company with a severely underfunded pension to join, notes DeFrehn. Or, if the company were allowed in, it might be allowed to bring its employees but not its old liabilities.

A Matter of Management

Whether or not a company in Chapter 11 should sweep everyone out of the executive suite, what qualities to seek in a new management team, how much to pay new management, and how active investors should be in managing the company are topics for a broader analysis of bankruptcy in general. However, there are management issues that relate specifically to the pension plan termination, which can provide key information for investors to consider in deciding whether a pension dumping company has a chance to survive.

The smilefest between Wilbur Ross and the textile union Unite Here points to one of those issues: the importance of owners and managers who understand how workers are affected when their pensions are pulled away. "You've got to get employees on board; you've got to end up convincing them that the short-term pain is beneficial. A lot of it is a trust factor—whether they trust management," says Marc Lasry of the hedge fund Avenue Capital.

That kind of rapport played a role at LTV and Bethlehem, where Ross and the USW negotiated virtually every step of the way. As Ross was pondering the acquisition, the union talked to a half-dozen other potential investment groups, including hedge funds, former managers at the two companies, and other steelmakers, says Dave McCall—the union's Ohio district leader who claimed he would have given his members pipe wrenches to keep the steel plants from being shut down. Unions in general are suspicious of private equity investors, whom they see as out for a quick buck, and the Steelworkers were looking for a long-term commitment. The USW also had unique leverage, because its contracts usually included a special clause requiring the acquirer to get the union's agreement on any new labor contract. "Some of [the investors] didn't want all of the company, some of them had different views about how they would run it, some didn't want to start it at all—they just wanted the inventory and assets to sell off," McCall recalls of the potential investors.

No one was a knight in shining armor, or a pushover for the unions, not even Wilbur Ross. "I preferred none of them," McCall says bluntly. After all, even under Ross's best-case scenario, thousands of workers would be laid off, work rules would change, and the pension plans would disappear. But Ross was the top of the lot, says Gary Hubbard, a spokesman for the union. "It's not that we love the man. It's a marriage of a lot of complicated forces. We understood him, we needed him, he needed us. We do know how to work with Wilbur Ross. He's a smart guy, and he will be pretty straight up with you. He'll wear a union hat; it serves a certain purpose."

Ross begins with a couple of advantages. He is the opposite of the archetypal cigar-chewing, screaming, fist-thumping Boss. Balding and bespectacled, he speaks quietly and precisely, even pedagogically, carefully sounding out each word in acronyms like VEBA. Although his successful bets are legend and *Forbes* estimated his net worth in 2006 at $1.2 billion, making him one of the four hundred richest people in America, he can be almost apologetic in his phrasing. After the third instance of answering "it depends" to questions about his investment criteria, he interjects, "You're probably going to think we don't have any ground rules at all."

He may also have learned some humility by venturing into politics, financing his then-wife Betsy McCaughey Ross's unsuccessful bid for governor of New York in 1998. "He has this very lowly demeanor that gets trust and respect," suggests Professor Altman of NYU, the expert who maintains the database on corporate debt. Altman has spoken at conferences and served on boards with Ross over the years and considers him a friend. "He has the demeanor and patience to sit down and negotiate effectively with all the various players to get agreement for the firm to emerge under his banner." Bruce Raynor of Unite Here had a similar reaction, tempered by his labor viewpoint: "He has been truthful and candid, which is not typical of owners. I find him a humble man." And, at least outwardly, Ross seems to sympathize with the employees and their need for retirement security, Altman and others say.

At the steel companies, Ross didn't merely put in the new retirement and health benefits. He worked with the United Steelworkers to negotiate drastic changes in the job rules and descriptions, eliminating a couple dozen bureaucratic classifications. He also hired back laid-off union members at LTV while cutting the managerial ranks. For proof that his management approach works, Ross pointed to the union members' overwhelming approval of the labor contracts. "Rather than attack wages as such, we try to change job descriptions, work rules, so you can use people more efficiently; then couple that with a buyout. As a result, we didn't have big morale problems, because nobody had been forced into layoffs. It was a voluntary thing," he claims.

His boast gets support from USW officials, including Dave McCall, who says that the union had been agitating for just those sorts of job changes for years. Actually, according to McCall, it was the Steelworkers who persuaded Ross to make the changes. "When LTV shut down," McCall says, "we called people that I'd known over a couple of decades who had worked at LTV, U.S. Steel, Bethlehem, National—a dozen shop-floor people who had experience with shop-floor job descriptions. We came together for month to discuss it. If we owned a mill, how would we design it?" As McCall describes their analysis, the old system had far too many nitpicking job categories, too much bureaucracy, and too much second-guessing by management. "They had people sitting around waiting for people to do their jobs. It used to be that the boss would come in in the morning and get a report from the night boss about eight different jobs that needed to be done. Then the assistant boss would go back to me. Now, [the union workers] just talk to the people they're relieving on the midnight shift and find out what's going on. The companies used to say to us, 'This is the way we always did it. You just leave your brain at the gate.' I think that impeded productivity, it impeded quality, and it impeded workers' sense of responsibility. If you broaden people's responsibilities, they don't have to work harder—they have to work smarter."

Mike Psaros of KPS Special Situations is even more devoted to empathizing with his workers. Good relations with unions is one of the four key elements in his investment decisions, along with the product line, the potential for cost reduction, and new management. He says that 90 percent of the companies in KPS's portfolio have unions, and in fact "the union has in most situations introduced us to the investment opportunity. We work in partnership with the union in bringing these companies out of bankruptcy." Buckner of the UMW, for one, tried to interest Psaros in bidding for Horizon Natural Resources as a relatively labor friendly alternative, but, says Buckner, "[Psaros] told me he didn't think he could compete with Wilbur Ross on the bid." In that case, obviously, Ross's relations with the union weren't as cozy as with the Steelworkers. Still, it wasn't his decision to shut down the pension plan at Horizon. Although Psaros does not try to preserve the old defined benefit plans in the companies he targets, he says a retirement plan of some sort is a must after he takes over. "All of our portfolio companies provide a pension benefit either through a 401(k) or through a Taft-Hartley vehicle," he points out. In addition, one of his companies, the fully funded coiling-equipment maker Genesis Worldwide II, maintained its traditional defined benefit plan.

The need to show some sensitivity to what the workers are going through when their pensions are terminated is one reason the huge pension grabs and payouts at Delta and United became so egregious. Pilots at Delta lost their shot at a lump-sum bonanza and had their potential pensions slashed by as much as half, on top of a previous 32 percent pay cut. So it was a slap in the face when CEO Leo Mullin and a crew of top managers were able to take their own, special executive pensions and skedaddle just before the bankruptcy hammer came down. A veteran pilot named Justin Pavoni, with twenty-two years at Delta, sent a blistering letter to Gerald Grinstein, the new chief executive, in August 2006, which was later posted on a self-styled "politically incorrect Delta pilots" website. Pavoni writes in the letter: "It would have been one thing if *all* employees had lost their pensions, from the CEO down the line, and if we all had taken a proportionate share of pay cuts in an effort to save this corporation from demise. . . . You have violated even the most basic principles of leadership."

At United, the problem was rich pay not to the suits who left but to those who stayed. As part of the carrier's reorganization and record-breaking pension terminations, the eight highest-ranking executives got promises of a total $3.5 million in annual salaries and more than $4 million in retention and signing payments, plus bonuses that in some cases doubled their salaries. Chief Executive Tilton alone raked in a base salary of $605,625, an equal-size bonus, a $3 million signing bonus, $4.5 million in pension and other benefits, $25 million worth of stock, and a further $6 million in stock options;

the top four hundred managers combined received $115 million in the new stock and options, equal to 8 percent of the company's equity. By comparison, one year later, Northwest's top four hundred executives would get just 4.9 percent of the equity. United was blasted in Congress and in news columns. The *New York Times*, for instance, called the compensation package "insanity squared" and a "share grab." Oregon Senator Ron Wyden grilled Tilton at a Senate hearing. The Association of Flight Attendants issued a statement proclaiming, "Employees have been forced to sacrifice annually over $4 billion in pay, pensions, work rules, and health care, while executives have richly rewarded themselves." For good measure, the statement pointed out, "In medieval times, people guilty of this kind of greed would have been boiled in oil." The pilots union began forming what it called a strike-preparation committee, and retired pilots appealed their plan termination to the U.S. Supreme Court— twice. What made the managerial payouts even worse was that the workforce had kept the airline alive a decade earlier by agreeing to huge wage concessions in return for a majority of the shares, to be held in an employee stock ownership plan—shares that of course lost all value when United filed for bankruptcy in 2002.

Whatever their intentions, even the most worker-sensitive vulture investors are not going to be loved by the unions. These investors are, from the workers' point of view, merely the least bad among a lot of bad choices. Given their druthers, most employees would rather the company not file for bankruptcy or impose any labor cutbacks at all. Wilbur Ross may have saved five steel companies and thousands of jobs, but thousands more workers were nevertheless laid off, and the pension plans disappeared.

Despite all these hazards, coming in as a new owner or manager— even when a pension plan may have to be dumped—does have its positive side. Even managers who don't make a point of reaching out to their employee base will generally enjoy a grace period when they start (as long as they don't look too greedy, as they did at United). That can be especially important if the owners' first step is to ax a major benefit, such as a pension plan. Because they don't carry the old management's baggage—such as previous cutbacks or poor decisions that got the company in trouble to begin with—the new crew may be able to shed the pension without rousing as much resentment. They wear the halo of riding in to save the company, albeit at the cost of jettisoning the pension plan. "Ross can negotiate with the union because the company is now providing a benefit where there was none," is the way Steve Kandarian, the former PBGC head, puts it. "Old Bethlehem management can't, because it cut existing benefits." That is, if Bethlehem cuts a $100 pension to $50, that stirs resentment because the company is decreasing the amount it used to provide. But if Bethlehem goes bankrupt and Wilbur Ross comes in and offers $50—or even $40—he's hailed because he kept the company from liquidating and giving zero. This was especially so at Bethlehem, because it was the PBGC that played the heavy by rushing in to close the plan before the shutdown benefits kicked in. On the other hand, new managers may not want to arrive and have their first act be to eliminate a perk that workers have enjoyed.

Remember too that top brass get—and lose—their own pensions. Certainly the defined benefit pension is not their only financial perk. Managers have their stock options, bonuses, and special "nonqualified" retirement plans (not tax-exempt but also not subject to ERISA) in addition to pay and standard pensions. But the irony is that now a company might regret terminating the maligned old defined benefit plan because that's exactly the kind of retirement benefit, far more than a 401(k), that is likely to appeal to the older, experienced managers found in the highest ranks.

Poisoned PR

"Whoops! There Goes Another Pension Plan," blared a headline in the *New York Times* on September 18, 2005. "The Broken Promise" shouted a cover story about pension terminations in *Time* magazine a month later. "The End of Pensions?" the *New York Times Magazine* asked that same month, October 2005. A PBS *Frontline* broadcast raised a similar question the following May: "Can You Afford to Retire?" And it's impossible to count all the references to "vulture investors" who buy up companies after—or because—they shed their pensions. This is not exactly the kind of publicity any business wants, but particularly not one fresh out of bankruptcy, struggling to improve its image among employees, customers, creditors, lenders, and investors.

When a company terminates its pension plan, says Phyllis Borzi, the George Washington University professor and former congressional pension counsel, "it changes the view of people in the community, who might have thought of this company as the anchor of the community, the good corporate citizen. People who would normally be willing to give the company the benefit of the doubt won't do so any more." Just as workers no longer trust an employer that breaks what was supposed to be a sacrosanct promise, the public also starts to have doubts. Many of these outsiders may be worried about their own pensions as well. All this comes amid a growing public skepticism about the trustworthiness of business in general, after the rash of scandals at Enron Corporation, WorldCom, and other headline-making corporations in the early 2000s. "No manager wants to be known as the guy that stripped away everyone's pensions," says Michael Kramer, the restructuring specialist at Perella Weinberg.

David Neigus, the Machinists' associate general counsel, suggests that such public suspicion was one reason the third group of airlines to file for bankruptcy—Northwest and Delta—did not dump their pension plans en masse as did United, US Airways, Pan Am, and TWA. (Neigus's union represents tens of thousands of machinists whose plans were shut down in some cases and saved in others.) Certainly, the two late filers had a range of motivations for hanging on to their plans. In large part, they were saved by the funding extension for airlines in the 2006 Pension Protection Act, which Congress passed just days before Delta would have had to throw in the towel (or so Delta claimed). But Neigus argues that there was another reason the first carriers shed more plans. They were able to slip their terminations under the radar, before all the headlines about retirees being thrown out in the cold. "US Airways was one of the first to terminate, and there was less pushback from some of the forces," he explains. "The public wasn't aware of it as much. The PBGC protected its interest, but it didn't become as big of an issue as it did when the PBGC's deficit skyrocketed and everyone started noticing." With the later terminations, by contrast, "there was a lot of pushback and pressure," says Neigus. "With United, it really came to a head. There was pressure from the unions; there was resistance from the PBGC; the politicians got involved. Perhaps Delta and Northwest were looking for a way of not confronting those forces." (For more on public pressure, see Chapter 14.)

Still, if hanging onto the pension plan is not financially feasible, what can a company do to preserve, or at least polish, its public image? Investor Michael Kramer, after pointing out that companies don't want to be seen as pension strippers, is clearly at a loss for suggestions about how to deal with such fallout. "You try to do the right thing. You have to continue to be professional, make decisions for the right reasons." It's the same kind of steps a company would take after any kind of disaster, like an oil spill or a product recall. The strategies that build employee morale, including good replacement benefits and some indication that management and the "vulture" investor care about the workforce and the community, can also help.

"Ultimately, what determines whether a company can reorganize has to be the soundness of the business," says Professor Gilson of Harvard. "There has to be a market for the product, you have to have a viable business. It would be measured by the same yardsticks you use for a business whether it's in bankruptcy or not"—and whether it sheds its pension plan or not.

10 | The Emergence of US Airways

"We were feeling some concerns about the strength of the franchise, but ultimately we believed that management could be successful. The termination of the pension plan was a condition."

—RICK SCHIFTER, PARTNER, TPG

I
F TED WESCHLER learns that a company has a serious problem with its pension plan, he usually keeps his billions in his wallet.

Weschler has been looking for undervalued investments "ever since I began trading baseball cards in second grade." He had a good chance to learn about a lot of baseball teams as well as a lot of distressed industries back then, moving from one Rust Belt city to another—Cleveland, Buffalo, Pittsburgh, and Erie, Pennsylvania—as his father, an executive with the A&P grocery chain, transferred between regions. After graduating from the Wharton School in 1983 with an undergraduate degree in accounting and finance, Weschler went to work for W.R. Grace & Co. for six years, in a series of jobs specializing in acquisitions and divestitures. He and a colleague then left Grace and established a firm called Quad-C in Charlottesville, Virginia, to do leveraged buyouts. But after ten years, Weschler decided "there was better value in public-sector investments." So in 1999 he went out on his own to launch a hedge fund, Peninsula Investment Partners—just down the road from Quad-C.

Almost from the start, Weschler has had opportunities to hone his thinking about unfunded defined benefit plans. Back in the mid-1980s, when he was still at Quad-C, "there were plenty of situations where an unfunded pension liability was so ugly you didn't want to get near owning the company. Some of the coal-mining operations in Pennsylvania or West Virginia, if you had a chance to buy these businesses for a dollar, you wouldn't, because you had a fundamentally aging population that was covered by a benefit that was underfunded."

149

Certainly, the prospect of walking straight into a business with a huge debt overhang that is inevitably going to get worse as the workforce ages and shrinks could chill an investor's enthusiasm, even an investor specializing in turnarounds. But why not just transfer the debt to the PBGC? Although that may seem to ease the financial strain, Weschler points out, it creates new problems of morale and management, which can undermine operations and erase any financial gain from dumping. Workers will become disgruntled with a company that has yanked back what they thought was a guaranteed benefit. "At the end of the day, a happy workforce is far more productive than an unhappy workforce," he says.

"The other thing that's spooky to me," Weschler adds, "is that it's a very complex accounting and a squishy accounting. All you need is a slight change in the earnings rate or the discount rate or interest rates. It's a number that can be wildly understated or overstated."

Given his concerns, Weschler ought to have been the last person to purchase a ticket on US Airways' second bankruptcy express in the spring of 2005, as the company faced an unfunded pension liability of some $2.5 billion. In fact, he was one of the first. He put in $50 million to buy about 4 percent of the reorganized airline's new stock and then a month later exercised an option to buy $10 million more. Apparently, this break with standard operating procedure paid off. A year and a half after his initial commitment, the value had soared fourfold, and US Airways was feeling strong enough to make an $8 billion bid to buy yet another bankrupt airline, Delta.

US Airways didn't fly straight to success, of course. Even after the second bankruptcy, it had its share of customer complaints and ill-conceived business decisions. To add to the mess, its CEO was hauled in for drunk driving. But the carrier has clearly emerged as a stronger airline than before, and Ted Weschler's out-of-character decision can be a model for the most skeptical investor.

Abandoning the Flight Plan

Airlines aren't Rust Belt dinosaurs like the steel companies, dragged down by a workforce top-heavy with retirees and outgunned by low-cost Chinese imports. By contrast, air travel is a relatively modern technology, and the workforce is young as well. Federal law shelters the U.S. industry from competition by generally blocking foreign-flagged companies from flying domestic routes. True, starting in 1960, pilots had to retire by age sixty, which might seem to create a huge, steel-industry-like pool of retirees. However, unlike steel-workers, they weren't retiring because the industry was contracting. The airlines would usually hire a fresh batch of younger replacement pilots and continue paying into the pension plan to cover their future benefits. (In any case, a new law in 2007 raised the retirement age to sixty-five.) In light of all those differences, airlines shouldn't be tumbling into bankruptcy like steel dominos.

Nevertheless, the PBGC has seen as many big airlines collapse as big steel companies, starting as early as Braniff International Airways in 1982. Their stories, moreover, run the gamut of every possible combination of financial and employee trouble. Five of the nation's all-time costliest pension terminations occurred at airlines, including the largest ever (as of 2007), United Airlines, with a total underfunding of over $7 billion at four pension plans. There have been repeat filings (TWA, US Airways), restructurings (US Airways, United, Delta) and complete liquidations (Braniff, Pan Am, Eastern, TWA). Between 1978 and 2005, 162 airlines filed for bankruptcy, the U.S. Government Accountability Office (GAO) stated in a special report in September 2005. Most were relatively small carriers, but four majors (United, US Airways, Delta, and Northwest) fell within less than three years. As Warren Buffett said in his chairman's letter to shareholders of Berkshire Hathaway in 1992, "Investors have regularly poured money into the domestic airline business to finance profitless (or worse) growth. For these investors, it would have been far better if Orville [Wright] had failed to get off the ground at Kitty Hawk."

How did such a modern business sector get into such bad shape? "The airline industry is characterized by intense competition, high fixed costs, cyclical demand, and vulnerability to external shocks. As a result, airlines have performed worse financially and are more prone to failure than most other industries," the GAO report summarizes. The first big external shock of the post-ERISA world was the Arab oil embargo of 1973–1974, followed soon after by the Airline Deregulation Act of 1978 and another devastating spike in oil prices during the Iranian hostage crisis of 1979–1980. Deregulation threatened the older "legacy" carriers because it opened up their long-protected routes and price structures to a theoretically unlimited swarm of new, largely nonunion fleets that, by definition, weren't dragged down by the legacy companies' huge, inherited costs—in particular, pensions and older, high-maintenance equipment. This new competition drove median round-trip prices down by 40 percent from 1980 to 2006, according to a GAO report issued in June 2006. The legacy carriers managed to fight back in a variety of ways, such as by controlling the all-important gates at major airports and retaining customers through frequent flyer programs. Thus, even as legacy carriers fell in a first round of bankruptcies, a slew of the small newcomers stumbled, too.

In the 1990s, the boom years of the Clinton presidency, the upward phase of the industry's cycle kicked in. Then the September 11, 2001, terrorist attacks socked the airlines with the biggest passenger drop in their history. Not only were people terrified of flying, but with the country in recession, they couldn't even afford a ticket. Carriers slashed their routes as much as 25 percent. Conditions got so bad that Congress passed special legislation giving the airlines $5 billion in direct aid plus up to $10 billion in loan guarantees and assorted insurance help. Just as the industry was trying to climb out of that disaster, the SARS epidemic hit Asia in the fall of 2002. Now people were scared to fly to Asia. On top of all that, the U.S. invasion of Iraq, which began in 2003, and Hurricane Katrina's pounding of offshore oil fields in September 2005 sent oil prices gushing again.

The airlines' managements contributed to the problem with their perennial tendency to bulk up on new jets during the good times, yoking the companies to long-term leases. "They make the same mistakes over and over," says Lisa Beckerman, the Akin Gump attorney, who was the counsel to Delta's creditors' committee. Moreover, many of the employees who had been hired during the roaring 1950s and 1960s were now reaching retirement age. And this time the legacy carriers bore the brunt. They simply couldn't cut their costs as nimbly as the regionals and newcomers could.

Bankruptcy No. 1

US Airways took off in 1939. Or, to be more precise, All-American Airways took off in 1939, carrying airmail for the U.S. Post Office in western Pennsylvania and the Ohio Valley, according to an official history on the carrier's website. Over the next sixty years, it would change names three times as it broadened its geographical reach, becoming Allegheny Airlines, US Air, and finally US Airways. Through a series of mergers and acquisitions, it absorbed Piedmont Airlines, Mohawk Airlines, Lake Central Airlines, Pacific Southwest Airlines, the Boston–New York City–Washington Trump Shuttle, and some prime TWA routes to London.

By most accounts, US Airways (its name by 1997) was particularly hard hit by deregulation and September 11. For one thing, its hub was in Washington, DC, which was closed longer than other airports after the terrorist attacks, and it relied heavily on the New York City–Washington shuttle it had obtained from Trump. Because of its route structure, US Airways also faced particularly stiff competition from newcomers like Southwest Airlines, JetBlue Airways, AirTran Airways, and Independence Air. It was also an awkward size, neither big enough to be a major carrier nor small enough to be a low-cost regional. Even before the September 11 attacks, the company had tried to prop itself up by merging with United, but the U.S. Department of Justice had blocked that for antitrust reasons. In August 2002, with losses of more than $500 million for the first half of the year, added to nearly $2 billion of red ink from 2001, US Airways filed for Chapter 11 reorganization in the Eastern District of Virginia.

For a value investor like the buyout firm TPG, that was the moment to take a serious look. Based in Fort Worth, Texas, TPG was cofounded in 1992 by David Bonderman, a former chief operating officer of the Robert M. Bass Group and one of the best-known and most aggressive turnaround artists in the business. He may also be one of the industry's most aggressive rock music fans, hiring the Rolling Stones to play at his sixtieth birthday party in Las Vegas — a little shindig that reportedly cost $7 million—and the group the B-52's for a celebration in San Francisco in 2000 when TPG raised its first $4 billion. Although TPG's holdings are eclectic, with stakes in the luxury department store Neiman Marcus, a Japanese toy manufacturer, and several tech firms at one time or another, it specializes in neglected, big-name consumer brands, including Del Monte, Metro-Goldwyn-Mayer, clothing company J. Crew, PETCO Animal Supplies, and Burger King. The Burger King acquisition caused some eyebrows to elevate after TPG and two other private equity firms shared $511 million in dividends, fees, interest, and expense reimbursement within less than four years, without giving up their 76 percent ownership. In another eye-catching deal, TPG teamed up with buyout giant Kohlberg Kravis Roberts in early 2007 to acquire a controversial Texas utility, TXU, for $45 billion. Not only would that be the largest leveraged buyout ever, but the two acquirers also set out to court environmental groups, attaching a number of unusual environmental requirements to the deal and forcing TXU to drop plans to build eight coal-fired plants. Typically, TPG takes an active role in management and maintains its holdings for twelve years. In 2007, *Fortune* magazine ranked TPG number four on its "Power List" of leading private equity firms, with more than $30 billion in assets at that point.

When US Airways filed, TPG had about $10 billion under management and some experience in the airline industry. The firm had made its reputation with a recapitalization of twice-bankrupt Continental Airlines in 1993—a deal that observers back then considered chancy because of Continental's unstable history but which ended up multiplying TPG's initial $66 million investment tenfold. Although TPG had sold off its Continental holdings at the time of the US Airways filing, it still owned what partner Rick Schifter calls "a small stake" in America West, one of the newer upstarts. "We historically believed the airline industry is cyclical. We figured there would be some rebound, but it wasn't clear when," says Schifter, a trim man of average height, with thinning hair, pale blue eyes, a cleft chin, and a speaking style that churns out words double-time.

For Schifter, the key to investing in US Airways was its management, including CEO David N. Siegel. "We felt satisfied with [the management in place]. They were working hard to reduce their costs. We were feeling some concerns about the strength of the franchise, but ultimately we believed that management could be successful." So TPG agreed to put in $200 million for a 38 percent share, with the rest to be publicly traded, presumably going to unions and other unsecured creditors. The bid was contingent on the filing of Chapter 11 and some serious cost cutting. One of those costs was the pension plan for approximately eight thousand active and retired pilots.

According to the PBGC, the pilots' plan had just $1.2 billion in assets to pay $3.7 billion in promised benefits, or a $2.5 billion underfunding. "The termination of the pension plan was a condition," Schifter says. That did not have to mean shifting it to the PBGC. For instance, US Airways was energetically trying to persuade the PBGC and Congress to let it stretch out its $2.5 billion payments over thirty years, more or less what LTV had done back in 1990. Legislators were also mulling a sweeping reform of the whole system of pension insurance that could include funding breaks for the airlines. Schifter would actually have preferred the legislative solution, because it would have avoided the risk of a bankruptcy court fight, as well as the hit to employee morale. And that hit would be especially hard because of the PBGC's cap on the maximum pension it pays, plus its early-retirement penalty. Together, those limitations would bring the US Airways pilots' pension below $28,000 per year if the PBGC were paying, compared with a probable $150,000 to $200,000 if the pilots could get their regular pensions. However, it would be another four years before Congress passed the 2006 Pension Protection Act giving airlines more time to fund their benefits. Facing reality, Schifter assumed there would have to be a typical distress termination.

So far, so good—at least for TPG. But as the firm began its due diligence on the deal, doubts grew. "We were getting cold feet," says Schifter. "We found that the industry took another turn for the worse in August through September, and we became concerned about how long it was going to take for the industry to recover." The White House under George W. Bush was clearly preparing for an invasion of Iraq, which added to TPG's anxiety because of the potential impact on the economy and oil prices. Just then, the Retirement Systems of Alabama made a counteroffer to pay $240 million for a 37.5 percent stake in US Airways, along with $500 million in cash financing. TPG could have gone into a bidding war. Instead, says Schifter, "we got out of the way"—with a huge sigh of relief.

Now a group of pension funds was bidding for a company that was dumping its own pension plan, but Alabama is not your ordinary pension fund. No stodgy 60/40 stock-bond allocation for Alabama. Under David G. Bronner, who became chief executive in 1973, the Alabama funds, which cover teachers, state employees, and judicial workers, earned a reputation for pushing the bounds of alternative investments. The funds' most famous moves involved creating the Robert Trent Jones series of golf courses through the middle of the state and rescuing one of Manhattan's largest office towers. As of 2002, when US Airways filed in bankruptcy court, Bronner had built the Alabama system from $500 million in assets to more than $20 billion. He saw the US Airways bid as part of a much broader project to make Alabama a major player in the airline industry. He would spend the next few years trying to persuade Airbus Industrie to build a manufacturing plant in Mobile, to relocate a US Airways maintenance plant to that city, and to hook up the carrier with local suppliers.

The US Airways deal went ahead. Alabama committed its $740 million, and the federal government agreed to $900 million in loan guarantees through its post–September 11, $15 billion bailout package for the industry. Mechanics, flight attendants, pilots, and other union workers gave back more than $1.5 billion worth of labor concessions. And the pilots lost their pensions. In return, pilots still on the job got a relatively generous 401(k) plan. US Airways triumphantly emerged from bankruptcy in March 2003, just seven months after filing.

Or so it seemed.

11

The Reemergence
of US Airways

*"The industry was going to be viable again. We were looking
for an opportunity to participate in that."*

—ED SHAPIRO, PARTNER, PAR CAPITAL MANAGEMENT

Even before US Airways emerged from bankruptcy in 2003, there were signs of trouble. The carrier's attempt to stretch out its pension funding over thirty years had created a lot of heavy waves in Washington, DC. Steve Kandarian, then the PBGC's executive director, flat-out said no. "Some cited the 1986 LTV Supreme Court case as precedent, but that case really didn't apply to the US Airways situation," he argues. The LTV arrangement had been part of a larger court battle centered on whether the steelmaker was trying to subvert the meaning of "termination" by shutting down its existing plan and putting in a new one that was substantially the same, without paying for the accumulated liabilities. The funding extension in LTV's case was a practical solution, because LTV could not afford to pay back the whole liability all at once after it lost in the Supreme Court. By contrast, US Airways was trying to establish a funding extension from the start for what would essentially be a sham termination.

"Congress sets the funding rules. If I as PBGC chief can set the funding rules for US Airways, I can do that for any company," Kandarian warns. "Do you really want the executive director of the PBGC setting the funding rules on a company-by-company basis?" In fact, his successor, Brad Belt, later took the opposite stand, asserting that this missed opportunity, with some financial protections for the PBGC, might well be the solution for avoiding future terminations.

Whether or not Kandarian was on solid ground legally, he was in quicksand politically. His denial infuriated Arlen Specter, the powerful senior senator from Pennsylvania. US Airways had been founded in western Pennsylvania and still maintained major hubs in Pittsburgh and Philadelphia, which meant that a lot of endangered employees and retirees were probably Pennsylvania voters. And Specter, a moderate Republican, knew he would be facing a tough primary against a more conservative opponent in 2004. (He ultimately squeaked by, 51 percent to 49 percent.) Specter had cosponsored the unsuccessful Senate bill that would have stretched out the pension funding. So in January 2003, Specter hauled Kandarian and Jim Keightley, then the agency's general counsel, to a hearing before the Appropriations Committee's Subcommittee on Labor, Health and Human Services, and Education and Related Agencies, which he chaired. He grilled them for over an hour.

But the airline didn't get its funding extension, either from the PBGC or Congress. And TPG's concerns came to pass: The U.S. invaded Iraq, sending oil prices way up. In 2004, US Airways was spending $300 million more on fuel than expected. Discounts reduced revenue by another $450 million. Employees refused to make $800 million in concessions demanded by management, beyond the $1.5 billion they'd already given up. The pilots' new 401(k) was costing almost as much as the terminated pension plan, at least in the short run. In September 2004, barely eighteen months after triumphantly exiting from bankruptcy, US Airways was grounded again. The Alabama Retirement System, the largest single shareholder, lost its $240 million equity stake (though not the $500 million loan). CEO Bronner refused to comment for this book, but in an interview with a reporter from the *Philadelphia Inquirer* conducted while the airline was still struggling to stay alive, he emphasized that the holding constituted only about 1 percent of the retirement system's entire portfolio. "You have to put it in perspective," he said. "I'm a big boy. I make my bets and take my losses."

This time, almost no one expected the aircraft doors to reopen.

Finding the Money

By the fall of 2004, Ed Shapiro was ready to start putting some more money in the airline industry. He had been specializing in that industry for more than a dozen years, first at Wellington Management in Boston—a firm founded in 1928 and one of the most venerable in the financial world—and since 1997 at PAR Capital Management, the $1.5 billion hedge fund at which he was one of four partners. PAR's philosophy is that each of its eight portfolio managers specializes in just a few fields, and Shapiro chose airlines plus media and entertainment. Earlier in 2004, PAR had trimmed its holdings in American Airlines by about two-thirds, to around 6.5 million shares, and shed its entire 15 percent share of America West. "We were increasingly concerned about the state of the industry," Shapiro recalls. "Capacity was out of whack, and costs were too high." Nevertheless, "it was a critical industry, and people were going to continue to fly." Therefore, he calculated, things were probably nearing bottom. He figured on one or two more bankruptcies. "The industry was going to be viable again. We were looking for an opportunity to participate in that."

Shapiro took a good long look at US Airways, which was desperately seeking financing to emerge from its second bankruptcy. It was hardly an obvious play; the track record for second bankruptcies is probably even worse than for second marriages. "We spent a lot of time analyzing the company and meeting with management and its advisers," Shapiro says. "We concluded that while it had accomplished a lot in terms of reducing its costs and restructuring its network, it still didn't have the scale to compete with the larger-network airlines and increasingly aggressive low-cost carriers." That wasn't the only problem. "There had been significant management turnover during the bankruptcy, and we were concerned that they didn't have sufficient management depth." In February 2005, he took a pass.

About a month later, US Airways's financial adviser came back with a new suggestion: Would PAR be interested if the company merged with another, unspecified airline? Shapiro signed a confidentiality agreement in order to find out more, since "it potentially solved our issues with regard to scale and management." In fact, the prospective merger partner was none other than PAR's old investment, America West. The new parent company would keep the US Airways name, but almost everything else would be from America West—the corporate culture, the type of retirement benefits, and, most important, the CEO.

America West had been one of those upstart, low-cost—and pensionless—airlines nipping at the profits of legacy carriers like US Airways. It had spent three years in bankruptcy itself in the early

1990s and come close to a second visit after the September 11 attacks, rescued only by $98 million in government cash, a $380 million federal loan guarantee, and the efforts of a new, young, charismatic chief executive named Doug Parker, then age thirty-nine. Since that time, the industry had been swooning over Parker like fans of his own favorite rock stars. A fast tracker who'd worked his way up the corporate ladder at American and Northwest airlines after business school, Parker rejuvenated America West by overhauling maintenance and easing travel restrictions such as mandatory Saturday-night layovers for discount flyers. He sent letters of apology to passengers whose travel schedules were disrupted. And he won the loyalty of his workforce by avoiding big pay cuts and by his personal style. Disarmingly casual and self-deprecating, he shed his tie, management jargon, even his full name. (For the record, it's W. Douglas Parker.) Ted Weschler recalls how Parker leaped to defend his rank and file against one investor's criticism of high labor costs at an annual meeting; later, in 2006, he would even forgo his own bonus. Presumably, he had a special bond with his workers because his wife, Gwen, was one of them—a former flight attendant and union activist at American. As Doug Parker told the *New York Times* in 2007, if he complains to Gwen about high labor costs and the need for wage givebacks, "it's not going to make for a nice evening at home."

The Parker myth went way beyond business decisions. There were tales of how he ran with the bulls in Spain and went bungee jumping on his honeymoon. Perhaps the quintessential Doug Parker story was the "smelly watch" example, as relayed by his communications director, Elise Eberwein, in *USA Today*: Driving to work one morning, Parker kept sensing a foul odor in his car. Then he smelled it at a staff meeting. Finally, he realized it was the dried sweat on his cloth-band wristwatch, which he'd worn that weekend while running a ten-kilometer race for charity. So he waved around the offending watch at the meeting, announcing, "Smell my watch!"

The wild-boy lifestyle had its downside, however. Two years after Shapiro pondered investing in Parker's airline merger, Parker was arrested for drunken driving in his home state of Arizona, at least the third time in his adult life that he'd been driving under the influence.

The knowledge that he'd really be investing in Doug Parker's operation (prearrest) clinched the deal for Shapiro. PAR committed

$100 million, with an option to increase the amount by 20 percent within thirty days of the closing. But the airline wanted to launch with $350 million to $550 million in initial capital before going to the public markets. Shapiro therefore went looking for more cash. Air Wisconsin Airlines was one obvious partner, since it already had ties with the bigger carrier—it provided short, regional tie-in flights to US Airways and also had made a $125 million debtor-in-possession (DIP) loan with an equity conversion kicker. Air Wisconsin agreed to convert the DIP to an equity stake, and another regional airline, Air Canada, committed $75 million. (It would later get a contract to do maintenance work for US Airways.) Next, Shapiro placed a call to Ted Weschler. As Weschler remembers the moment, "It was an out-of-the-blue phone call." But the two men had heard of each other because they were among the few people in the finance world to share an oddly linked interest in airlines and satellite TV. They had other things in common, too. Both had known since they were kids that they wanted a career in finance. Both had done undergraduate work at Wharton. And both were pleasantly disposed to any company run by Doug Parker.

Weschler had one key question for Shapiro: "How are they dealing with the pension situation?"

Taking the Bullet

That concern over pensions was something else Weschler and Shapiro shared. As it happened, US Airways CEO Bruce R. Lakefield (who had replaced the prebankruptcy chief, Siegel) had already made the decision to terminate the carrier's three remaining pension plans—for flight attendants, machinists, and "certain employees" (Henry Rose's clients, the executives)—which were underfunded by a total $2.5 billion. Then he turned his airline over to Doug Parker.

It was an alternative version of the classic new-manager honeymoon. "You have a very interesting dynamic," as Weschler sees it. "Whoever it is that oversees the rejection of the pension plan is not going to be viewed as exactly a white knight by the rank and file, and labor relations are so important in the airline industry. Bruce Lakefield was very pragmatic. He wanted to do whatever it took to make US Airways survive. He wasn't looking in any way, shape, or form to entrench himself as the CEO going forward. What made it work, in effect, was that he was willing to take the bullet in association with shutting down the pension and the grief of the rank and file that would go with it, because that was the necessary medicine for US Airways to survive at all. The America West team that was coming in was not immediately burdened with the perception of being the new guys that come in and destroy the pension." In other words, Weschler could invest in his cake and eat it too: US Airways could terminate the pension plans without some of the morale problems that usually go with that move.

Lakefield also declined to be interviewed for this book, but did say, "None of us liked the hand we were dealt, but we put the people of the airline first and did our best to save their jobs."

For his part, Shapiro was a little more open to investing in a pension-laden airline than Weschler was. He still would have taken a look at US Airways if it had maintained the underfunded plans, "but we likely would have concluded that it was not viable, given the magnitude of the liability. Given the increase in the low-cost carriers that don't have defined benefits, it is increasingly difficult if not impossible to remain competitive with that disadvantage."

Shapiro and Weschler made their moves. Shapiro's PAR invested $160 million for 10.7 million shares at $15 to start and then picked up a further $100 million worth of holdings, or 2.75 million shares, at about $37 per share from Air Canada and Air Wisconsin when the original holders' six-month lockup ended in March 2006. (The two carriers had come into the deal for strategic reasons rather than as pure investors and were happy to cash out after more than doubling their investments, according to Shapiro.) That made PAR the carrier's largest single stockholder, with 15 percent of the shares. Meanwhile, Weschler initially committed $50 million for an ownership stake of about 4 percent, adding $10 million worth from Air Wisconsin and Air Canada.

In September 2005, once again, US Airways pulled itself out of Chapter 11. Less than a year later, Congress would finally pass the new pension law—the one that Rick Schifter of TPG had hoped would save the pilots' pensions in the first bankruptcy—giving airlines extra time to fund their pension plans.

US Airways lasted just a year and a half after emerging from its first bankruptcy; within the same amount of time, a year and a half, after emerging from bankruptcy number two, the company was widely viewed as a success. The merged US Airways–America West finished

2006 with a $304 million profit, the third-best showing among the big carriers, versus a $46 million loss for the two airlines combined in 2005. The stock price, which had launched at around $19 per share in September 2005, more than doubled within the first year and a half. Investors like Shapiro and Weschler, who came in early at $15 a share, did even better, of course. (Their price was fixed in May 2005, at the time they committed to purchase, although they didn't actually buy the shares until September.) The stock hit as high as $63 in November and December 2006, though it slid into the high $40s and low $50s by the eighteen-month anniversary, probably because of rising fuel prices plus the collapse of US Airways' hostile bid for Delta. In February 2007 PAR sold nearly half of its holdings—6.5 million of 13.5 million shares—in a private transaction with Goldman Sachs at $57.80 a share, or nearly triple the purchase price. By then, Shapiro says, the position's market value of approximately $800 million represented more than half of PAR's total assets, and, he implies, the firm simply didn't want any single holding to constitute such a big percentage.

There was another set of early investors who also did well. In June 2005, a month after signing up Weschler, Air Canada, and Air Wisconsin, Shapiro had added two more investors at $16.50, in order to get more of the initial capital that US Airways–America West felt was needed. He brought in his old firm, Wellington, which put in $125 million with an option for 20 percent more, and the hedge fund Tudor Investment Corp., founded by the swashbuckling futures trader Paul Tudor Jones II, with $65 million plus the 20 percent option. Jones, by the way, could outmatch Doug Parker in amazing life anecdotes. A college welterweight boxing champion, he made a fortune trading cotton and playing European interest rate futures and currencies, predicted the 1987 market crash, chaired the New York Cotton Exchange (NYCE), set up a celebrity-studded antipoverty organization with *Rolling Stone* magazine publisher Jann Wenner, pleaded guilty to environmental violations in filling a wetlands on his Maryland estate, and married an Australian fashion model after a rollicking time on the dating scene.

The Secret Formula

What made this reorganization not merely work but indeed beat the long odds against emerging from a second bankruptcy? Certainly, the new airline was able to seize some efficiencies from its merger by eliminating unneeded gates, cutting management overlap, shedding unprofitable routes, and grounding five dozen planes. The number of seats was slashed by more than 15 percent, and overall costs were cut by $340 million. Management estimated that, once the two carriers' operations were fully fused, expenses could be trimmed by $600 million more per year. And don't forget those pension savings.

Like the rest of the industry, moreover, US Airways got a boost from an improving economy and an up cycle in the cyclical airline business. Emerging from the rolling wave of bankruptcies during the previous few years, carriers had reduced routes and seats by some 20 percent, and bottom lines began to improve by the summer of 2006. A big setback came in August of that year, with the announcement that a terrorist plot had been foiled at London's Heathrow Airport. Throughout the world, airports clamped on even more rigid regimens for screening passengers, and travelers waited in endless, angry lines while their water bottles and toothpaste tubes were confiscated as potential flight hazards. Eventually, travel volume picked up again, the boarding restrictions were loosened slightly, and US Airways and other airlines were able to raise fares about 15 percent for the year. The industry as a whole ended 2006 with its first profit since 2000, although the trend started to weaken in 2007.

But the real secret of US Airways' success was the way it dealt with its workforce. Employee morale is always crucial, and particularly so in a service business like commercial aviation, where flight attendants, counter personnel, reservations agents, and even pilots are talking directly with customers. "If you want to keep flying in a service industry, you can't keep basically cutting off your employees at the knees," David Neigus, the Machinists union lawyer, warns.

Because of the employee-friendly corporate culture that Parker brought from America West, supported by the US Airways management, the new US Airways managed to avoid the morale and PR disasters that Delta and United top brass inflicted on their own companies. Instead of a Leo Mullin at Delta bailing out with his $16 million pension intact, Bruce Lakefield gave up his job. Instead of a Glenn Tilton at United collecting nearly $40 million worth of salary, bonuses, stock, stock options, pension, and other benefits, Doug Parker skipped his own bonus and defended his workers at the annual meeting.

The apparent fairness of US Airways' management's approach went a long way toward solving the perennial problem of throwing-Grandma-on-the-street headlines. "You need the right kind of CEO, and a lot of communication," Ted Weschler explains. "You need to share data with people, make them part of the process, don't let them be surprised. One of the things Doug Parker is so good at [is that] he's got incredible empathy for the folks that took a hit. He really believes in saving the company." Parker held a number of town meetings to explain the route, seat, and other cost cutbacks to the staff and issued press releases to the outside, Weschler says. Of course the employees weren't thrilled about losing their pensions, and they started pushing harder in contract negotiations as the stock price rose. Still, there was little, if any, animosity toward the Parker management team. Gary Richardson, head of the chapter of the flight attendants union that represents former America West attendants, was quoted in the *New York Times* in January 2007, saying of Parker: "He's a great guy. An incredible man." It also helped that the old US Airways had managed to save most of the workforce's pensions during the first bankruptcy. The workers could have a certain level of trust that management wasn't gunning for them from the start.

Of more direct importance to the staff, they weren't left penniless for retirement. US Airways and the Machinists union had negotiated a multiemployer pension plan in the midst of the first bankruptcy, with the airline contributing one dollar for each hour the forty-five hundred machinists worked, according to Beth Almeida, the union's assistant director for strategic resources. That was untouched by the terminations of the second round. "Right now the Machinists union is probably one of the best spokespersons for US Airways because the company agreed to bring people into the multiemployer plan," says Christian Weller of the Center for American Progress, the liberal think tank. (Weller ought to know, since he is married to Almeida.) Meanwhile, the pilots who remained got what by all accounts was a generous 401(k).

Not everyone was flying high on US Airways, of course. Shelley Greenhaus of Whippoorwill invested in Delta and Northwest but not US Airways, because "we never liked their route structure." Pilots still lost one-third to one-half of their pensions, on average, and by 2007 they were itching to restore some of the $100-an-hour in wages they'd given back in the first bankruptcy and get more flexible work rules. Flight attendants, too, were pushing for big raises. In fairness, at that point workers at almost every carrier were agitating for a return of some of the wages they'd forfeited at various points to save their companies, now that the industry's profits were improving, and the US Airways pilots' pension losses were typical of airline bankruptcies. Even US Airways' culture couldn't completely counter the industry-wide morale drag from the general cuts in pensions, other benefits, jobs, and wages.

The nice new 401(k), meanwhile, didn't help the pilots who had already retired. Furthermore, it was widely acknowledged that the merged carrier was having trouble with the practical details of amalgamating the two airlines' staff seniority lists, their reservation systems, and their websites. The new US Airways mishandled more baggage in 2006 than any of the other majors (7.82 reports of mishandled bags per 1,000 domestic passengers), according to the federal Department of Transportation. When the company finally combined the two reservation systems the following March, the self-service kiosks at its hubs in Philadelphia and in Charlotte, North Carolina, didn't work, leading to delays of up to two and a half hours for thousands of passengers. A month later, US Airways admitted that its cost cutting had gone too deep and announced that it would bring in more than one thousand new hires to help with the summer rush.

I saw that organizational confusion firsthand in the summer of 2006, when my family took a US Airways flight from New York City to Phoenix. Having booked the reservation online, I wanted to follow up with a phone call about the seat assignments. Since the reservation was listed as a US Airways flight, I called the US Airways toll-free phone number. I was put on hold for a long time, until the operator determined that I actually should be transferred to America West. Accordingly, when I needed to call again, I used the America West toll-free number—at which point, I was transferred back to US Airways. Then, when we arrived at the airport, which happened to be just as it was opening for business at 4 a.m., we joined a line of passengers at an empty US Airways gate that had our flight number prominently displayed. After waiting about ten minutes with no indication that any employee from any airline was actually going to show up at the counter, I went searching for information. Oh no, I was told; our flight was actually checking in at an America West counter around the corner—which did not list our flight on its signboard. But the trip itself was smooth, and the attendants on board were perfectly friendly—even as I read a book about bankruptcy.

A Too Happy Ending

The ultimate proof of US Airways' success may be its bid in November 2006 to acquire Delta, an airline that was a little further behind in bankruptcy and had terminated only one of its pension plans. The $8 billion hostile offer, later raised to $10.2 billion, was ultimately withdrawn because of opposition from Delta and its creditors. Nevertheless, it proved that going bankrupt and terminating a pension plan or two need not be the kiss of death. One could even argue that it proved that terminating four plans is better than terminating one, since the four-plan terminator (US Airways) would have gobbled up the one-plan terminator (Delta).

Or maybe the bid proves that US Airways was *too* successful. The five senators who in January 2007 asked the PBGC to restore the pension back to US Airways cited that bid, along with the carrier's dramatically improved financial picture and the restoration precedent established by LTV. "Indeed, it is striking that the $5 billion in cash being offered as part of the hostile Delta offer exceeds the full amount of the unfunded liabilities recently transferred to the PBGC. Certainly, neither the PBGC, other employers paying premiums to the PBGC, innocent pensioners, nor taxpayers should bear billions in costs to enable companies to buy out their competitors," wrote Senators Frank R. Lautenberg (Democrat of New Jersey), Johnny Isakson and Saxby Chambliss (both Republicans from Georgia), and Maria Cantwell and Patty Murray (both Democrats from Washington state).

Parker also came in for a personal grilling on the pension issue from Senator Lautenberg at a Senate Commerce Committee hearing. His response: "Senator, the $5 billion is not our money. That money is Citigroup's money and Morgan Stanley's money, and that money only comes to us if we acquire the airline, because they know full well the value that can be created by putting these two companies together, and they know that they will be paid back," referring to the financing US Airways had lined up to provide the $5 billion in cash it was offering for Delta and also to refinance two loans for Delta and US Airways.

The airline business is a tough arena for investors. In addition to the financial and business factors like recession and foreign competition that batter most industries, these companies are also subject to the vagaries of political and social trends. (Will another terrorist attack scare off travelers?) They will soon have to fork up part of the cost to revamp the nation's antiquated air traffic control system, which could run to $40 billion—and that's if they're lucky. The unlucky alternative is that the system doesn't get revamped, delays increase, and sooner or later a big plane crashes. Given all these negatives, US Airways' survival—reservation mess-ups, failed bid for Delta, and all—looks even more impressive.

Part Four

The Future

12 | The Problem Continues

"DB plans' problems run far deeper than the snapshot of their financial health conveyed by today's or even tomorrow's funding gap."

—RICHARD BERNER, CHIEF U.S. ECONOMIST, MORGAN STANLEY

FEW STEEL companies in the United States still have traditional defined benefit plans. The same is true for textile manufacturers. Several big airlines maintain their plans, but they got special help from the 2006 Pension Protection Act, which gave that industry more time to fund its obligations.

So is the problem of pension dumping played out? Have all the companies that could possibly shed their pensions done so by now? Is this a pool of opportunities that has dried up for investors?

Hardly. With nearly twenty-nine thousand private-sector defined benefit plans still in operation as of 2007, logic and history alone dictate that some percentage will fail in coming years. Dozens of large plans are short by tens of millions of dollars. In fact, depending on what the markets happen to be doing during the month and year in which an observer chooses to analyze the data, the majority of large company plans may be underfunded. Industries like autos, auto parts, utilities, metals, consumer durables, and other heavy equipment in particular are under intense and growing pressure from foreign competition, deregulation, demographics, and all the other factors that have already brought down so many plans. What's more, the Pension Protection Act might help the airlines, but it will probably make things worse for everyone else by accelerating the rate at which plans must be funded.

And if all that wasn't troubling enough, hedge fund and private equity investors have been inadvertently creating a whole slew of new investment possibilities for vulture investors by their desperate rush to pour money into companies—almost any company, no matter its bond rating, financial prospects, or leverage. Too many of

171

those companies are simply not seaworthy. They will fail, dragging their pension funds down with them.

So vulture investors who like companies with vulnerable pensions needn't worry. They will have plenty of business. It's just a matter of predicting which industries will generate it.

Follow the Economy

To get a sense of how many plans are likely to fail, the PBGC is as good a place as any to start. It has the most data on funding status and the most pessimistic definition of "well-funded." In 2005, the agency estimated that plans with a total of nearly $10.5 billion in claims faced a "probable termination," a classification so dire that the company essentially has to be in bankruptcy or on the verge of terminating. Another $108 billion worth were listed as "reasonably possible" to face underfundings, but that definition goes to the other extreme, including plans that are on the PBGC's early warning list and might have only a $5 million underfunding plus a bond rating below investment grade. In its five-year strategic plan for 2008 through 2013, issued in fall 2007, the agency announced that it would crack down on potential deadbeats and "improve risk monitoring."

Data from the annual survey of the one hundred largest plans by Watson Wyatt and *Pensions & Investments* magazine show that in 2006 seventy-three were underfunded, compared with just twenty-seven that had enough money. Also, McKinsey & Co., in a report issued in May 2007, predicted that companies holding 10 percent to 20 percent of all U.S. pension assets would terminate their plans by 2012, although the report also said many of those would be well funded, terminating simply because the parent company wanted out of the pension business.

True, the number of companies that are underfunded is less important than the size of the funding gap, but there, too, several indicators are worrisome. Nearly half of the underfunded companies in the *P&I*/Wyatt survey were short by $1 billion or more—and that calculation used the companies' financial assumptions and methods, not the PBGC's, which may underestimate the real liability and may rely on overly optimistic market predictions. What's more, in an article for the winter 2006 edition of Morgan Stanley's *Journal of Applied Corporate Finance*, Michael Peskin and two fellow managing directors at the firm (chief U.S. economist Richard Berner and Bryan Boudreau, head of the asset liability strategies group in North America) calculated that about 15 percent of the 360 companies in the Standard & Poor's 500 that have defined benefit plans had pension liabilities that came to more than 30 percent of their market capitalization. The trio warned that "when a plan['s obligation] starts to become significant relative to market capitalization, the pension economics become a more urgent matter." And Ron Gebhardtsbauer, the former chief actuary at the PBGC, points out that as of early 2005, the size of the underfunding had been getting worse over the years. Although the average terminated plan used to be around 60 percent funded, he says, the rush of airline and metals failures has dragged the average below 50 percent. Overall, the funded status of plans covered by the PBGC dropped almost steadily downward year after year from the high reached in 1985 of 162 percent: That is, back then the plans had 62 percent more assets than they needed. By 2003, the funding ratio had plummeted to almost half of what it had been: 84 percent.

Although the overall trend line sags downward, there are plenty of zigs and zags within it, because pension funding is vulnerable to the greater economy. During the 1990s, the roaring stock and bond markets boosted returns so high that most companies didn't even need to contribute a penny to their defined benefit plans to meet their funding requirements. Then the economy crashed in 2001, and so did funding. In just the four years from 2001 through 2004, 577 plans tumbled, including six of the ten all-time biggest. Matters picked up during the next few years as the stock and bond markets and the overall economy improved. By year-end 2006, both the Watson Wyatt and Towers Perrin consulting firms estimated that in aggregate American defined benefit plans were slightly better than fully funded again. Eight months later, however, after the credit markets dried up and the stock market plunged, the situation reversed. In general, and not surprisingly, Professor Altman's data banks at NYU show that the bankruptcy rate closely tracks the path of economic recession, jarred by the occasional large bankruptcy like Delta's during an otherwise slow 2005. "It's nice that we were 100 percent funded as of the end of 2006," says Alan Glickstein, a senior consultant with Watson Wyatt. "I don't think it will stay that way. It's going to be a roller coaster. It's not going to be a flat train."

Of course, the parallels aren't exact. Even in the boom years of 1996 through 2000, 390 plans went under. And even in the worst economic season, not every company with an underfunded pension plan will dump. Chapter 8 describes a number of factors influencing that decision, starting with the fact that different companies use actuarial assumptions, interest rate assumptions, asset allocations, and benefit formulas that may raise or lower their funding level and their ability to fund.

Each company is also buffeted by the particular economic cycles of its own industry. Airlines like Delta, United, and US Airways dove into bankruptcy and jettisoned pension plans in the early 2000s because the September 11, 2001, terrorist attacks scared people away from flying, and then oil prices shot higher than their own cruising altitudes. With profits down, they couldn't afford to put enough money into their pension plans. Steelmakers were hurt in the early 2000s by a different set of trends, including competition from low-cost domestic mini-mills, other competition from foreign rivals, antiquated workplace bureaucracies, and the switch to aluminum and plastic by their biggest customers. When CIT Group considers which companies are likely to need debtor-in-possession loans, "we always look for companies that are dependent upon a volatile commodity, so that they have absolutely no control," managing director Deirdre Martini says.

Investor Frenzy

The explosion in the investor universe in the early 2000s added another kind of cyclical pressure. Between 2000 and 2007, some seven thousand new hedge funds were launched, and that industry's assets more than doubled, to about $1.3 trillion. Private equity firms were sitting on a total war chest estimated at anywhere from $750 billion to $2 trillion by year-end 2006. Where would they put all that money? By late 2005, savvy investors were getting worried. They were simply running out of good investments. "There are more hedge funds than there are stocks in the U.S. That's crazy," Jay Vivian, managing director of IBM's retirement funds, told

Institutional Investor magazine that December. The only place these investors could go was down—toward investments in ultrashaky properties, including subprime mortgage pools, junk bonds, and highly leveraged buyouts.

Private equity firms overpaid for their target companies, they got into bidding wars, and as the prices skyrocketed, they borrowed to the hilt to cover the deals. Lenders were happy to join the gold rush, doling out loans without the usual covenants—such as requiring borrowers to have certain cash cushions—to protect themselves. Or, if some fusty old bank insisted on being cautious, hedge funds were happy to step in. They snapped up the junk bonds issued by the target companies, and they provided financing to the private equity funds at five, six, even seven times cash flow, according to finance experts like Psaros of KPS and Miller of Weil, Gotshal. Junk bond issuance hit a record $148 billion in 2006.

Inevitably, gravity had to take over. As the default rate on subprime mortgages began to rise in July 2007, investors in junk debt got nervous about their own holdings. They demanded higher yields on new issues and yanked their money out of hedge funds, forcing the funds to dump some of their loans and bonds in order to raise the cash to pay them. Lenders pulled back from new buyouts—including, temporarily, Chrysler.

Vultures sat back and grinned. Savvy investors and other experts like Psaros, Miller, and Professor Altman of NYU had seen it coming. Once the dust settled, there would be a whole new crop of bankrupt and distressed companies to pick through at fire-sale prices—companies that couldn't meet the tougher credit standards, abandoned buyout targets, and holdings jettisoned by panicky private equity and hedge funds. "It's not going to take much of an economic downturn for these companies to end up filing for bankruptcy," Psaros said a full year before the crunch. "We're very grateful to Wall Street for manufacturing these opportunities." And among those bankruptcies would undoubtedly be a cohort with pension troubles.

Even if all those cyclical roller coasters flattened out—even if every industry in America was skimming along on an economic cruise that included muscular stock markets, high interest rates, no particular catastrophes, a roaring macroeconomy, and reasonable restraint by hedge funds—many pension funds would still be in serious trouble. That's because some of the causes of underfunding and termination are ongoing, if not permanent, regardless of the particular point in the overall economic cycle: Among them are low-cost foreign competition for Rust Belt industries, airline deregulation, Wall Street's focus on short-term profits, rising oil prices, the trend toward 401(k)-style retirement plans and away from pension plans, increased longevity, the advent of mini-mills, and the switch to replacement materials in the steel industry. None of these trends is likely to change in the next few economic cycles—if ever—and all of them put pressure on pension plan funding.

Wall Street's "what have you done for me this quarter" attitude, for instance, makes companies afraid to "waste" spare cash by being conservative in their actuarial assumptions and putting a little extra in the pension plan. Increased longevity means that retirees will be collecting pensions for more years than the actuaries assumed when the plans started. Most of the company-specific factors mentioned in Chapter 8 are also long-term phenomena. If it turns out that the best way to keep a pension plan properly funded is to invest in bonds that are matched to its liabilities, an investment manager who has followed the traditional 60/40 asset allocation can't just dump the 60 percent stock portion overnight. Or, to cite another possible cause, if the company's main problem is a generous benefit formula, it can alter that formula for the future, but it cannot rescind what it has already promised.

"DB plans' problems run far deeper than the snapshot of their financial health conveyed by today's or even tomorrow's funding gap," Berner of Morgan Stanley warns in an official publication of his firm's research department, cowritten with managing director Trevor Harris. The inexorable demographic timeline alone, the paper adds, "will swamp the impact on plans' long-term funding gaps of almost any plausible rise in interest rates or in equity prices."

Pension Reform: From Bad to Worse

As more and bigger pension terminations hit the headlines in the busy years of the early 2000s, the federal government came under tremendous public pressure to *do something*. There were demands to rescue impoverished retirees, save the pension system, and replenish the PBGC's shrinking coffers. Thus, in August 2006,

Congress passed the Pension Protection Act, or PPA, a mixed bag of incentives, punishments, and varying deadlines, with the stated intention of improving the financial situation at ailing companies and at the PBGC.

The optimistic reaction among pensions experts was that the new law would help somewhat, but it wouldn't end all terminations. The pessimistic response: It would make things worse.

Perhaps the key provisions of the new law were that most plans had to be fully funded in seven years, rather than the previous maximum of thirty years, and full funding was now defined as having enough money to cover 100 percent of liabilities, not 90 percent. (Only in politics and the arcane realms of economics could "full" have ever been defined as 90 percent.) Airlines, however, got an extra three to ten years to catch up, which was the exemption that saved Delta and Northwest. The length of the extension depended on whether a carrier allowed employees to continue accumulating benefits. To keep the financial hole from getting deeper, plans that were "at risk"—less than 80 percent funded—could not improve their pension benefits for the workforce as a whole unless the improvements were funded immediately, and plans that were severely underfunded couldn't add to executive benefits either, even though those benefits don't count as part of the pension plan. Meanwhile, restrictions were placed on two tactics—"smoothing" and the use of credit balances—that can hide a pension plan's underfunding. With smoothing, companies average out their plans' losses and gains in their financial reporting, rather than marking the assets to market. The new law shortened the smoothing period to two years from five and allowed it only within a narrower range of values. As for credit balances, which are the excess contributions from prior years, underfunded plans could no longer apply the balances to tide them over for a lean year.

Other portions of the act tightened the rules on the interest rate assumptions that could be used in calculating future liabilities and required even healthy plans to start paying the extra PBGC premiums that had previously been owed only by underfunded ones. The law also made permanent a provision that had been part of a tax bill a year earlier and which was supposed to expire in 2010. The provision levied a special premium of $1,250 per employee for three years on any company that terminated its underfunded pension plan and then managed to emerge from bankruptcy. On the promising side, if a company had spare cash and wanted to prepare for a rainy day, it could get a tax break for contributing 50 percent above its funding requirement. The PPA also included a number of measures affecting multiemployer plans, 401(k)-style plans, and hybrid plans, which combine elements of both defined benefits and defined contributions plans. To add one more complication, different provisions were phased in at different times.

In signing the bill in August 2006, President George Bush declared, "The message from this administration . . . is this: You should keep the promises you make to your workers. If you offer a private pension plan to your employees, you have a duty to set aside enough money now so your workers will get what they've been promised when they retire." And in theory, the Pension Protection Act would get pension plans into better shape by forcing companies to stop playing games with their numbers: no more shading the truth by smoothing, which disguised how badly underfunded a plan was in a bear market. No longer could companies buy off their unions with promises of richer benefits when they couldn't even pay for what the plans already included. If companies followed the law and took proper care of their pension systems, there should be little reason for a plan ever to be terminated.

Bankrupt airlines clearly gained from the new law. Companies in halfway decent shape might also be better off in the long run. "If companies that are underfunded today actually can make those contributions to shore up the plan, the probability of having an underfunded plan in the future obviously goes down," says Steve Kerstein, the benefits consultant from Towers Perrin.

So much for the good news. The most serious problem was that the Pension Protection Act changed few of the flaws in ERISA that had caused so much underfunding to begin with. It had no answer to the basic dilemma: If a company is in such bad financial shape that it hasn't paid its pension contributions, how can it be expected to pay an even bigger contribution faster? Indeed, the law *increased* the pressure by speeding up the payment schedule, raising the bar on the definition of "full funding," and eliminating the tricks companies used to disguise their true funded status. That was one reason Senator Benjamin Cardin of Maryland voted against the measure while he was in the House of Representatives. "I'm concerned that more companies will find this onerous and therefore terminate their defined benefit plans," he says. Congressman Earl Pomeroy of North Dakota cites similar worries. It might be proper and reasonable to take some of the steps required by the new act—few would argue against telling shareholders and employees the true status of the pension plan's funding—but companies shouldn't kid themselves that this law would make their financial situations any better.

Moreover, the legislation did not base PBGC premiums on the plan's level of risk, as many experts advised. It did not alter the PBGC's lowly status in bankruptcy court. Nor did it—or could it— do anything about the economic and financial pressures that push companies into bankruptcy. As for the provision allowing more rainy day funding, Sherwin Kaplan, the veteran pilots' lawyer, scoffs, "If you are sitting there as a CFO and you have a choice, do you declare a dividend to your stockholders, do you declare more stock options for senior executives, do you go out and acquire another company? Funding the pension plan may not be number one."

"I think that the bill makes the situation worse, not better, as it relates to defined benefit plans," Dallas Salisbury, the head of the benefits research center EBRI, declares, his anger evident. "It essentially takes those enterprises that have underfunded plans, which generally occurs because of business issues, and puts in place a regime that has greater volatility to it and more intense funding requirements." Or, in the words of Beth Almeida of the Machinists union: "We don't have a lot of confidence that it will prevent termi- nations. The law brings in a lot of new sources of volatility that make planning for pension funding less predictable, with the elimination of smoothing. It doesn't enable a good-faith employer to forecast out and develop business objectives around defined benefit plans." In its annual "High-Risk Series" update for 2007—a regular audit of federal programs that "in some cases, are at high risk due to their greater vulnerabilities to fraud, waste, abuse, and mismanagement"— the Government Accountability Office warns that as a result of flaws in the law, the "PBGC may be exposed to additional terminations of large underfunded plans . . . as stricter funding requirements and higher premiums may lead sponsors to terminate or freeze their plans."

Consultant Kerstein of Towers Perrin points out that it wasn't just plans in shaky shape that would be likely to terminate thanks to the PPA. Even a company that seemed well on the way to full funding could be knocked into bankruptcy by the law's toughened standards. He lays out this scenario: "In the future, you have to ask what happens if there's a significant downward trend in terms of the funded ratio of plans. Let's say a company has funded its plan reasonably well. It's close to 100 percent funded. Then you get a year when the stock market tanks and interest rates go down. All of a sudden that funded percentage goes a lot lower. [The funding] could drop from 100 percent to 80 percent [the law's at-risk level] really fast. Interest rates go down 1 percent; that'll change the liabilities by 10 percent or more. Then let's say the stock market drops 10 percent. You've got to make it up pretty quickly now. Can a company afford to do it? If it didn't have to make it up quickly [as was the case under the old law], it wouldn't be such a big deal. This law will make the contribution requirement more volatile. If you get negative volatility at the wrong time, what's going to happen? If a company's funding ratio drops to 80 percent and the plan is big relative to the size of the company, that could be a significant issue."

Would that penalty of $1,250 per eligible employee prompt companies to hang onto their plans? Not necessarily. It depends in part on the size of the workforce covered by the program and the value of the overall claims. Since the penalty didn't take effect until January 2006, after the big rush of airline, steel, and other terminations, it was too early as this book went to press to gauge the impact it has had. However, the penalty obviously didn't stop Northwest from threatening to terminate; only the funding extensions of the PPA did that.

To backtrack and try to see what the penalty might have done in hindsight, consider Weirton Steel, which had the smallest workforce—about 9,200 vested employees—and thus the smallest potential fine of the top ten terminations in PBGC history. Had the law been in effect when Weirton dumped its plan in 2004, the fine would have come to about $34.5 million. By contrast, Weirton needed to contribute about $100 million annually to catch up with its underfunding of nearly $700 million under the PPA's seven-year amortization rule. Unless Weirton had some reason to think that it would soon be in better financial shape and able to fund its pension program properly, it would be cheaper to pay a fine of $34.5 million than a contribution of $100 million, especially if that contribution merely delayed the fine for a year. The hit would have been even worse for TWA, with a slightly smaller underfunding of $668 million and nearly four times as many participants.

Anyway, it's unlikely the $1,250 per capita penalty would ever be paid in any bankruptcy. It would probably just be added to the whole pool of outstanding claims for the unsecured creditors to fight over. If the amount is too burdensome, "you may see more liquidations instead" of Chapter 11 filings, suggests Lisa Beckerman, the lawyer for Delta's creditors committee. She is the only person I spoke with who even thinks the fine is worth mentioning.

Yet more pressure was looming from the Financial Accounting Standards Board (FASB), the quasi-independent body that writes the accounting rules for U.S. businesses. Hoping to give investors better information and to harmonize with international standards, FASB in the early 2000s began a multiyear review of pension accounting. At year-end 2006, it took its first action, requiring companies to show the amount of pension underfunding or overfunding on their balance sheets, not just in the footnotes of their financial statements.

Next on the agenda: perhaps mark-to-market accounting of investment returns and liability changes. Analysts did the recalculating and found that the new rules and proposals could increase debt and drag down shareholders' equity by billions of dollars, even turning some bottom-line black ink to red. In a paper issued in January 2006, Towers Perrin estimated that if the proposals for mark-to-market accounting were implemented, "immediate recognition of a 10 percent change in retirement plan obligations would have changed 2004 pretax income for the 78 *Fortune* 100 companies studied by 26 percent. For eight of these companies, a 10 percent increase in obligations would have turned pretax income into losses." With all the rules put together, David Zion, an analyst at Credit Suisse, told *Institutional Investor*, shareholders' equity for 2004 would have fallen by more than 25 percent at eighteen of the Standard & Poor's 500 companies—wiping out the value at two of them.

If this litany of prospects scared away investors and caused the rating agencies to lower the companies' bond ratings, it was certainly possible that the higher cost of borrowing and lower equity value could push some companies into Chapter 11. At that point, what loyalty could management possibly have to the pension plan that had gotten the company into so much trouble?

13 The Next to Fail

"Today's profitable, prosperous industry could be tomorrow's bankrupt industry."

—Lawrence Sher, director of retirement policy, Buck Consultants

IF MORE pressure lies ahead for companies with pension plans and more plan terminations are in the cards, which of these companies should investors be watching? Which of them would be most likely to dump?

The Auto Industry

Ask almost anyone paying close attention to corporate America's fiscal health which business sector is likely to generate the next pension terminations: The most common answer is the auto industry. Automobile manufacturers, auto-parts makers, tire and rubber companies—anything connected to a car. Norman Stein, a professor at the University of Alabama School of Law who specializes in pensions, sums up the sentiment, "The auto industry is next. I don't know who comes after that."

Auto manufacturing meets almost all the criteria spelled out in Chapter 8: First, it's a Rust Belt industry facing serious foreign competition. Indeed, Toyota and GM spent 2007 battling for the title of world's largest automaker, measured by the number of vehicles sold, while the French-Japanese alliance of Renault-Nissan threatened to knock Ford down yet another notch to fourth place.

As for financial weakness, by the early 2000s, the erstwhile Big Three's North American auto operations were leaking red ink like a busted gas tank. DaimlerChrylser, which had acquired Chrysler back in 1998 (when it was Daimler-Benz) amid great fanfare, sold off the money loser to Cerberus Capital Management less than a decade later.

Ford's situation was so bad that it mortgaged its North American assets and was considering selling off its Volvo division. Moreover, with GM, Ford, and Chrysler combined shedding tens of thousands of jobs through layoffs, buyouts, and early retirements, their ratios of active workers to retirees were getting more and more off balance. By 2007, the industry could count 180,680 active workers and 540,340 retirees, or just one worker to support the pension of every three retirees—in other words, a negative worker-retiree ratio instead of a positive one.

The troubles didn't end there. Size was also a factor. GM, for example, has always had the largest private-sector pension plan in the nation. Although size needs to be taken in context, the GM context was staggering: By the early 2000s, its pension assets were more than five times the entire company's market capitalization.

The design of the benefits program was a further problem for the industry. The carmakers tended to provide the flat-dollar type of benefits that are least likely to be properly funded. They argued that their legacy health and pensions benefits cost them $1,000 per vehicle, adding to their cost disadvantage against Japanese and Korean rivals. The Americans might have won a reprieve with their 2007 deals with the UAW to transfer the health care liability to VEBAs, or voluntary employee benefit associations, run by the union. However, that didn't solve the long-range problems of unpopular gas-guzzling cars, tough foreign competition, inefficient facilities, and a warped employee-retiree ratio. Moreover, what if the VEBAs were to run short, as happened with a similar trust for Caterpillar workers in 2004? Caterpillar claimed the shortfall wasn't its problem, but the union sued. To top it all off, if any industry could be hurt by rising oil prices, it's the auto industry.

It's no surprise, then, that auto and auto-related companies rank high on almost every list of companies with funding problems. Goodyear Tire & Rubber was arguably in the worst shape of the 360 large companies that Gordon Latter of Merrill Lynch analyzed in his "Pensions and Endowments" reports in the fall of 2006, measured by all the criteria he used. Moreover, the company had come close to bankruptcy in 2003, and it ended 2006 with a $2.2 billion pension deficit, even after contributing more than $650 million that year. (One caveat: Latter put together his list before Goodyear settled a three-month strike at year-end 2006, which was expected to help its financial situation by shifting future liabilities to the union.)

In Latter's industry-by-industry analysis, autos virtually tied for the third-largest funding deficit. In the *Pensions & Investments* roster, DaimlerChrysler logged the eighth-biggest funding gap by dollar size, at $3 billion (below Delta, Northwest, and American Airlines, among others), while Ford was number thirteen and Goodyear, fifteen. Just how big the underfundings truly are is debatable, depending on whether the PBGC's more pessimistic method or the companies' optimistic one is used. By the most optimistic measure, Ford at year-end 2005 had an underfunding of more than $2 billion in the *P&I* chart, whereas according to the PBGC, its deficit was $12.3 billion. GM actually claimed to be *overfunded* by $6 billion in 2005, after issuing bonds two years earlier solely to feed some $18.5 billion into the plan. The PBGC argued that GM was $31 billion underfunded. Even with the supposed overfunding, GM itself warned, in its 2006 annual report, "Our extensive pension and [post-employment] obligations to retirees are a competitive disadvantage for us."

But where does bankruptcy fit into these troubles? To terminate a plan without going through incredible hoops and giving up control to the PBGC, a company needs to be bankrupt. Industry watchers are waiting to see if the health care VEBAs that the UAW agreed to will be enough to save the automakers. Before those deals, the prospect of bankruptcy certainly did not seem so far off the map. Professor Altman of NYU in summer 2006 gave GM a 20 percent chance of filing for bankruptcy before 2008 and a 50 percent chance by 2011. Morgan Stanley, in its analysts' reports of December 19, 2006, and January 24, 2007, warned of a risk of bankruptcy at Ford and GM, respectively, perhaps five years off. About Ford, analysts Jonathan Steinmetz and Jane Park write, "We view bankruptcy risk as low in the next 2–3 years but high longer term if cash burn [running through cash too fast] does not improve." As for GM, "we also believe that bankruptcy risk is present longer-term (5 years out or more) if the company cannot reduce its health care payments/other expenses and/or start generating much more contribution margin selling its vehicles." They did not change those predictions after the Chrysler sale to Cerberus.

Although Chrysler's new owner presumably wasn't going to rush the automaker into Chapter 11, after paying $7.4 billion for the company, some observers wouldn't dismiss the prospect altogether down the road. The day after the deal was announced, Peter Morici, a business professor at the University of Maryland, was quoted in the *Wall Street Journal*, saying that the ex–Big Three had only a one-in-five average chance of surviving under the best of circumstances. In any case, Chrysler's pension and health care underfundings, which together totaled about $18 billion in early 2007, were a major issue in the sale. To win the auto union's grudging acceptance, Cerberus had to pledge to put $200 million into the Chrysler pension fund, and Daimler promised to pay $1 billion if the plans terminated within five years.

Not everyone is so convinced that the big carmakers will go into bankruptcy and shed their pensions. For all of Ford's problems, an analyst at a major Wall Street firm predicts that the Ford family members, with their control of 40 percent of the voting shares, would never agree to a filing that wiped out their stock holdings. GM lacks that protection. But in light of its employee buyouts and the sale of a controlling share in GMAC, its consumer finance arm, "basically GM is going through an out-of-court restructuring right now," says Deirdre Martini of CIT. "What would bankruptcy even give them?" Before she went to work at CIT in July 2006, Martini says, friends teased her that she wanted to stay as the U.S. Trustee in New York City because that was where GM would be likely to file. "I said, 'That's a long wait.'" Still, even GM optimists admit that a number of things could upend any hopeful predictions, including drops in the stock market or interest rates that hike the carmaker's liabilities and slash its fund's asset value.

Auto Parts

When it comes to auto parts companies, even the optimists sound dreary. Collins & Aikman, Dana, Delphi, Dura Automotive Systems, Federal-Mogul, Jernberg, and Tower Automotive had all filed for bankruptcy by the end of 2006, and vulture investors like Wilbur Ross, Carl Icahn, Cerberus, and Appaloosa Management were busy scrounging for bargains, figuring that consolidation would strengthen the hand of the survivors. Investors were also counting on growing demand from non-U.S. carmakers. As for the pensions, Jernberg had dumped its plan, Collins & Aikman was talking to the

PBGC, and the only reason Delphi was able to keep its program, most observers point out, is that GM had agreed to maintain responsibility for an estimated $7 billion in retiree pension and medical obligations when it spun off the auto parts arm in 1999. If other managements hadn't yet terminated plans, suggests the auto analyst quoted on page 186—the one who expects the Ford family to keep that company alive—they might be holding the threat in reserve, as a bargaining chip with their unions.

One investor with a small holding in Dana describes an unusual deal between the creditors' committee and management that had kept the pension intact for at least a year. Management got bonuses for keeping total unsecured claims below certain limits, with the size of the bonus varying according to which limit was met. The bonus had a "soft maximum" of $2.85 billion, but that could be breached, the investor adds. Thus, managers could get bigger bonuses if they could avoid adding the pension plan to the pile of claims.

The parts sector is susceptible to bankruptcy and termination because it suffers from a double whammy. Not only does it face the same problems as its customers, the auto industry—namely, growing competition from Asia, high oil prices, rising costs for raw materials, huge legacy costs for an aging work force, and overcapacity—but also the carmakers turn around and try to pass their troubles on to the parts makers by squeezing them on price. The parts companies have historically had little clout with which to fight back, although Collins & Aikman briefly cut off deliveries to Ford in 2006 over a pricing dispute. "It really is a domino-like chain reaction," Martini says. "If the demand for American-made vehicles is decreasing, then the supply chain from those particular vendors will slow down." Nell Hennessy, the former PBGC deputy executive director, says the suppliers are more vulnerable than the auto giants are because "there's more commodity-like pricing, so there's more competition based solely on price."

All parts companies are not in the same predicament, however. In general, investors and analysts consider bigger companies, diversified companies, and those with an important niche to be in stronger shape. "Because there's so much technological change, companies that apply new technology first can earn premium returns," says John Casesa, the analyst-turned-investor, pointing in particular to BorgWarner in power trains and United Technologies in turbo

chargers and fuel delivery as being strong bets. Another analyst fa-
vors higher-value electronics makers like Johnson Controls. For his
part, Wilbur Ross—using a different barometer to test for troubled
companies that have a relatively good chance of revival—began
delving into makers of plastic parts.

Metals and Heavy Manufacturing

There's no real consensus among analysts on which industry takes
second place after autos in terms of pension trouble. The most popular nominations for most-likely-to-fail rankings include the remaining airlines, metals, heavy-equipment manufacturing, and paper and
pulp. Looking solely at the magnitude of underfunding, the PBGC
in 2005 cited the broad fields of "transportation, communication,
and utilities" as having by far the worst probable exposure—nearly
$9.6 billion.

In Gordon Latter's industry-by-industry list, the largest pension
deficits were found in capital goods manufacturing and energy, with
materials and automobiles virtually tied for third place. Meanwhile,
on the 2006 P&I ranking of companies by size of underfunding, Delta
naturally topped the list, which was put together before the pilots'
plan was terminated. After that, the ten biggest were at Lockheed
Martin (nearly $5 billion), ExxonMobil ($3.93 billion), Raytheon
($3.9 billion), Northwest Airlines (nearly $3.7 billion), American
Airlines ($3.2 billion), DuPont ($3.1 billion), DaimlerChrysler
($3 billion), United Technologies ($2.8 billion), International
Paper ($2.3 billion), and Dow Chemical (nearly $2.3 billion). The
following year's list was similar: Delphi (nearly $4.2 billion), North-
west (a bit over $3 billion), Delta (nearly $3 billion—after it junked
its obligations to the pilots), Raytheon ($2.795 billion), Lockheed
Martin ($2.79 billion), American Airlines (nearly $2.5 billion),
Johnson & Johnson ($2.1 billion), FedEx ($2 billion), ExxonMobil
($1.55 billion), and Alcoa ($1.5 billion).

Still, the absolute size of the deficit may not be all that significant unless it's considered in the larger context of the company's
overall financial health (see Chapter 8). When Latter homed in on
specific companies, he used what he considered the key measure of
that context—pension deficit as compared with free cash flow—to

list them in order of worst-to-best shape. Top rankings went to Raytheon, International Paper, DuPont, ConocoPhillips, Alcoa, Kimberly-Clark, Air Products and Chemicals, and Goodyear, which more or less match the general industry sector predictions.

Even putting the underfunding in context doesn't dig deep enough, however, because the underfunding itself may be based on false assumptions. That goes back to the hazy accounting rules that pension plans are allowed to follow. Consider one key assumption: the discount rate that is used to transform future payments into current dollars. An overly high rate could underestimate the actual liability by assuming lower costs in the future. The average discount rate for the one hundred largest funds in the 2005 *P&I* chart was 5.6 percent, but among the worst ten, Dow, American, Northwest, and Raytheon were all a bit high at 5.7 percent or above, as was the supposedly well-funded General Motors. Similarly, the following year, nine of the ten worst funded had rates higher than the 5.8 percent average. The risks of setting a wrong rate are so strong that the Securities and Exchange Commission even jumped in to investigate.

Also fodder for manipulation is the return on assets (ROAs) and future interest rates. In 2005 the SEC reportedly told several big companies to justify ROAs of more than 9 percent, and Olivia Mitchell of the Pension Research Council considers even that too generous. The companies on the *P&I* list for 2006 generally used a rate of 8 percent to 9.5 percent. In the ranks of the worst funded, Delta, ExxonMobil, and American Airlines all had a 9 percent rate, and Northwest used a whopping 9.5 percent. Thus, their underfundings will likely turn out to be even more dire than they seem on the surface.

American is in an odd situation because it uses the liability-driven investing strategy advocated by Mitchell and others—buying bonds whose maturities match the timing of its obligations. So, on the one hand, it shouldn't have to worry about market returns. Yet, on the other hand, it is almost impossible for such a bond-laden portfolio to achieve the 9 percent ROA.

Airlines like American are at risk for yet another reason. Congress in 2007 surreptitiously gave a special funding deal to American and the remaining carriers that hadn't yet dumped their pensions in bankruptcy. This was not done through the Pension Protection

Act, as it was with Delta and Northwest, but, nine months later, was tucked away in a spending bill for the war in Iraq. The new law allowed the not-yet-dumping carriers to use a higher discount rate, which could artificially improve their funded status. According to the PBGC, these airlines would now be able to pay their pension funds a total of $2 billion less over ten years. The justification that the bill's sponsors gave for this favorable treatment was that Delta and Northwest had already gotten funding breaks, and the "good" airlines that had kept their plans going shouldn't be penalized.

Very nice, except now these airlines would join the ranks of the underfunded and be at risk of dumping. In fact, critics said American and the others would be even more likely to dump. That's because Delta and Northwest were required to freeze their plans, preventing employees from building up further benefits and increasing the liability. But the "good" airlines didn't have to freeze. As the debate continued, congressional critics proposed new bills to water down the funding break.

Utilities and Less-Likely Prospects

Which other industries might be candidates for bankruptcy and pension dumping? Some interesting speculation swirls around electric utilities, one of the industries high on the PBGC's worry list. Historically, these were seen as rock solid, thanks to government regulation that assured a steady stream of profits while transferring costs, including pension costs, to the ratepayers. Although the companies might take on a high level of debt, "it's a smart choice" for risk-averse investors, Professor Gilson of Harvard says. "They have a lot of hard assets that can serve as collateral and very stable cash flows." From the 1930s until 1988, no utility had ever gone bankrupt.

Things began to change when Public Service Company of New Hampshire filed in January 1988. PSNH might be seen as a special case because of its controversial Seabrook nuclear power plant. But then the tremors spread. Starting in the 1990s, the federal government and about half the states and the District of Columbia opened up the industry to more competition. Under a 1996 federal law, states could let unregulated producers compete to sell power to utilities, which would merely deliver it to customers. Many utilities were swamped by the sudden freedom. Rates went haywire: Some states set caps on rate increases, which shot up after the caps expired. In other cases, the expected competition among producers never materialized. Customers screamed; in California, electricity delivery failed in rolling blackouts. At the same time, the cost of natural gas—one of the main fuels used to generate electricity—also skyrocketed. Some utilities thrived, and investors like Goldman Sachs and the Carlyle Group made sizable profits buying and selling power plants. But other utilities collapsed into bankruptcy.

Some analysts and pension experts saw a possible replay of the way deregulation had battered the airlines, even to the extent of soaring fuel prices as another shared vulnerability. Facing pressure on all sides, the newly deregulated utilities would have to cut spending where they could, and that might well include their pension plans. Nothing was protected any more. "It was easy for them to overpromise [pension benefits] because they thought they never had to pay the piper," says Phyllis Borzi, the former House Labor subcommittee counsel. "They could pass on to the ratepayers the cost of their benefit plans. They could afford to be quite generous. Management never focused on the fact that there might come a day that they, not the ratepayers, might actually have to figure out how to pay for these benefits."

Vultures were also circling the housing sector, as home prices in most parts of the country faltered in 2006 and then slid further after the subprime credit crunch the following year. Construction companies themselves wouldn't be termination candidates, because they have almost always had multiemployer plans. But there's a whole subgroup of industries that suffer when home construction slows, such as manufacturers of washing machines and refrigerators, and those are exactly the kind of Rust Belt industries likely to have defined benefit plans. They would also fit into Gordon Latter's most-vulnerable classification, capital goods manufacturers.

Oil companies and defense contractors are found high in the underfunding rankings as well, but their pensions enjoy particular safeguards. Oil companies are so profitable that investors are confident they can afford to cover any funding gaps. The pension liability is just a blip in the vast expanse of earnings and expenses. Kerstein of Towers Perrin says oil company officials have told him, "One dry hole costs much more than this pension plan could ever cost." Brad Belt, the former investment banker and former PBGC chief, nevertheless keeps a wary eye on the sector, pointing out that oil prices are cyclical.

Defense contractors, for their part, are basically safe because the bulk of their business is with the government, and the common practice is for government contracts to include reimbursement for pension costs. It's a bit like the utilities before deregulation: Even if the pension deficit looks big for the moment, everyone knows it can just be billed to a third party. In April 2006 the Department of Energy tried to change the time-honored practice in its own dealings, announcing that for all future contracts it would pay only for defined contribution plans, but not defined benefit programs. The public outcry was so furious—the House of Representatives even tacked an amendment on to the department's budget appropriation barring any money to carry out the new policy—that the department backed down less than two months later. If that wasn't enough protection, the Pension Protection Act gave defense contractors extra time to meet the new funding requirements.

Chemical companies also show up toward the top on both the *P&I* and Latter lists, but there's an interesting reason why investors consider them unlikely to terminate their pension plans. They are in one of the industries (along with the aerospace sector of defense) where, experts say, a defined benefit plan makes far more sense than a 401(k). Chemical companies have put years into training their scientists, and they want these highly skilled professionals to stick around for long-term projects. An ongoing defined benefit plan whose payout jumps dramatically over time is a great lure for keeping these people. If the plan is terminated, so is their inducement to stay; the scientist can't accumulate any more credits. Making the need for retention even more crucial is an overall shortage of engineers. "When you have highly technical chemical engineers and a lot of senior people who will be retiring, and there are not necessarily a lot of replacements behind them, there is tremendous focus on keeping the people you have. You also want to make it attractive to have people come to you mid- or late-career," points out Alan Glickstein, the Watson Wyatt consultant. Thus, even if their funding deficits are big, basic HR needs may keep chemical companies from terminating their plans.

Despite all these logical explanations, however, investors know that any predictions are ultimately unreliable. "You come to the conclusion that it could happen in any industry," says Lawrence Sher, director of retirement policy at Buck Consultants, another big benefits consulting firm. "Today's profitable, prosperous industry could be tomorrow's bankrupt industry."

14 | The Politics

"There's a lot of economic insecurity these days, and part of that picture is pensions. People are worried."

—CONGRESSMAN EARL POMEROY, DEMOCRAT, NORTH DAKOTA

PENSION TROUBLES have a hard time competing with other national issues for political attention. How can "actuarial assumptions" and "asset allocation" stand up against headliners like taxes, immigration, gay marriage, or abortion? "This is very dry, hard-to-understand stuff," points out Judy Schub, the PBGC's former assistant executive director for legislative affairs.

But when the pressure is strong enough and the stories are heartbreaking, pensions have been known to gain political moxie. "The history of old-age pensions suggests that [the issue] is a very powerful political force," muses Steven Sass of the Center for Retirement Research in Boston. "Social Security was passed because of pressure from the grass roots. The passage of ERISA was stalled in Congress for years and years, until Javits's office finally organized a network to see if local TV stations could find some worker in their districts who had been ripped off." After Studebaker hit the headlines in the early 1960s for shutting down its Indiana plant, leaving thousands of workers without the pensions they'd expected, "the Finance Committee members went home for their break, and they were excoriated." Political pressure also surfaced back in the 1980s, when the problem was overfunding, not underfunding, and companies were terminating pension plans in order to grab their "excess" assets. Either a staff member for Ohio Senator Howard Metzenbaum, who had a particular interest in pensions and a reputation as a populist, or the senator himself "was calling us virtually every day," recalls Bill Beyer, the longtime PBGC attorney.

The question now is whether bankruptcy terminations will lead to a similar political backlash. Will the public pay attention and bombard their senators and representatives with letters or e-mails?

Will that pressure move the politicians to write new laws making it so onerous to terminate a pension plan that struggling companies will keep their pensions going? Will this phenomenon, in short, have the political power of Studebaker?

Attacked from All Sides

Starting around 2005, it was hard to walk past a newsstand or turn on the television without seeing headlines that shouted, "The Death of Pensions." Greedy airline executives raked in millions of dollars worth of stock options and bonuses while pilots' pensions were sliced in half. Flight attendants just a few years short of retirement were looking for new jobs, and mining towns were becoming ghost towns as the plants where so many had worked closed down. Even employees whose companies were rock solid started to get nervous when they saw these stories, wondering if their pensions could be next.

Jonathan Carson, the Los Angeles lawyer who does bankruptcy claims back-office work, spends part of his time alerting retirees and other creditors about significant pending deadlines and court dates in bankruptcy cases. Each time he sends out a notice—whether or not the pension is actually being terminated—he says, "We get hundreds of calls a day: 'My name is Mary, I'm seventy-four, my husband is eighty-one; he's in the hospital now. Will he still get his pension?'"

In the early 2000s, as more and more plans began to drop like dying autumn leaves, political interest perked up. To many in Congress it was a classic case of the rich hurting the little guys, and vulture investors were stealing Grandma's pension, pure and simple. One investment banker with a long history of working in pensions and benefits recalls talking in 2005 and 2006 with staff members on the House and Senate labor committees—the supposed congressional pensions experts—during the negotiations over the Pension Protection Act. They were particularly suspicious of Wilbur Ross's outsize bonanza in the steel industry, the banker says. "People on the Hill have the idea that because in hindsight it worked, there was a systemic problem—that Ross found a way of ripping off the pension funds, ripping off employees, the retirees, and the government," he explains. Because Ross bought the steel companies for around $2 billion and sold them for $4.5 billion and the pension plans were terminated at the same time, the congressional skeptics felt that somehow the employees were cheated out of $2.5 billion worth of retirement pay. Investors like Ross, the banker adds, "are not easy to sympathize with. Nobody likes people who make a ton of money. [Those people also] have to do things that create more suffering [to keep the company going], even if it benefits people in the long run."

Politicians attacked the pension-termination demon from a variety of angles, offering a range of fixes, many of which found their way into the Pension Protection Act. Furious at the United Airlines payouts to CEO Tilton and others, Republicans and Democrats united to include a ban on improving special executive benefits if the rank-and-file pension plan was underfunded. "Retirement security" was one of the Democratic Party's "Six for '06" priorities in its candidates' victorious congressional campaigns in 2006. The AFL-CIO that same year listed ten principles for reforming the Bankruptcy Code, including strengthening workers' claim to their pensions. Two members of Congress—House Judiciary Chairman John Conyers of Michigan and Senator Richard Durbin of Illinois—introduced a bankruptcy reform bill in September 2007 that would make it harder to throw out union contracts in bankruptcy while making it easier for workers to win claims for wages and benefits. Even President Bush, in an interview with the *Wall Street Journal* that January, warned carmakers not to duck their pension obligations. "That's not how the market works and that's not corporate responsibility as I see it," the newspaper quoted him as saying. Although ERISA is supposed to preempt state laws, California Assemblyman Johan Klehs, a Democrat from San Leandro in the northern part of the state, found a narrow loophole and introduced a measure that would prohibit any dividend payments to shareholders if a company missed a pension payment. The measure passed the state Assembly in 2006 but stalled in the Senate, and then Klehs had to leave office because of term limits. He didn't expect anyone else to pick up his banner.

The momentum continued into the 2008 presidential election. Mark McKinnon, a media adviser to President Bush and then to Arizona Senator John McCain's presidential campaign, told the *Wall Street Journal*, "The old indicators that we reliably counted on—unemployment, the stock market—don't seem to matter much anymore. And other things do—health care and pensions."

"There's a lot of economic insecurity these days, and part of that picture is pensions," says North Dakota Congressman Earl Pomeroy, a Democrat and one of the members of Congress most knowledgeable about pensions. "People are worried about losing their job, and they're worried about losing their pension."

The PBGC felt the pressure, too, but it was attacked from starkly opposite directions. On the one hand, when the agency jumped in to terminate the Bethlehem Steel pension plan in 2003, Ohio Congressman Ralph Regula demanded a meeting with then Executive Director Steve Kandarian. Regula, a Republican, chaired the House subcommittee with jurisdiction over the PBGC, and he was upset that the Bethlehem workers in his district wouldn't get their shutdown benefits.

Two years later, a different set of politicians would put the heat on a different PBGC executive director, Brad Belt—this time to *allow* Aloha Airlines to terminate. California supermarket mogul Ronald Burkle and former football star Willie Gault had said they were willing to invest $100 million to rescue the Hawaii-based bankrupt airline, but only if it dumped its four pension plans. The PBGC argued that the airline had the financial wherewithal to maintain at least one of the plans. "I had entreaties from the mayor of Honolulu, members of Congress from Hawaii, the governor of Hawaii, the Department of Transportation," Belt recalls. "They wanted me to stand down on aggressively pursuing the PBGC's economic and legal interests"—that is, not to appeal the bankruptcy judge's ruling that allowed the airline to shut down all the plans. "The assertion was that otherwise Burkle wouldn't buy, and the airline would have to liquidate, and jobs would be lost," says Belt. "Well, that's not part of the statutory criteria the PBGC is supposed to look at."

These pressures were piled on top of the scores of mundane political demands that the PBGC, as a federal bureaucracy, was routinely experiencing. "Like any government agency, we'd get congressional letters every day," usually questioning why a constituent's pension had been terminated, Bill Beyer says with a shrug.

Forces Converging

Pension terminations don't happen out of the clear blue sky. They are part of a much bigger set of trends—some of them contradictory—

in demographics, health care, taxation, politics, business, labor-management relations, international trade, the Internet, and the role of government. People are living longer, spending more money on evermore varieties of medical treatments, thus raising businesses' cost of providing defined benefit pensions. But some businesses will spend much less on pensions because employees switch from job to job, not staying long enough at any single place to build up a large benefit. To cut immediate payroll expenses, old-line industrial companies are pushing their staffs to retire early. But that shift will most likely hike pension costs down the road because of the incentives usually required to get people to leave. Other employees are retiring later than they had planned because their pensions are too small and they can't afford to stop working. Government as well as business has stepped back, taking less of a role in providing direct social services (such as defined benefit plans) to citizens and workers. More and more companies are switching to 401(k) plans, in which employees have to save their own money for retirement and make their own investment decisions. Some experts claim that Americans are happy with that trend because they want to take more control of their own lives. No, other experts retort, they are not happy, because they want more services. They don't want to be responsible for making investment decisions in their 401(k)s. Whatever workers may want, unions have less and less power to get it for them. A company might avoid the whole problem by shuttering its U.S. plants and outsourcing to Eastern Europe or China. However, other countries are facing some of these same demographic and pension dilemmas—including some of those supposed havens of low-wage outsourcing.

With so many forces converging, it's hardly surprising that the pension termination controversy has gotten drawn into some far bigger political debates.

The most controversial was probably the wrangle over Social Security—which is truly the ultimate defined benefit program. According to the most widely cited predictions, unless some drastic changes are made in income or outgo by the middle of the twenty-first century, the system will not have enough money to pay retirees their full benefits. President Bush's solution was to convert Social Security into the equivalent of a 401(k) plan. He made that goal his top domestic priority after the Republicans' strong showing in the 2004 elections, advocating that some of the money that employers historically contribute to the Social Security trust fund be put instead into individual accounts that workers would invest themselves. The idea was wildly unpopular across the political spectrum, and Bush had to retreat.

Even when companies don't dump their pension plans on the PBGC, they are killing their defined benefit plans in slow motion. They shut the door to new employees and block even the existing staff from building up any new benefits. Everyone is shunted to a 401(k) or some other alternative instead. That means, as soon as the last existing covered worker is gone, so is the plan.

Another key issue intimately tied in with pensions has to do with health care for retirees. Most of the old-line companies that provide defined benefits also promise to pay part of their retired workers' medical costs. Typically, they fill in some of what Medicare doesn't cover, up to a limit that the companies themselves set. Both pensions and retiree health benefits share many of the same woes: The beleaguered industrial companies that offer them are having trouble meeting the costs, rising life expectancy is pushing their tab higher, and weakened unions have less clout to keep the benefits from eroding.

There's a crucial difference, however. Health care benefits have no ERISA, no PBGC, and no funding requirement. That means companies can reduce their coverage or require employees and retirees to pay a bigger share of the cost any time they want, unless the benefits are offered as part of collectively bargained union plans. It also means that money is rarely set aside for these benefits, which is one reason the VEBA pool that Wilbur Ross established at his steel companies was so striking. To make matters worse, medical costs regularly rise faster than inflation. While overall inflation increased less than 4 percent through the late 1990s and early 2000s, for example, the cost of health insurance premiums shot up by two or three times as much. So the financial hole in corporate medical benefits kept getting deeper. Although GM might have had a nicely funded pension plan (at least, by its own accounting), it owed $50 billion for retiree health care, according to Morgan Stanley. Ford was an estimated $26 billion in the red. The United Auto Workers over the years agreed to billions of dollars in concessions such as higher employee premiums, but by 2007 both sides were getting frustrated.

And businesses are not alone in their pension purgatory. Retirement plans run by the state governments had a combined underfunding of $381 billion in 2006, according to the National Association of State Retirement Administrators. When the pension programs covering approximately 20 million municipal, county, and local agency employees and retirees are added in, estimates of the total shortfall reach as high as $800 billion.

These plans suffer from some of the same problems plaguing their corporate counterparts, including retirees' longevity and stock market gyrations, as well as their own unique issues. Public funds are not governed by ERISA or the Financial Accounting Standards Board; nor are they backstopped by the PBGC. Even the SEC has no jurisdiction over these entities unless there's outright fraud. Public benefit plans operate under much looser governmental accounting standards, with oversight largely from politicians—whose mandate is to keep contributions low so as to avoid hiking taxes—and from union leaders, whose goal is to keep benefits high. Besides, generous pensions and other benefits are part of the unwritten labor bargain, to compensate for the public sector's historically skimpy wages. Unions then hopscotch each other's benefits, threatening to withhold endorsements of governors, mayors, and legislators who won't agree to big increases in benefits.

Eventually, government promises in some jurisdictions outstrip revenues. San Diego, California, for example, hid its problems for years with accounting gimmicks while publicly proclaiming its financial health, until a pension trustee blew the whistle in 2003; it turned out that the retirement fund was an amazing $1.4 billion in the red. Only *then* did the SEC have the authority to investigate. The Federal Bureau of Investigation and the local U.S. Attorney's office also jumped in, while the mayor resigned and the bond markets shut their doors. Meanwhile, an investigation by the *New York Times* in 2007 found that "New Jersey has been diverting billions of dollars from its pension fund for state and local workers into other government purposes over the last fifteen years, using a variety of unorthodox transactions authorized by the Legislature and by governors from both political parties" and also "overstated even what it has claimed to be contributing." The SEC investigated that, too. Arthur Levitt Jr., a former SEC chairman, warned of the dangers in late 2007. Conditions overall got so bad that a few states and cities tried to cut benefits, which, like those of their corporate counter-parts, are supposed to be untouchable.

The Ripple Effect

For all the headlines and political interest, skeptics argue that only about 13 percent of Americans could ever be directly affected by companies dumping their pension plans. That's the percentage of the private-sector workforce that had defined benefit pensions as of 2005, according to the Employee Benefit Research Institute. And of course, far fewer than that 13 percent will actually have their plans terminated. Why should the rest of the population care about something that's going to happen to so few? In any case, should people who have never had a pension plan be expected to cry for those whose pensions might be cut? At least they were lucky enough to work at a place that made an attempt to provide guaranteed pensions. "The average worker either has no pension or a defined contribution pension," says Olivia Mitchell of the Wharton School's Pension Research Council. "Pilots were paid $80,000, $90,000, $100,000. Their pensions were $150,000, $200,000. The average worker is not going to see anything like that. So there's a lot of jealousy but not a lot of sympathy."

Unfortunately, it's not just the 13 percent with defined benefit plans who would be hurt. When benefits lawyer Deene Goodlaw warns her students at Boalt Hall, the law school of the University of California, Berkeley, about the disappearance of pension plans, the message doesn't sink in with the twenty-somethings at first—until she hits home: "When your parents show up with their moving van to move in with you because they can no longer afford to live on their own, you will appreciate defined benefit plans."

Moreover, unions may have fewer members than they did in their prime, but they still know how to get those few voices heard. Shelley Greenhaus of Whippoorwill points out that labor leaders, who are inherently wary of buyout firms like his, could easily aim their PR against the buyers if a pension plan is dumped. "A lot of unions can legitimately turn around and say, 'The predecessor company mismanaged the business, and the LBO firm took out hundreds of millions of dollars [to cover fees, dividends, interest, and expenses]. Why should the rank and file have to pay for that?" A lot of times they're right," Greenhaus adds. "That's a very difficult and emotional issue."

Big pension funds, which often invest in private equity, also represent their workforces' interests, in a way. They have historically not taken an active role in fighting pension dumping (or any other labor issue, for that matter). But after the Cerberus-Chrysler deal, labor experts such as the Service Employees International Union began talking up the potential for pension-investor muscle. On the positive side, notes Christian Weller of the Center for American Progress, if a company provides decent replacement benefits, as US Airways did, the union can be one of the "best spokespersons."

So the start of the twenty-first century might be one of those turning points, like 1974 with ERISA, when pensions have political charisma. Karen Ferguson, director of the Pension Rights Center in Washington, DC, an advocacy organization for employees and retirees, claims that the same worry and anger generated in the Studebaker days are out there, just waiting for something specific, like a piece of legislation, to rally around. "It's a question of getting it focused and organized and coming up with a solution," says Ferguson. "The level of sophistication and the level of organization of affected employees are new. It might take one more big termination."

Brad Belt, the former PBGC chief, comes from a different end of the political spectrum from Ferguson. He was a staff lawyer for Republicans on the Senate Committee on Banking and then an investment banker before heading the PBGC from 2004 to 2006. Still, his view on the issue's potential volatility is surprisingly similar: "There was a lot of outcry over United and Northwest and Delta. That's largely dissipated. But if there is a new round of defaults, I expect outrage to surface again."

And if public outrage were truly ready to boil, in what direction would that energy be channeled? There is no shortage of likely targets. The obvious ones are the corporate executives who mismanaged a company into bankruptcy or failed to fund a plan properly. A subset of that comprises the particularly egregious managers, like the brass at United Airlines who walked off with their multimillion-dollar salaries, bonuses, stock options, and pensions. "Where you look at significant increases in nonqualified [non-ERISA] retirement plans for highly paid executives and some of the strategies that have been employed to provide protection when plans for rank and file are terminated," notes David Walker, the U.S. Comptroller General, "that's where we are seeing some criticism."

Another target is the new investors who insisted on terminating a plan before they would fork over any dollars. That would tie in nicely with the congressional outrage that flared in 2007 over the tax breaks enjoyed by private equity fund investors. Managements, meanwhile, might try to persuade their angry constituencies that it's really the fault of labor leaders who kept pressing for rich benefits even after times got tight. The least likely, but possible, target for public fury is the politicians who wrote the loophole-filled laws that allow companies to escape their pension promises.

"The assault on defined benefits is one issue in a whole network," says Sass of Boston College's Center for Retirement Research. "It will hit when people realize they don't have enough money to survive in retirement. People who are retiring will not have defined benefit plans." As he sees it, they might sue their company, saying something like, "You took away my defined benefits. I had this implicit contract." They might also sue regarding their 401(k) plans over issues like high fees and poor investment choices. "They're going to work longer. In the next five to ten years, we'll see the transition."

Solutions

Even as he signed the Pension Protection Act in August 2006, President Bush acknowledged that it would not wipe out pension dumping. "The problem of underfunded pensions will not be eliminated overnight," he said. "In the end, the primary responsibility rests with employers to fund the pension promises as soon as they can."

If the PPA is not to be the final legislative word, critics of the bill have plenty of proposals for what they would like to see in real pension-bankruptcy reform. There are, for starters, the long-standing goals of matching PBGC premiums to the risk of default, encouraging companies to invest in bonds correlated with the pension payouts, and boosting the PBGC's claim to a higher priority level in bankruptcy court. Another idea comes from Congressman Pomeroy: "We could move to require a company to exhaust every other reasonable alternative, in the financial reorganization—

strategies that don't have dumping the pension as the first step." No one predicts an outright ban on ever terminating a pension plan, or limitations so strict that the choice would become impossible outside of liquidation, but if some truly outrageous bonus grabbing and Grandma trashing occurred in a big bankruptcy, Congress could clamp on some severe restrictions.

To a number of people in Washington, on Wall Street, and in the pension world, the best solution would be to give more companies the kind of moratorium that the PPA allowed for the airlines and which US Airways had tried, unsuccessfully, to get from Congress and the PBGC—but with tighter oversight. "[We need] some way that companies coming out [of bankruptcy] could work out their plans, stretch them out," suggests Senator Cardin of Maryland, who for years sat on the House Judiciary Committee, which has jurisdiction over bankruptcy, and then switched to the Senate Judiciary Panel. As Norman Stein of the University of Alabama law school explains the overarching theory, "You take the current unfunded liabilities, put them in one pot, and give the companies a lot more time to fund them, maybe fifteen years. For future liabilities, I would have a separate pot, and I would require that extraordinarily conservative actuarial assumptions be used." The leniency would also work for companies in financial trouble but not in bankruptcy, and even for companies that wanted to let employees continue to grow their benefits—as long as the moratorium was under tight control, Stein says.

"If the PBGC had this power, they could have said to United, 'Nope, we're not taking over your pension plan. We're going to keep you responsible, but we'll lower your contributions for a while. Then, when you come out of reorganization, you'll gradually have to increase your contributions,'" Ron Gebhardtsbauer of the American Academy of Actuaries argues.

Brad Belt contends that the PBGC actually had such power, although it is hard to find anyone other than US Airways' previous management that agrees. He envisions the PBGC making a deal: "Rather than use [cash-flow problems] as an excuse to go into Chapter 11, I would rather sit down with a company and be able to say, 'If you need some additional time and you want to stretch out the payments, we can do that.' If the alternative is that the plan is going to be off-loaded on the PBGC, let's avoid that. But there's got to be a cost to doing that. The PBGC would get covenant protection, maybe fallback warrants if the company rebounds. The PBGC would move up the capital structure."

The closest thing to a funding moratorium on the books is a hardship waiver under the tax code. Companies that prove hardship can request a one-year waiver of their pension contribution as many as three times within any fifteen years. Northwest did that in 2003. However, Bill Beyer, the veteran PBGC lawyer, dismisses the waivers as "very narrow and not much help." Because the waived payment is amortized over five years, not forgiven completely, "you're just stacking up your problem over the next five years. It's a loan, basically." Also, the IRS will usually demand in return a secured claim to some interest.

By and large, the various pension-saving proposals are good ideas. Some of them might even preserve retirement payments for some workers. First, however, it's important to distinguish which proposals would actually bolster pension funds and which ones would merely bolster the PBGC. Those two goals are not necessarily the same.

The single most effective measure to preserve more pensions would be to change bankruptcy law so that the debtor company doesn't automatically get whatever it wants. One way to do this would be to put some teeth into Section 1113, the provision that requires the company to negotiate in good faith with unions and prove that termination is "essential to the continuation of the debtor's business" before reneging on any negotiated benefits. Congress could write a clear and strict definition of *essential*. It could also declare that *necessary* and *essential* within the wording of the law mean the same thing. Even better, a new law could extend these protections to pensions even where there is no union, mandating that the company convince the bankruptcy trustee or another third party that the termination is essential.

Practically speaking, however, none of that is going to happen—which is one reason no one even suggests it. Any changes would have to go through the House and Senate judiciary committees, which oversee bankruptcy laws, and "historically the judiciary committees have been unwilling to delve into pension issues," says Randy Hardock, the Delta benefits lawyer and former Senate Finance Committee staffer. The judges' bias in favor of the debtor company is too strong, and the bankruptcy bar and other creditors like things the way they are now.

For similar reasons, there is no chance of giving the PBGC higher priority in bankruptcy. As pointed out in Chapter 6, there's no love lost between the other creditors and the PBGC. Boosting the agency's status would only lower their own, so why should they? In any case, that step probably wouldn't save a single pension plan. By the time a case gets to court, the PBGC most likely has already agreed to a termination. If it had higher status, it would merely be arguing for a bigger piece of the pie.

In theory, a company could solve the whole problem by switching to a liability-driven investment strategy in its pension trust. From the day someone is hired, the company would buy bonds that matured exactly when pension payments needed to be made. The money would be on hand to pay the pensions, safe and sound. But reality has a nasty way of intruding on nice theories. As soon as a company encountered serious financial pressures, whether because of low-cost foreign competition, recession, or any other reason, it would be sorely tempted to make a bet on the stock market with its pension assets, hoping for a big win that would save it the cost of buying a fresh lot of bonds. Stocks outperform bonds over the long run, so the odds are that the gamble would pay off.

Congress could try to nudge companies to stay on the liability-matching path by tying PBGC premiums to the pension fund's risk profile. Such risk-based premiums were seriously considered as part of the Pension Protection Act of 2006. Again, this is a case in which the solution might help the PBGC's bottom line, but it wouldn't save any pensions. Companies will not base their asset allocation decisions on whether they can save a few bucks in PBGC premiums, because the premiums are simply too small, relative to the funding hole, to matter.

So the best approach is some sort of behavioral modification, combining the stick of Congressman Pomeroy's "last resort" idea with the carrot of funding extensions—under strict conditions. Of course, termination is already supposed to be the last resort—that's the point of Section 1113 and the PBGC's review—but obviously there are plenty of loopholes in the definition of *last* right now. A new law would need more specific requirements, with enforcement mechanisms. The standards that the PBGC now uses in its review could be codified. "I would argue that termination should be a last-resort option, unless the company has exhausted all other options," says Brad Belt, listing among those options the IRS hardship waiver and an ERISA exemption allowing cash-short companies to contribute hard assets instead of cash. No doubt a company could fudge any requirement, even a stricter one, if it wanted ("Your Honor, we tried a waiver, truly we did, but the amortization costs would just be too much"). Still, finessing two laws (this new one plus Section 1113) rather than just one might give a company more pause.

As for the carrot—stretching out the funding—the pension world already knows that it works. Funding extensions saved most of the pensions at Delta and Northwest and arguably might have helped US Airways' pilots too. Yes, this tactic rewards deadbeats, which isn't fair. But to get an extension, a company would have to submit to tough oversight, with constant monitoring and reporting. No benefits improvements would be allowed in nonqualified executive plans, and there would be limits on improving benefits in the rank-and-file pensions. The PBGC would also set a tight cap on the financial assumptions, such as the discount rate and return on assets, that these companies could use. Hanging overhead would be the threat that the PBGC could withdraw the extension and demand full funding immediately if the company strayed.

Of course, no bill gets written overnight. In the thirty-two years between ERISA and the 2006 Pension Protection Act, Congress passed five major changes to ERISA (including the PPA). At that rate, it takes Congress about six years to approve a pension law. Any measure that affected pensions' role in the bankruptcy process would have to go through extra legislative bureaucracy because it would come under the jurisdiction of the congressional labor committees, which oversee pensions, as well as the judiciary committees. The good news for companies and their investors is that the built-in delay gives them time to counter their lousy public images. Investors can push managements to tone down their bonuses and work with their unions to come up with good replacement benefits. Investors can even refuse to invest in companies that they fear will sink from their own morale problems.

Ultimately, even if some changes in ERISA and bankruptcy law are passed, the government will not force companies to keep their unaffordable pension plans, nor will it ban terminations completely.

None of these proposals, even in combination, can guarantee the preservation of every pension fund against the macroeconomic, technological, global, and demographic pressures pushing on them. Companies with shaky finances that really want to dump their plans will be able to.

For many companies, the hundreds of millions of dollars in apparent savings will be tempting. Others will find that it's not, in fact, worth the hassle. As Wilbur Ross, who probably knows more than anyone about how to make money by investing in companies that shed pensions, points out, "It isn't that you can just say, 'Aha, there's the pension—zap! That solves all my problems.'" Keeping a pension plan can drain the purse; terminating can drain morale and public image. Terminating, in any case, does not wash away all of the other problems—from poor management to high interest rates to cutthroat foreign competition—that got the business in trouble to begin with.

Whatever paths companies choose, the size of their retirement plans and their funding gaps are too big for investors to ignore. Pension funds are no longer just a source of income for retirees. In recent years, they have become an assumed factor in corporate finance, especially since the Sarbanes-Oxley Act has forced companies to be more aware of every financial nook and cranny. "A more recent trend among corporations is to incorporate the pension plan directly into corporate finance decisions," Richard Berner of Morgan Stanley wrote in the *Journal of Applied Corporate Finance* in winter 2006. And now investors are learning that pension funds—or rather their demise—might also provide a financial lifeline to companies struggling out of bankruptcy. Freed from the huge pension debt burden, these struggling companies can channel the tens of millions of dollars that would have gone into the pension fund toward other aims instead, like technology upgrades, salaries, or acquisitions—aims that might help the company revive. Terminating the pension by itself won't save a company; it must be combined with significant steps to rebuild trust and morale, such as decent replacement retirement benefits and honest communication, along with the kind of smart business practices every successful revival needs. But termination is now solidly in the restructuring arsenal. In other words, by dumping the pension plan that was supposed to provide a stipend for workers *after* they retire, a company might have enough money to stay in business and provide respectable wages for those workers *before* they retire.

That isn't what Congress intended when it passed ERISA. But it could provide a paradigm that might work.

Notes

Any quotes, direct or indirect, attributed to an individual are from interviews I conducted with that person between May 2006 and May 2007, unless otherwise indicated in the text. Also, sourcing is not provided for information widely in the public domain, such as provisions of the Pension Protection Act of 2006 or the bankruptcy filing of United Airlines.

Introduction

Page xiv—*The basic philosophy of investing*: Hilary Rosenberg, *The Vulture Investors* (New York: John Wiley & Sons, 2000), 7–10.

Page xvi—*By 2000, defined benefit systems*: Mary Williams Walsh, "Corporate Pensions Face Pressure Despite Stock Rally," *New York Times*, Dec. 31, 2003, C1.

Part 1: The Reasons

Chapter 2: Last in Line: The Retiree

Page 15—*however, most judges were still allowing*: Floyd Norris, "Pay Plan at Dana Ruled Illegal," *New York Times*, Sept. 6, 2006, C1.

Page 17—*Consider the example of a reorganizing debtor*: Lynn M. LoPucki, *Courting Failure: How Competition for Big Cases Is Corrupting the Bankruptcy Courts* (Ann Arbor: University of Michigan Press, 2006), 163–164.

Page 18—*At Delta, the retirees were granted*: "Delta Retired Pilots to Get $800 Million in Claims," *Reuters*, Nov. 27, 2006.

Chapter 3: Pension-Free and Ready to Compete—Or Not?

Page 24—Journalist Hilary Rosenberg: Rosenberg, 137–139.

Page 24—the average pay in China: "How Rising Wages Are Changing the Game in China," *BusinessWeek*, March 27, 2006.

Page 28—Edwin C. Hustead, a former chief actuary: Edwin C. Hustead, "Trends in Retirement Income Plan Administrative Expenses," chap. 8 in *Living with Defined Contribution Pensions: Remaking Responsibility for Retirement*, edited by Olivia S. Mitchell and Sylvester Schieber (Philadelphia: University of Pennsylvania Press, 1998), 166.

Page 31—As BusinessWeek *magazine saw things*: Dean Foust, "Now Boarding: Merger Mania," *BusinessWeek*, Nov. 27, 2006.

Page 32—And many of them felt a perennial resentment: Dean Foust, "Flight Plan," *BusinessWeek*, Dec. 4, 2006.

Part 2: The Laws

Chapter 4: Writing the Rules

Page 37—Pension plans had been toppling: Steven A. Sass, *The Promise of Private Pensions: The First Hundred Years* (Cambridge: Harvard University Press, 1997), 56.

Page 37—the typical plan in 1974: Richard A. Ippolito, *Pensions, Economics and Public Policy* (Homewood, IL: Dow Jones-Irwin, 1986), 71.

Page 39—It could be argued that Americans have been enjoying: Sass, 6.

Page 39—After the Civil War, Union veterans: Ibid., 12.

Page 40—"Managers believed they could reduce": James A. Wooten, *The Employee Retirement Income Security Act of 1974: A Political History* (Berkeley, Los Angeles, and London: University of California Press, 2004), 21.

Page 40—*"Railroads were the first modern enterprises"*: Sass, 19.

Page 40—*Some leading universities set up a retirement system*: Ibid., 52.

Page 40—*Andrew Carnegie did the same*: Ari Jacobs and Mike Johnston, "Response to CIEBA Request for Impact Analysis of Emerging Issues," Hewitt Associates paper, March 12, 2004, 6.

Page 40—*By 1919, about 15 percent*: Sass, 38, 53.

Page 41—*Wooten also notes in his book*: Wooten, 34.

Page 41—*In 1945, according to Sass*: Sass, 217.

Page 43—*Kaiser-Frazer closed*: Wooten, 55.

Page 43—*Studebaker-Packard, a nine-year old*: Ibid., 54–76.

Chapter 5: Failure's Fallout: LTV and Other Precedents

Page 58—*The first prominent company*: Fran Hawthorne, "Raiding the Corporate Pension Fund," *Institutional Investor*, December 1983, 101.

Page 59—*During the next seven years*: Karen Ferguson and Kate Blackwell, *Pensions in Crisis: Why the System Is Failing America and How You Can Protect Your Future* (New York: Arcade Publishing, 1995), 127.

Page 59—*Vincent Blake, vice president and controller*: Hawthorne.

Chapter 6: The Bankruptcy Court Minuet

Page 62—*Wavering back and forth*: Kevin J. Delaney, *Strategic Bankruptcy: How Corporations and Creditors Use Chapter 11 to Their Advantage* (Berkeley and Los Angeles: University of California Press, 1998), 19–21; and David A. Skeel Jr., *Debt's Dominion: A History of Bankruptcy Law in America* (Princeton and Woodstock, UK: Princeton University Press, 2001), 25–26.

Page 69—*The inquiry must go beyond evaluating*: William G. Beyer, "Pensions, Bankruptcy, and the Pension Benefit Guaranty Corporation," chap. 30 in *Annual Survey of Bankruptcy Law* (Thomson/West, 2005), 128.

Page 69—*the* International Herald Tribune *put the value*: Lawrence Malkin, "Who Will Share TWA's Future?" *International Herald Tribune*, Dec. 8, 1992.

Page 69—*In a smaller case in the spring*: Mary Williams Walsh, "Steel Maker's Pension Plan to Continue," *New York Times*, April 1, 2006, C1; and Mary Williams Walsh, "U.S. Moves to Seize Bankrupt Steel Maker's Pension Plan," *New York Times*, Feb. 4, 2006, C4.

Page 73—*starting with a case under*: Beyer, 139.

Page 74—*There was no question*: Delaney, 110.

Page 75—*Starting as early as 1985*: Marcia L. Goldstein, an attorney with Weil, Gotshal & Manges in New York, has been collecting a running list of contradictions among the circuit courts decisions.

Page 77—*In one of the first big fights*: Rosenberg, 101.

Part 3: The Investors

Chapter 7: How Investors Play the Game

Page 87—*In June 2005, when Jernberg Industries*: The information about Jernberg comes from a variety of sources, including author's interview with Michael Psaros, PBGC press releases, KPS documents, and also the article by Jeffrey McCracken, "How Financiers Pursue Profit at Skidding Auto-Parts Maker," *Wall Street Journal*, Dec. 21, 2006, A1.

Page 87—*and a third of $1.2 billion in 2007*: Shawn Tully, "Why the Private Equity Bubble Is Bursting," *Fortune*, Aug. 20, 2007, 30.

Page 90—*In acquiring LTV's remains, Ross*: Daniel Gross, "Is Wilbur Ross the Next Andrew Carnegie?" *Slate*, Jan. 16, 2003.

Page 90—*In acquiring LTV's remains, Ross*: The information in this paragraph comes from my interview with Greenhaus as well as from Rosenberg, 106–108.

Page 94—*Senior secured debt like the kind*: Praveen Varma and Richard Cantor, "Bond Prices at Default and at Emergence from Bankruptcy for US Corporate Issuers," Moody's Investors Services Special Comment, June 2005, 6.

Page 97—*This time there would be*: Jeffrey McCracken, "The Man Who Would Be King of Auto Parts," *Wall Street Journal*, Nov. 3, 2005, B1.

Page 97—*According to an article in* Fortune *magazine*: Alex Taylor III, "Bankruptcy Raider Moves in on Auto Parts," *Fortune*, Dec. 11, 2006.

Page 97—*meshed with one of Ross's publicly*: Nick Bunkley, "Big Investors Breathing New Life into Gasping Auto Parts Suppliers," *New York Times*, Jan. 31, 2007, C4.

Page 97—*He was also looking for niches*: Taylor.

Page 98—*After missing its required 2005*: "Pension Talks in Planned Plant Closures," *Associated Press*, Jan. 11, 2007.

Page 98—*The* Wall Street Journal *in a November 2005 article*: McCracken.

Page 98—*He told* Fortune, *as well*: Taylor.

Page 99—*since Max Heine pretty much*: Rosenberg, 8.

Page 99—*the amount of defaulted debt doubled*: Ibid., 16.

Page 99—*Distressed investing in the 1990s*: Ibid., 19.

Page 100—*Amazingly, the Congressional Research Service*: William Klunk, "Pension Funds Investing in Hedge Funds," Congressional Research Service Report for Congress, June 15, 2007.

Chapter 8: The Signs of Failure

Page 101—*Every big U.S. player in the industry*: Rosenberg, 100.

Page 102—*Bethlehem's numbers track the decline*: Malcolm Gladwell, "The Risk Pool," *The New Yorker*, Aug. 28, 2006; and Carol J. Loomis, "The Sinking of Bethlehem Steel," *Fortune*, April 5, 2004.

Page 102—*Between 2000 and 2004, more than forty*: Jeffrey McCracken and Paul Glader, "New Detroit Woe: Makers of Parts Won't Cut Prices," *Wall Street Journal*, Mar. 20, 2007, A1.

Page 106—*Towers Perrin over the years has*: For this book, Towers Perrin ran an extra set of tables from its database showing the median in each category measured.

Page 107—*Latter developed some charts*: The data come from Latter's "Pensions & Endowments 15" report, particularly tables 5 and 6, October 4, 2006.

Page 108—*Not surprisingly, Delta led the chart*: Rob Kozlowski, "Top Plans' Liabilities Keep Tumbling," *Pensions & Investments*, July 10, 2006, 1.

Page 109—*Whereas in 2000 there were more than five*: Pete Engardio and Carol Matlack, "Now, the Geezer Glut," *BusinessWeek*, Jan. 31, 2005, 44.

Page 110—*Thus, Eli Lilly and Co. enjoyed one of the best*: Kozlowski, 1.

Page 110—*For instance, the average projected long-range*: Ibid.

Page 111—*When Watson Wyatt surveyed*: *2005 Survey of Actuarial Assumptions and Funding*, Watson Wyatt Worldwide Research Report, 3.

Page 111—*In the June 2006 issue of*: Karen Wiltsie and John Stokesbury, "What Audit Committees Don't Know Can Hurt Them," *Directorship*, June 2006.

Page 112—*The Congressional Research Office study in 2007*: Klunk.

Page 114—*A final-average system is the most*: Watson Wyatt survey, 26.

Page 114—*EBRI has calculated that*: Jack VanDerhei, "Defined Benefit Plan Freezes: Who's Affected, How Much, and Replacing Lost Income," EBRI Issue Brief #291, March 2006.

Page 115—*The median final-average-pay*: Watson Wyatt survey, 10.

Page 116—*Richard A. Ippolito, a former pensions official*: Ippolito, 168.

Page 120—*As Kevin J. Delaney*: Delaney, 161.

Page 120—*Similarly, another book on bankruptcy*: Skeel, 221.

Page 121—*Professor Delaney contends that the*: Delaney, 60–97.

Chapter 9: Pensionless Restructuring

Page 126—*The results were similar for Diane K. Denis*: Diane K. Denis and Kimberly J. Rodgers, "Chapter 11: Duration, Outcome, and Post-Reorganization Performance," *Journal of Financial and Quantitative Analysis* 42, no. 1 (March 2007): 101–118.

Page 126—*Of the 65 percent of the companies*: Here's the full breakdown: Of the 718 companies in the database as of October 2006, 47 were still unresolved. Of the remaining 671, there were 436, or 61 percent, that had emerged from Chapter 11, and 235, or 39 percent, that failed to emerge. Then, of the 436 that emerged, 280 had been out for at least five years, which Professor LoPucki considers an important yardstick. So of those 280 that had been out at least five years, 53, or 19 percent, refiled for bankruptcy within their first five years, and 28 refiled at some point later.

Page 126—*Another study—this one by Edith Hotchkiss, an associate professor*: Edith Hotchkiss, "Postbankruptcy Performance and Management Turnover," *Journal of Finance* 50 (1995): 3–21.

Page 126—*The Denis-Rodgers report*: Denis, 18.

Page 127—*When he and a colleague*: LoPucki and his colleague, Joseph Doherty, director of the Empirical Research Group at the UCLA School of Law, calculated the data for pension terminations specifically for this book. The full data are these: Sixty-five companies terminated their pensions, of which thirty-four failed to emerge, thirty emerged, and one case was still pending. Of the thirty that emerged, twenty-three lasted more than five years, seven refiled within five years, and five refiled after five years.

Page 129—*a fight with the Steelworkers union*: John Stucke, "Kaiser Seeks $60 Million for Top Brass," *SpokesmanReview*, July 19, 2002.

Page 129—*including stakes in an Australian refinery*: "Bankruptcy Court Approves Kaiser Sale," *Houston Business Journal*, Nov. 8, 2004.

Page 135—*By contrast, the most common*: "Survey Findings: Trend and Experiences in 401(k) Plans 2005," survey by Hewitt Associates, 28.

Page 135—*whereas most of the companies surveyed by Hewitt*: Ibid., 7.

Page 139—*The pooled setup is exactly*: Gladwell.

Page 140—*The USW also had unique*: Bernard Wysocki Jr., Kris Maher, and Paul Glader, "A Labor Union's Power: Blocking Takeover Bids," *Wall Street Journal*, May 9, 2007, A1.

Page 141—Forbes *estimated his net worth*: "The Richest People in America," *Forbes*, Oct. 9, 2006, 80.

Page 142—*He also hired back laid-off union*: Nicholas Stein, "Wilbur Ross Is a Man of Steel . . . and textiles and optical networking and anything else in deep, deep trouble," *Fortune*, May 26, 2003.

Page 143—*the eight highest-ranking executives got promises*: Details on the United executives' pay come from a number of sources, including Gretchen Morgenson, "Gee, Bankruptcy Never Looked So Good," *New York Times*, Jan. 15, 2006, Section 3, 1; and "Airline Mergers Can Lead to Labor Conflict," cnn.com, Dec. 14, 2006.

Page 144—*The* New York Times, *for instance*: Morgenson.

Chapter 10: The Emergence of US Airways

Page 151—*Between 1978 and 2005, 162 airlines*: "Commercial Aviation: Bankruptcy and Pension Problems Are Symptoms of Underlying Structural Issues," U.S. Government Accountability Office Report to Congressional Committees, September 2005, 3.

Page 151—*"The airline industry is characterized"*: Ibid., 3.

Page 152—*This new competition drove*: "Airline Deregulation: Reregulating the Airline Industry Would Likely Reverse Consumer Benefits and Not Save Airline Pensions," U.S. Government Accountability Office Report to Congressional Committees, June 2006, 18.

Page 152—*The legacy carriers managed*: Ibid., 16.

Page 153—*hiring the Rolling Stones*: Greg Ip and Henny Sender, "In Today's Buyouts, Payday for Firms Is Never Far Away," *Wall Street Journal*, July 25, 2006, A1.

Page 153—*a little shindig that reportedly cost $7 million*: Andrew Ross Sorkin, "In Defense of Schwarzman," *New York Times*, July 29, 2007, Sunday Business, 6.

Page 153—*and the group the B-52's*: Carol Matlack, "Texas Pacific: Ready, Set, Buy!" *BusinessWeek*, Oct. 22, 2001.

Page 154—*The Burger King acquisition*: Ip and Sender.

Page 154—*In 2007, Fortune magazine*: Katie Benner, Telis Demos, Corey Hajim, and Jia Lynn Yang, "The Power List," *Fortune*, March 5, 2007, 63.

Chapter 11: The Reemergence of US Airways

Page 158—*In 2004, US Airways was spending*: Chris Isidore, "US Air Files Chapter 11—Again," CNNMoney.com, Sept. 13, 2004.

Page 158—*but in an interview with a reporter from the* Philadelphia Inquirer: Tom Belden, "Awaiting US Airways' Profits," Retirement Systems of Alabama *Advisor*, July 2004, 2.

Page 160—*later, in 2006, he would*: Sally B. Donnelly, "Now Arriving: Mergers," *Time*, Nov. 19, 2006.

Page 160—*As Doug Parker told the* New York Times: Jeff Bailey, "An Updraft for the Airlines," *New York Times*, Jan. 12, 2007, C1.

Page 160—*There were tales of how*: Melanie Trottman and Evan Perez, "Surprise Hostile Bid for Delta May Spur Airline Merger Wave," *Wall Street Journal*, Nov. 16, 2006, A1.

Page 160—*Perhaps the quintessential*: Ben Mutzabaugh, "'Regular Guy' Steers Brand New Airline," *USA Today*, Nov. 27, 2005.

Page 163—*The merged US Airways–America West finished*: Jeff Bailey, "The Cycle Turns, and Airline Shares Have Fans Again," *New York Times*, April 3, 2007, C3.

Page 163—*versus a $46 million loss for the two airlines combined*: Dawn Gilbertson, "US Airways' Profit Soars," *Arizona Republic*, July 28, 2006.

Page 163—*in a private transaction with Goldman Sachs*: Ruth Mantell, "US Airways Major Holder Sells Almost Half of Stake," *MarketWatch* from Dow Jones, Feb. 13, 2007.

Page 163—*Jones, by the way, could*: The background on Paul Tudor Jones comes from several sources, including his biographies in *Financial World* magazine's rankings of "The Wall Street 100" for 1990 through 1995; *Forbes* magazine's "The 400 Richest Americans," 2006 edition; and the website for his charitable organization, the Robin Hood Foundation.

Page 164—*overall costs were cut*: Barney Gimbel, "Onboard the Wild Ride of Doug Parker," *Fortune*, April 30, 2007, 137–141.

Page 165—*Gary Richardson, head of the chapter*: Bailey, "Updraft."

Page 166—*and by 2007 they were itching to restore*: Jeff Bailey, "As Airlines Surge, Pilots Want Share," *New York Times*, Jan. 30, 2007, C1.

Page 166—*When the company finally combined*: Melanie Trottman, "US Airways' Check-In Shutdown," *Wall Street Journal*, March 5, 2007, A18.

Page 168—*His response: "Senator, the $5 billion"*: Gimbel.

Part 4: The Future

Chapter 12: The Problem Continues

Page 172—*Also, McKinsey & Co.*: "The Coming Shakeout in the Defined Benefit Market," McKinsey & Company report, May 2007, 7.

Page 173—*What's more, in an article*: Richard Berner, Bryan Boudreau, and Michael Peskin, "'De-risking' Corporate Pension Plans: Options for CFOs," *Journal of Applied Corporate Finance* 18 (winter 2006): 25–35.

Page 173—*Overall, the funded status*: *Pension Insurance Data Book 2005*, Pension Benefit Guaranty Corporation, 69.

Page 175—*"There are more hedge funds"*: Steven Brull, "Hedge Fund Holdouts," *Institutional Investor*, December 2005, 22–30.

Page 176—*"DB plans' problems run"*: Richard Berner and Trevor Harris, "Pension Missiles: Is the Cure Worse than the Disease?" published by Morgan Stanley Equity Research in its *Accounting and Economics* series, March 25, 2004.

Page 179—*In its annual "High-Risk Series" update*: "High-Risk Series: An Update," U.S. Government Accountability Office report, January 2007, 85.

Page 181—*In a paper issued in January 2006*: "Assessing the Impact of the Planned Changes in Accounting for Pensions and Other Postretirement Benefits," Towers Perrin white paper, January 2006.

Page 181—*With all the rules put together*: Steven Brull, "Pension Peril," *Institutional Investor*, January 13, 2006, 21–23.

Chapter 13: The Next to Fail

Page 183—*while the French-Japanese alliance*: Gail Edmondson, "Putting Ford in the Rearview Mirror," *BusinessWeek*, Feb. 12, 2007, 44.

Page 184—*Moreover, the company had come close to bankruptcy*: "Goodyear Strike Keeps Akron Quiet," *Associated Press*, Oct. 7, 2006.

Page 185—*"Our extensive pension and [post-employment]*: Ellen E. Schultz and Theo Francis, "As Workers' Pensions Wither, Those for Executives Flourish," *Wall Street Journal*, June 23, 2006, A1.

Page 185—*"We view bankruptcy risk as low*: Jonathan Steinmetz and Jane Park, "Ford: New Year's Resolution: Trim the Fat," Morgan Stanley research report, Dec. 19, 2006, 1.

Page 185—*As for GM, "we also believe that bankruptcy"*: Jonathan Steinmetz and Jane Park, "General Motors: No Man's Land," Morgan Stanley research report, Jan. 24, 2007, 1.

Page 186—*The day after the deal was announced*: Gregory Zuckerman, Serena Ng, and Dana Cimilluca, "Cerberus Finds Luster in Detroit," *Wall Street Journal*, May 15, 2007, C1.

Page 189—*In 2005 the SEC reportedly*: Mary Williams Walsh, "A Pension Rule, Sometimes Murky, Is Under Pressure," *New York Times*, Nov. 8, 2005, C2.

Page 190—*From the 1930s until 1988*: Rosenberg, 44.

Page 191—*Some utilities thrived*: David Cay Johnston, "Competitive Era Fails to Shrink Electric Bills," *New York Times*, Oct. 15, 2006, A1; and David Cay Johnston, "In Deregulation, Power Plants Turn Into Blue Chips," *New York Times*, Oct. 23, 2006, A1.

Chapter 14: The Politics

Page 197—*Even President Bush*: Christopher Cooper and John D. McKinnon, "Bush Plays Down Bailout Prospects for GM and Ford," *Wall Street Journal*, Jan. 26, 2006, A1.

Page 197—*Mark McKinnon, a media adviser*: Greg Ip and John D. McKinnon, "Bush Reorients Rhetoric, Acknowledges Income Gap," *Wall Street Journal*, March 26, 2007, A2.

Page 201—*Retirement plans run by the state governments*: Nanette Byrnes, "Can Retirees Afford This Much Risk?" *BusinessWeek*, Sept. 17, 2007, 30.

Page 201—*estimates of the total shortfall*: Mary Williams Walsh, "Public Pension Plans Face Billions in Shortages," *New York Times*, Aug. 8, 2006, A1; and Ibid.

Page 201—*Meanwhile, an investigation by the* New York Times: Mary Williams Walsh, "New Jersey Diverts Billions, Endangering Pension Fund," *New York Times*, April 4, 2007, A1.

Page 202—*Conditions overall got so bad that*: Mary Williams Walsh, "Once Safe, Public Pensions Are Now Facing Cuts," *New York Times*, November 6, 2006, p. A1.

Page 209—*"A more recent trend among corporations"*: Berner, "De-risking," 25–35.

Index

About the Author

For more than twenty years, Fran Hawthorne has followed the rise of 401(k) plans, the fall of old-fashioned pensions, and the ins and outs of Wall Street's dance with Washington, as an editor and writer at *Fortune*, *BusinessWeek*, and *Institutional Investor* magazine, where she is now a senior contributing editor. She is the author of three books on health care and investing, including *Inside the FDA: The Business and Politics Behind the Drugs We Take and the Food We Eat* (published by John Wiley & Sons, 2005) and *The Merck Druggernaut: The Inside Story of a Pharmaceutical Giant* (Wiley, 2003). Hawthorne writes regularly for *The New York Times*, *Newsday*, *Worth*, *Crain's New York Business*, and other publications. She graduated Phi Beta Kappa from the University of California at Berkeley.

About Bloomberg

Bloomberg L.P., founded in 1981, is a global information services, news, and media company. Headquartered in New York, Bloomberg has sales and news operations worldwide.

Serving customers on six continents, Bloomberg, through its wholly-owned subsidiary Bloomberg Finance L.P., holds a unique position within the financial services industry by providing an unparalleled range of features in a single package known as the Bloomberg Professional® service. By addressing the demand for investment performance and efficiency through an exceptional combination of information, analytic, electronic trading, and straight-through-processing tools, Bloomberg has built a worldwide customer base of corporations, issuers, financial intermediaries, and institutional investors.

Bloomberg News, founded in 1990, provides stories and columns on business, general news, politics, and sports to leading newspapers and magazines throughout the world. Bloomberg Television, a 24-hour business and financial news network, is produced and distributed globally in seven languages. Bloomberg Radio is an international radio network anchored by flagship station Bloomberg 1130 (WBBR-AM) in New York.

In addition to the Bloomberg Press line of books, Bloomberg publishes *Bloomberg Markets* magazine.

To learn more about Bloomberg, call a sales representative at:

London:	+44-20-7330-7500
New York:	+1-212-318-2000
Tokyo:	+81-3-3201-8900